Instructor's Manual with Test Items
for Myron H. Dembo's
Applying Educational Psychology in the Classroom

Fourth Edition

Instructor's Manual with Test Items for Myron H. Dembo's
Applying Educational Psychology in the Classroom

Fourth Edition

Prepared by
Gay Goodman
University of Houston

Test Items Written by

Sydney Blake

Brenda Sugrue

Also available with the Fourth Edition:
*Study Guide for Myron H. Dembo's Applying Educational Psychology
in the Classroom, Fourth Edition.* Prepared by William J. Gnagey.
Computerized Test Bank. Macintosh/IBM. Available to adopters only.
IBM available on 3½" and 5¼" disks.

Longman
New York & London

Instructor's Manual with Test Items for Myron H. Dembo's
Applying Educational Psychology in the Classroom, Fourth Edition

Longman, 95 Church Street, White Plains, N.Y. 10601

Associated companies:
Longman Group Ltd., London
Longman Cheshire Pty., Melbourne
Longman Paul Pty., Auckland
Copp Clark Pitman, Toronto

ISBN 0-8013-0484-9 (Text); 78317
ISBN 0-8013-0677-9 (Study Guide); 78682
ISBN 0-8013-0678-7 (Instructor's Manual); 78683
ISBN 0-8013-0679-5 (Macintosh Test Bank); 78684
ISBN 0-8013-0680-9 (IBM Test Bank); 78685

2 3 4 5 6 7 8 9 10-VG-9594939291

CONTENTS

PREFACE

The <u>Instructor's Manual with Test Items</u> for Dembo's <u>Applying Educational Psychology in the Classroom</u> is designed to assist instructors in delivering both didactic and experiential instruction for undergraduate and graduate classes. In addition, the manual provides numerous suggestions for observational activities and out-of-class assignments as well as evaluation strategies.

The first section of this manual is organized sequentially and by chapter. Each chapter presents information in six different areas. The content and uses of information are described below for prospective manual users. The second section provides test items for each of the 13 chapters in the book.

SECTION ONE

CHAPTER OBJECTIVES

The Chapter Objectives which are provided in the text are repeated in the manual for the instructor's convenience. The objectives are organized around the major focal points of each chapter and provide a general overview of chapter content.

FOCUS QUESTIONS

The second section in each chapter restates the Focus Questions which are included in the text. Each question is answered in detail for the instructor's convenience. Answers to the focus question, for the most part, are based directly on material presented in the text. As such, they represent specific, correct answers rather than debatable issues which are subject to interpretation or value judgments.

CHAPTER OUTLINE

Following the Focus Questions is a brief Chapter Outline. The outline is intended to acquaint the instructor with chapter content and sequence so that additional textbook information can be easily located.

KEY TERMS

Key Terms for each chapter are included in the Glossary of the text. They appear in bold print in the text of each chapter. Each of these terms is listed in the <u>Instructor's Manual with Test Items</u> and referenced to the page in the text on which it is defined.

CHAPTER GUIDELINES

The section providing Chapter Guidelines opens with a brief overview of chapter content. The overview is followed by several suggestions which can be used to supplement the information provided in the text. In some cases the supplementary material builds on material which is included in the chapter. In other cases, new information is suggested which is a logical extension of chapter material. The section on Chapter Guidelines also includes discussion questions. These questions do not appear within the body of the text. They can be used to stimulate group discussion during class time, or they can be easily adapted as essay exam items. For the most part, discussion questions do not have a right or wrong answer which is directly stated in the text. Often they require practical application of textbook material. In other cases they address issues for which there is no clear cut, defensible answer. The final section in Chapter Guidelines lists audiovisual aids which are suitable for use with the content provided in each chapter.

FOLLOW-UP ACTIVITIES

At the end of each book chapter several Follow-up Activities are listed for the students. Under the Follow-up Activities section of the manual, specific suggestions are provided to help the instructors adapt these activities for use with the class. In some cases, activity sheets are available. These can be reproduced and distributed directly from the manual. After each Follow-up Activity in the book has been discussed, additional Follow-up Activities are provided.

CHAPTER ONE

THE TEACHER AS DECISION MAKER

CHAPTER OBJECTIVES

Students mastering the content in Chapter One will be able to:

- Use a model of the teaching-learning process to analyze a teacher's instructional behavior.

- Observe student behavior in classrooms.

FOCUS QUESTIONS

1. How do the major variables in the teaching-learning process impact the effectiveness of instruction?

   Hunter identifies six variables in the teaching-learning process. These are:

   - instructional objectives
   - principles of learning
   - individual differences
   - teacher behavior
   - methods of instruction
   - evaluation of learner's behaviors

   Isolating each of these variables allows the teacher to consider major teaching responsibilities before teaching is begun. By examining them individually, the teacher is able to increase teaching effectiveness by making more valid instructional decisions concerning the selection of the learning task and the determination of appropriate teacher behaviors.

2. What type of problems do beginning teachers confront?

   A review of literature on the topic of beginning teacher concerns indicates that there are eight problems most frequently encountered by beginning teachers. These are:

   - classroom discipline
   - motivating students
   - dealing with individual differences
   - assessing students' work
   - relationships with parents
   - organization of classwork
   - insufficient and low or inadequate teaching materials and supplies
   - dealing with problems of individual students

CHAPTER OUTLINE

I. ORIENTATION

    A. Focus Questions

II. INSTRUCTIONAL DECISIONS MADE BY TEACHERS

    A. The Learning Task
    B. The Behavior of the Learner
    C. The Behavior of the Teacher

III. DECISIONS, DECISIONS. . .

IV. USING THE TEACHING-LEARNING MODEL TO ANALYZE INSTRUCTION

    A. An Elementary School Classroom
    B. A High School Classroom
    C. A Final Comment

V. THE COMPLEXITY OF CLASSROOM LIFE

VI. PROBLEMS ENCOUNTERED BY BEGINNING TEACHERS

KEY TERMS

teaching (p. 2)   instructional objective (p. 5)

learning (p. 2)   entry behavior (p. 5)

CHAPTER GUIDELINES

Chapter 1 addresses the personal hypotheses and beliefs that perspective teachers have about the teaching-learning process. It emphasizes the fact that this belief structure serves as the basis for making important classroom decisions which, in turn, affect how students learn. The chapter encourages teachers to examine the beliefs that they hold and the effects their beliefs have on the educational decision-making process. It stresses the importance of evaluating the effects of their beliefs and practices and modifying their teacher behavior when necessary. The field of educational psychology is presented as a body of content which teachers can use to test their personal beliefs about teaching and learning.

Madeline Hunter's model of the teaching-learning process is introduced. This model identifies individual differences, teacher behavior, instructional objectives, theories and principles of learning, teaching methods, and evaluation of student behavior as major variables in the teaching-learning process.

The chapter stresses the fact that some teachers become discouraged because they are unable to make effective decisions about the problems that arise in their classrooms. Teachers need to learn to analyze their problems so that they can effectively use their knowledge of educational psychology.

Teachers are encouraged to develop systematic strategies for observing student behavior. The need to separate a description of behavior from personal feelings and inferences is emphasized. The anecdotal method of recording student behavior is presented.

Concerns of beginning teachers and their feelings of inadequacy are explored. The chapter identifies such concerns as classroom discipline, motivating students, dealing with individual differences, assessing student work, handling relationships with parents, and organizing the classroom.

Supplementary Materials

Instructors seeking to expand on the material included in Chapter 1 might review models of teaching and learning other than the one proposed by Hunter. Joyce and Weil discuss 23 different models. They classify the models into four categories, or types:

- information-processing models
- social interaction models
- personal models
- behavior-modification models

Introducing the student to these models provides a contrast and comparison to the work provided by Hunter. It also provides an excellent introduction to the theories which are presented in many of the subsequent book chapters.

Joyce, B., & Weil, M. (1980). Models of teaching (2nd ed.). Englewood Cliffs, NJ: Prentice-Hall.

Another teaching model developed by John Carroll emphasizes five elements which he feels contribute to instructional effectiveness.

CARROLL'S MODEL OF SCHOOL LEARNING

- Aptitude: Ability of students to learn
- Ability to understand instruction: Readiness of students to learn lesson content
- Perseverance: Willingness or motivation of students to spend time learning
- Opportunity: Time devoted for student learning
- Quality of instruction: Effectiveness of lesson presentation

---

Adapted from: Carroll, 1963

Carroll, J. (1963). A model of school learning. Teacher's College Record, 64, 722-733.

In 1987, Slavin adapted the work of Carroll to incorporate a new model. He calls his model the QAIT Model of Effective Instruction. This model focuses on four variables.

QAIT MODEL OF EFFECTIVE INSTRUCTION

- Quality of instruction
- Appropriate levels of instruction
- Incentive
- Time

Slavin, R. E. (1987). A theory of school and classroom organization. Educational Psychologist, 22(2), 89-108.

Another possibility for expanding the content of Chapter One is to include data-based systems for observing and recording student behavior. These data-based techniques could be presented as an extension of the presentation on anecdotal recording. A thorough introduction to data-based techniques is provided by Kazdin in her discussion of collecting baseline data.

Kazdin, A. E. (1980). Behavior modification in applied settings. Homewood, IL: Dorsey Press.

Additional topics to include in Chapter One are teacher evaluation and retention. Also, information related to teacher stress and job satisfaction could easily be related to teacher decisioning and increased teacher effectiveness. Finally, Hunter's Clinical Supervision model for evaluating teaching effectiveness could be presented.

Hunter, M. (1973). Appraising teacher performance: One approach. The National Elementary Principal, 52, 62-63.

Discussion Questions

1. As a classroom teacher, you formulate the following instructional objective for your ninth grade English class:

   "Given a compound sentence, the student will diagram the sentence, correctly labeling all eight parts of speech."

   Relate this objective to Hunter's model. Which of the nine decisions have been made either implicitly or explicitly by the teacher during the formulation of this objective?

2. Dembo suggests that adequate instructional models should be diagnostic, prescriptive and normative. Which of the nine decisions that Hunter identifies as making up the teaching learning process contribute diagnostic, prescriptive and/or normative information?

3. As a sixth grade physical education teacher, you have a girl in your third period class who seems always to be fighting with other children. You don't know exactly what the dynamics of this behavior are, but it is really irritating you. Design a procedure of anecdotal recording for systematically observing this behavior. What information would you hope to gain from your anecdotal records?

4. Consider that you are a third grade teacher and want to teach multiplication. In order to plan your lesson what instructional decisions do you need to make? Formulate the questions you would ask. Be sure you relate them directly to the multiplication curriculum, your learner population and your teaching style.

Audiovisual Aids

Who Did What to Whom (Research Press, color, 1974, 16 min.).
Forty scenes in various settings illustrate the kinds of interactions that occur between people. Many of them are based on school-related problems, and provide excellent vehicles for developing decision-making skills in human relations.

Teacher Decision Making - Part 1 (MP 402, Camput Film Distributors, 1971, 30 min.). This film identifies the most important daily teaching decisions that are the foundation of learning efficiency and effectiveness.

Teachers Make a Difference (614-135V2, Association for Supervision and Curriculum Development, 10 min.). This video presents testimonials from the people who relate how they were inspired by their teachers. It provides an excellent motivational strategy.

FOLLOW-UP ACTIVITIES

1. Analyze Common Myths About Teaching

   Instructors can adapt this activity to group use by reproducing and distributing the questionnaires contained in Follow-up Activity Sheet 1-1. Each class member can then be requested to complete the questionnaire. Results of class responses can be informally tallied and discussed in terms of the impact of each belief on teaching behavior.

2. Thinking About Teaching Problems

   This activity can be readily adapted to a debate topic. One possibility is to have the class focus on instructors they currently have or have had in the past. Have them reflect on the following questions:

   - What problems has the teacher had?
   - Did the teacher realize that a problem existed?
   - What strategies did they use to solve the problem?

This activity could also be personalized to the individuals in a given class. They could be asked:

- What kinds of teaching problems do you anticipate?
- Why do you think these problems will arise?

3. Use Library Reference Sources to Identify Information About Teaching and Learning

This activity could be expanded and adapted as an out-of-class assignment, for either small groups or individuals. The assignment contained in Follow-up Activity Sheet 1-3 might be helpful for instructors who want to make this adaptation.

4. Analyze the Teaching-Learning Process

Instructors can distribute Follow-up Activity Sheet 1-4 which is based on the work of Madeline Hunter (1973). This activity requires that class members observe in a classroom while the teacher is presenting a lesson. They can then make anecdotal records and evaluate the lesson on a number of variables.

Additional Follow-up Activities

5. Observing Teacher Beliefs During Instruction

Organize the class into groups of four to six according to age level or subject matter area they plan to teach. Have each group generate an appropriate instructional objective. Then have the group role-play the actual teaching of the specified task while the remainder of the class observes. As the class observes, have them take notes on the teacher's assumptions or beliefs which can be implied from observing the lesson.

6. Study Beliefs About Teaching

Have all members of the class generate a list of beliefs that they hold in the areas of classroom management, discipline, relationships with students, instructional methods, and teaching materials. Then organize them in groups to compare their beliefs. Have them propose methods of testing or validating their beliefs with students in actual classroom situations.

MYTHS ABOUT TEACHING QUESTIONNAIRE

DIRECTIONS: Read each item and mark the response that best describes your belief.

	Strongly Agree	Not Sure	Strongly Disagree
1. A person needs to feel some pressure to be motivated to learn			
2. Children have a natural desire to learn			
3. Younger children need more structure than older children			
4. Competition is a great motivator			
5. Human intelligence is fixed by the time a child begins school			
6. Failure is helpful in motivating children			

CONDUCT A LIBRARY SEARCH

Following is a series of hypothetical beliefs that could influence instructional decisions:

- Boys are better at math than girls.
- Boys are more difficult to manage than girls.
- Discovery learning promotes higher achievement than didactic teaching strategies.
- Drug and suicide prevention programs greatly reduce the incidence of these problems.
- Teachers generally favor children who are bright and creative.

Have your group choose one of these beliefs, or generate another belief which you want to explore. Have each group member go to the library and locate a research article which investigates this topic. Each group member should then summarize the research article according to 1) author, 2) title, 3) journal, 4) purpose of study, 5) subjects, 6) procedures, 7) results, and 8) conclusions.

Your group will be reconvened during the next class meeting to share the research article summaries and answer the following questions:

1. Based on research findings, what conclusions can you draw with regard to your belief?

2. How could this information be utilized to influence instructional decisions?

TEACHING-LEARNING RATING FORM

DIRECTIONS: As you observe the teacher presenting the lesson, rate the teaching performance on variables 1 through 4. Then write anecdotal records for items 5 through 8.

VARIABLE	Definitely Yes			Definitely No	
1. Was the objective clear?	X	X	X	X	X
2. Did teaching focus on a learning target?	X	X	X	X	X
3. Was the difficulty level of the lesson appropriate?	X	X	X	X	X
4. Was the objective achieved?	X	X	X	X	X

5. What did the teacher do to facilitate learning?

6. What did the teacher do that interfered with learning?

7. What problems arose during the lesson and how were they handled?

8. What suggestions do you have for improving the lesson?

Adapted from: Hunter, M. A. (1973). Appraising teacher performance: One approach. The National Elementary Principal, 52, 62-63.

CHAPTER TWO

INTELLIGENCE AND COGNITIVE DEVELOPMENT

CHAPTER OBJECTIVES

Students mastering the content in Chapter Two will be able to:

• Identify the psychometric, Piagetian, and information-processing approaches to intelligence.

• Explain how the theory of intelligence a person adopts can influence intervention strategies designed to enhance intellectual development and academic achievement.

FOCUS QUESTIONS

1. Is intelligence a unitary trait or a composite of traits?

   Intelligence is viewed as the capacity or set of capacities that allows any individual to learn, to solve problems, and/or to interact successfully with the environment. For the most part, theories of intelligence have been viewed from one of two perspectives. The first takes the position that one general factor accounts for most of our mental ability. The second approach to intelligence takes the position that there are many different factors or aspects of human intelligence abilities as they relate to success in various subject areas. Depending on the perspective of the theorist, intelligence is considered either a single or multifactor trait.

2. How is intelligence measured?

   The most widely used measures of intelligence are the Revised Stanford-Binet and the Wechsler Intelligence Scale for Children-Revised (WISC-R). These tests are administered to a single student at a time by a trained examiner. Each test consists of a variety of items which sample several areas of ability. An individual student's performance on these items is then compared to the performance of other students the same age. Individually administered intelligence tests are most frequently used for making decisions about educational placement.

3. Are intelligence tests fair to all students?

   The issue of the fairness of intelligence tests has been debated for years. White students tend to score higher than black students, and middle-class students tend to score higher than lower-class students. Some critics argue that the poor performance on IQ tests by some black students stems from bias in the test items and administration procedures. Intelligence tests are also criticized for emphasizing verbal ability over other types of mental ability. Some teachers use intelligence test scores to label children as poor students. Also, intelligence tests are often a basis for discriminatory practices in schools, especially in the placement of poor and minority students. Educators as well as the courts disagree as to whether or not intelligence tests provide bias scores for minority students. Intelligence tests may not adequately measure the academic potential of minority-group children, but attempts at developing "culture-free" intelligence tests have not been successful.

4. Is intelligence fixed, or can it be changed?

There is considerable evidence that IQ test scores fluctuate widely during childhood and adolescence. This evidence speaks in favor of the theory that intelligence can be changed. Both the Head Start Program and the Follow Through Program were educational preschool interventions designed to increase the intelligence and academic performance of children from impoverished backgrounds. It is important to note, however, that students' IQ's and/or achievement gains diminished once they left the program. Although there were many benefits from these programs, the implication of these findings is that intelligence must be maintained once it is established.

5. Is intelligence determined by environment or heredity?

Although there is evidence that inheritance plays an important role in determining intelligence, there is also evidence that environmental factors play an important role. Authorities disagree on the extent to which they believe one or the other of these factors influence individual intelligence. It is impossible to determine the exact contribution that each of these factors makes because the environment begins to interact with heredity at the moment of conception.

6. According to Piaget, what are the major characteristics of children thinking at the preoperational, concrete, and formal operation stages?

The preoperational child has a difficult time with classification tasks and is capable of formulating primitive concepts. The preoperational child:

- is capable of manipulating symbols.
- does not have the ability to deal with problems that necessitate reversible thinking.
- cannot focus back and forth between details.
- has difficulty stating another person's point of view.
- focuses on the static aspect of an event rather than on the transformations from one state to another.
- sees some relationship between particular instances when there is none.

The concrete operations stage marks the beginning of operational thought. A child at concrete operations:

- acquires logical thought processes that can be applied to concrete problems.
- opts for logical decisions instead of the perceptual decisions of a preoperational child.

- is still unable to deal with abstract material such as hypotheses and verbal propositions.
- develops an awareness of the principles of conservation.
- ranks in order a series of objects.
- becomes more sociocentric in communication.
- takes another's point of view when requested.

At approximately 11 years of age, the child can use concrete operations to form more complex operations. The formal operator:

- formulates many alternative hypotheses in dealing with a problem.
- thinks abstractly.
- deals with statements or propositions that describe concrete data.
- accepts contrary-to-fact propositions.
- isolates individual factors and possible combinations of factors that may contribute to a solution or a problem.

7. What are the criticisms of Piaget's theory?

Although Piaget's theory has made important contributions toward the understanding of cognitive development, there are a number of criticisms of his theory. His critics argue that he has underestimated the intellectual abilities of preschool children and has overestimated the formal operational thinking of adolescents and adults. Also, he fails to explain in detail the changes in the structure of thinking. Finally, some critics argue that the sequencing from one stage to another may be only an artifact of the evaluation procedure Piaget used.

8. What instructional practices would Piaget recommend?

There are two major aspects of Piaget's theory which have implications for instructional practice. One is that children are active thinkers who construct their own understanding of the events in the world around them. This notion implies that the school curricula should involve students as active participants in the learning process rather than requiring them to absorb knowledge by passively listening to the teacher. The development of the open classroom which allows students to work on projects in different learning centers is one attempt to apply Piagetian concepts to instruction. The use of discovery learning which encourages students to acquire concepts on their own rather than by explanation from the teacher is another teaching strategy consistent with Piaget's theory of cognitive development. The classroom teacher must also be able to assess a child's level of cognitive development and determine the type of abilities the child needs to be able to understand the subject matter. A teaching strategy developed from Piaget's theory is to confront the child with other points of view contrary to the child's thinking. The confrontation strategy can take many forms including questions, demonstrations, and/or environmental manipulations.

9. How do neo-Piagetian theories modify Piaget's theory?

Fischer is a neo-Piagetian who places greater emphasis on the role of the environment in explaining cognitive development than Piaget did. Another neo-Piagetian researcher, Pascual-Leone, believes that the development of memory capacity is the major reason why children demonstrate different thinking at different ages. He believes that mental space and its growth is an alternative approach to explaining cognitive development. Case also uses the notion of mental space in formulating his theory of cognitive development, but reemphasizes that working memory is not the only constraint on the quality of children's thinking.

10. How do information-processing theorists criticize the psychometric approach to intelligence?

Information-processing theorists criticize the psychometricians by suggesting that there is more to intelligence than that which can be measured numerically. They maintain that one must also take into account the underlying mental processes that contribute to individual differences in intelligence.

11. How do information-processing theorists approach the study of intelligence?

The information-processing psychologists begin with the question "What are the basic psychological processes involved in solving a particular problem?" Next, these researchers attempt to propose a theory to explain how these processes are performed and executed, the sequence of the processes, the length of time needed to solve each problem, and which items are more difficult. Finally, they attempt to determine how individuals differ in the speed and accuracy of executing separate mental processes.

CHAPTER OUTLINE

I. ORIENTATION

    A. Focus Questions

II. THE PSYCHOMETRIC PERSPECTIVE

    A. The Composition of Intelligence
    B. Individual Intelligence Tests
    C. Uses of Intelligence Tests
    D. Some Misconceptions about Intelligence Tests
    E. Intelligence Test Bias and Fairness
    F. Educational Interventions to Increase Intelligence and Academic Performance

        1. A critique of compensatory education programs

III. THE PIAGETIAN PERSPECTIVE

    A. The Process of Cognitive Development

IV. PIAGET'S DEVELOPMENTAL STAGES

    A. Sensorimotor Stage (0-2 years)
    B. Preoperational Stage (2-7 years)
    C. Concrete Operations Stage (7-11 years)
    D. Formal Operations Stage (11 years and above)

V. CRITICISMS OF PIAGET'S THEORY

VI. IMPLICATIONS OF PIAGET'S THEORY FOR EDUCATION

    A. Teaching Strategy
    B. Discovery Learning
    C. Curriculum

VII. THE INFORMATION-PROCESSING PERSPECTIVE

    A. Neo-Piagetians
    B. Information Processing and Human Abilities

        1. Sternberg's triarchic theory of intelligence

VIII. THINKING ABOUT THE TEACHING-LEARNING MODEL

KEY TERMS

psychometric (p. 34)

information processing (p. 34)

intelligence (p. 35)

factor analysis (p. 36)

Structure of Intellect (p. 36)

contents (p. 36)

operations (p. 36)

products (p. 36)

mental age (p. 38)

intelligent quotient (IQ) (p. 39)

individual intelligence tests (p.39)

mentally retarded (p. 40)

gifted and talented (p. 40)

socioeconomic status (SES) (p. 43)

heritability (p. 45)

organization (p. 48)

adaptation (p. 48)

assimilation (p. 48)

accommodation (p. 48)

disequilibrium (p. 48)

equilibration (p. 49)

sensorimotor stage (p. 50)

object permanence (p. 50)

preoperational stage (p. 51)

reversibility (p. 51)

conservation (p. 52)

decenter (p. 53)

egocentrism (p. 53)

transductive reasoning (p. 54)

concrete operations stage (p. 54)

combinativity (p. 54)

associativity (p. 54)

identity (p. 55)

serializing (p. 56)

formal operations stage (p. 56)

hypothetico-deductive reasoning (p. 56)

propositional reasoning (p. 56)

combinatorial reasoning (p. 56)

open education (p. 60)

discovery learning (p. 61)

enactive (p. 62)

iconic (p. 62)

symbolic (p. 62)

CHAPTER GUIDELINES

Chapter Two begins by presenting several perspectives on the nature of intelligence. The psychometric approach is presented as one theory which attempts to identify the content and structure of mental abilities. Some proponents of the psychometric approach view intelligence as a single-factor trait. Others believe that intelligence is a multifactor trait. Guilford's model comforms to the multifactor theory of intelligence. He has identified 180 characteristics which he feels contribute to the intelligence construct.

Intelligence testing is discussed from an historical perspective beginning with the early work of Alfred Binet and the concept of mental age equivalents. The Stanford-Binet and the Weschler Scales are discussed as two types of individually administered tests which are often used for making educational placement decisions. Caution is advised for teachers in the interpretation of intelligence test scores. Factors which may affect the reliability and validity of test scores are presented.

Some common misconceptions concerning intelligence tests are dispelled. These include the fact the intelligence tests do not measure "innate" ability, and that they are not an exact indicator of all the mental abilities which a learner might possess. The changeable nature of I.Q. scores as well as their heavy reliance on verbal rather than other types of abilities is stressed.

Performance profiles of groups of students with various demographic characteristics are presented. Data indicating that white students and students from high socioeconomic backgrounds tend to score higher than minority students and students from low socioeconomic backgrounds are discussed. Content in Chapter Two expresses the prevailing opinion that intelligence tests may not adequately measure the potential of minority students. It acknowledges, however, that attempts to develop culture-free intelligence tests have not been successful.

Preschool programs designed to increase the intellectual development and academic performance of low socioeconomic students are discussed, along with Arthur Jensen's controversial theory of intelligence. He believes that members of low-SES groups have inherently lower conceptual ability than members of middle-SES groups.

Following the discussion on theories of intelligence, Piaget's theory of cognitive development is presented. Piaget's theory is recommended as a guide in the structuring and sequencing of subject matter in the curriculum. Teachers are encouraged to be conscious of the cognitive-developmental level of their students and to analyze tasks in the curriculum to determine the level of reasoning required for the successful completion of each task. Piaget's theory implies that teachers should use concrete learning experiences whenever possible and not move into abstract levels of thinking too quickly. Critics of Piaget question the validity of distinct stages of development. They believe he overestimated the ability of adolescents and adults to move into formal operational thinking. They also challenge his methodology.

Information processing is discussed as another theory of cognitive development. Proponents of this theory believe that children can be taught problem solving at an earlier age than Piaget's theory would predict. They disagree with Piaget's notion that each stage of development involves a totally new form of thinking. The information-processing approach emphasizes the processes and strategies which individuals employ when they engage in intelligent behavior. As a result of this focus, information processing is particularly useful in suggesting directions for training intelligent performance.

Finally, Sternberg's triarchic theory of intelligence is presented. It focuses on three different aspects of intelligence which are exercised in different domains. According to this theory, current intelligence tests measure only a small part of intelligent behavior.

Supplementary Materials

Instructors wishing to elaborate on the material presented in Chapter Two could demonstrate the administration of actual test items from one of the Wechsler scales or the Stanford-Binet. Such a demonstration could serve as the basis for illustrating the relationship between achievement and background experiences and various methods of measuring aptitude. Also, "hands-on" experience with IQ test items helps to dispel many of the myths that students may have regarding IQ measures.

Thorndike, R. L., Hagen, E. P., & Sattler, J. M. (1986). <u>Stanford-Binet Intelligence Scale</u> (4th ed.). Chicago: Riverside Publishing.

Weschler, D. <u>Weschler Adult Intelligence Scale</u> (1955). New York: Psychological Corporation.

Weschler, D. <u>Weschler Preschool and Primary Scale of Intelligence</u>. (1969). New York: Psychological Corporation.

Weschler, D. <u>Weschler Intelligence Scale for Children-Revised</u>. (1974). New York: Psychological Corporation.

In addition to the tests mentioned in Chapter Two, instructors might wish to expose the students to other measures of ability which are often used in school assessment and placement. One of these is the Peabody Picture Vocabulary Test-Revised which provides a quickly administered estimate of ability. Also, a group I.Q. test such as the Otis-Lennon Mental Ability Test could be used as could the Vineland Social Maturity Scale, which offers a measure of adaptive behavior.

Doll, E. (1965). <u>Vineland Social Maturity Scale</u>. Circle Pines, MN: American Guidance Service.

Dunn, L., & Dunn, L. (1981). <u>Peabody Picture Vocabulary Test-Revised</u>. Circle Pines, MN: American Guidance Service.

A resource which is useful in helping students understand conservation tasks as well as Piagetian interviewing and evaluation techniques is the <u>Concept Assessment Kit - Conservation</u> by Goldschmid and Bintler. The kit includes three standardized forms for measuring various conservation tasks. A manual is included which contains scoring procedures as well as normative data. Children of various ages can be tested and compared.

Goldschmid, M. L., & Bintler, P. <u>Concept Assessment Kit - Conservation</u>. San Diego, CA: Educational and Industrial Testing Service.

Another suggestion for supplementing material provided in the text is to provide concrete suggestions of how teachers might apply Piaget's theory to educational decision-making in their classrooms. Wadsworth is an excellent source for providing practical applications in both the math and reading content areas, as well as for expanding the presentation on Piaget's theory.

Wadsworth, B. J. (1989). <u>Piaget's theory of cognitive and affective development</u>. White Plains, NY: Longman.

Discussion Questions

1. Consider the stages of language development for a preschooler. First, the child learns to identify his cat. He calls him "kitty." Soon all cats are referred to as "kitty." Later the child sees a friend's pet rabbit. He says, "I want to hold the kitty." The friend replies, "That's not a kitty; it's a rabbit." Soon, the child visits a petting farm. He identifies the rabbits by name. How are the characteristics of assimilation and accommodation evident in this exchange?

2. Many professionals as well as lay persons feel that intelligence tests discriminate against low SES and minority students. How do you think schools would be changed if the practice of administering IQ tests was eliminated?

3. In an effort to standardize the school curriculum offered to children across various districts, many states have mandated Curriculum Guides. These guides specify exactly what material will be taught to children at each grade level and in each subject matter area. The purpose of Curriculum Guides is to insure that each child has an equal opportunity to be taught appropriate age- and grade-level skills. How do you think Piaget would respond to this practice?

4. One criticism of intelligence tests is that they depend too heavily on verbal skills. This could be because we live in a society that values and rewards these types of skills. Consider that you relocate in a culture whose livelihood depends on hunting. What skills would be valued in this new culture. How might you construct an "IQ" test to measure these skills?

5. Consider that you present ten-year-old students with the following word problem and monitor their performance as they work. Then you make a note of each child's ability to solve the problem correctly .

    "Each box of crayons has a dozen different colors.
    How many boxes of crayons would you have to
    buy to get 80 crayons?" How many crayons of
    each color would you have?

How would the psychometric perspective, the Piagetian perspective and the information processing perspective differ in their reactions to the children's responses? What questions would be of interest to proponents of each theoretical perspective?

Audiovisual Aids

Information Processing (MP32509, McGraw-Hill Films, 1965, 29 min.). This film examines and explains some of the information processing that occurs in a stimulus-rich, complex environment.

Piaget: Cognitive Development (MP2576, CR/McGraw-Hill Films, 1973, 20 min.). In this film, Piaget's maturational stages of development are contrasted with behavioristic learning theory and practices.

Intelligence: A Complex Concept (CR/McGraw-Hill Films, color, 1978, 20 min.). This film explores some of the varied definitions of intelligence, including Guilford's and Piaget's. The problems associated with testing are also discussed, including differences between individual and group tests.

Cognitive Development (CR/McGraw-Hill Films, color, 1973, 20 min.). This film describes both Piaget's position and behavioral positions on the development of cognitive ability.

Piaget's Developmental Theory: Conservation (Davidson Films, color, 1966, 28 min.). This film describes and demonstrates the development of logical intelligence in the preoperational, concrete, and formal operations stages. It includes suggested teaching programs.

Piaget's Developmental Theory: Formal Thought (Davidson Films, color, 1971, 33 min.) This film shows a variety of distribution, placement, and measurement activities to demonstrate the capacity of high school students to reason on a formal or concrete level and to discover whether their reasoning abilities evidence a transitional period.

Piaget on Piaget (Yale University Media Design Studio, color, 1979, 42 min.) This film depicts an interview with Piaget, in which his comments are interwoven with presentations of his classic research with children.

Memory (McGraw-Hill Films, color, 1980, 30 min.) This film introduces through a series of vignettes the short-term, long-term, and sensory memory of the brain, then concentrates on how to improve long-term memory. It shows methods for categorizing and referencing memory to facilitate fast, efficient recall, stressing that organization is the key to memory.

Memory: Fabrics of the Mind (Films for the Humanities and Sciences, color, 1980, 20 min.) This videotape examines various areas of research on memory and the brain. Included are the topics of different types of memory and their location, brain chemistry, the process of forgetting, and explanations for prodigious feats of memory.

FOLLOW-UP ACTIVITIES

1. Compare and Evaluate the Psychometric, Piagetian, and Information-Processing Perspectives of Intelligence

   Follow-up Activity 1 could be adapted to a group activity by dividing the class into three equal groups. Each group could then represent one of the perspectives on intelligence and present how psychologists from the perspective they choose would train and view the task. Some of the issues which might emerge from such a comparison are as follows:

Psychometric Perspective. These psychologists would be interested in knowing whether or not the student had the ability to deal with content at this level of abstraction. They would be very interested in a correct response or product. Also, they would want to know how the students' abilities in this area compared with others the same age. They would be likely to set up a standard teaching format and view success or failure as a function of aptitude and ability. Success would be contingent upon a correct answer.

Piagetian Perspective. Piagetians would be far more interested in how the student arrived at a solution to the problem and how his thinking progressed in terms of assimilation, disequilibrium, and accommodation. The way the student approached the problem would provide the Piagetian with an index of the level of cognitive development. The structure of the teaching task would be open ended with an emphasis on discovery learning and creativity.

Information-Processing Perspective. Information-processing psychologists would also be interested in how the student approaches the problem. Their concern, however, would be with the problem-solving strategies and reasoning processes the student employs in deciding how to approach the problem and execute the necessary steps for its solution. They would structure the teaching task so that the maximum number of strategies are given to assist the student in remembering the steps in the process.

2. Analyze a Piagetian Quotation

Instructors adapting Follow-up Activity 2 to group use would want to elicit from the class concepts that serve as the basis for Piagetian thinking. Piagetians, for example, might believe that:

- fast-paced, diadactic teaching interferes with the natural evolution of the student's cognitive structures.

- good teaching involves creating opportunities for new structures to develop, not just transmitting new structures.

- by forcing a child to learn too much too fast, inventiveness and creativity are stifled.

3. Assess a Child's Level of Cognitive Development

Instructors could easily adapt Follow-up Activity 3 to an out-of-class assignment by assigning the Piagetian classification experiment contained in Follow-up Activity Sheet 2-3. To do so, class members would need to make arrangements to interview four different children. During the interviews they could assess each individual child's ability to classify across two dimensions. Interview data could be recorded on a copy of Follow-up Activity Sheet 2-3. They could then compile their data in class by age level of child interviewed to see the shift in developmental level from the preoperational stage to the level of concrete operations.

4. Try a Piagetian Experiment

Follow-up Activity 4 could be adapted as an out-of-class assignment by having the class construct similar experiments to determine children's ability to conserve not only quantity but also numbers, weight and volume. The experiments could be conducted using students in grades kindergarten through five. Compiling the data in class would demonstrate the development of conservation abilities from the initial level of conserving numbers through the more advanced level of conserving volume. A clear pattern of development should emerge as student ages range from five to eleven.

Additional Follow-up Activities

5. Identify Children's Developmental Stages

Reproduce and distribute Follow-up Activity Sheet 2-5 to everyone in the class. Have them read each statement and determine which of Piaget's developmental stages is characteristic of the child's thinking.

Key: 1. b   2. a   3. b   4. c   5. a   6. b
      7. b   8. c   9. b

PIAGETIAN CLASSIFICATION EXPERIMENT

DIRECTIONS: Conduct the following experiment with four children between the ages of five and ten.

          Materials: A box containing 20 small blocks (beads, balls, or candies may be substituted). All 20 must vary only in color. Include 18 red ones and 2 green ones (any color may be substituted for red or green).

          Presentation: Show the child the box and ask the following series of questions. Say:

      #1: "In this box, which are there more of, wooden blocks" (or substitute appropriate classifier) "or red blocks?"

           Record answer. Then say:

      #2: "Are all the red ones made of wood?"

           Record answer. Then say:

      #3: "If I take away all the wooden beads, will there be any beads left?"

           Record answer. Then say:

      #4: "If I take away all the red ones will there be any left?"

Child 1

Age: years _____ months _____

Question #1 _____

Question #2 _____

Question #3 _____

Question #4 _____

Level of Cognitive Development _____

Child 2

Age: years _____ months _____

Question #1 _____

Question #2 _____

Question #3 _____

Question #4 _____

Level of Cognitive Development _____

Child 3

Age: years _____ months _____

Question #1 _____

Question #2 _____

Question #3 _____

Question #4 _____

Level of Cognitive Development _____

Child 4

Age: years _____ months _____

Question #1 _____

Question #2 _____

Question #3 _____

Question #4 _____

Level of Cognitive Development _____

PIAGET'S DEVELOPMENTAL STAGES

DIRECTIONS: Read each example below. Mark whether the child's thinking is characteristic of the:

a. Sensorimotor Stage

c. Concrete Operations Stage

b. Preoperation Stage

d. Formal Operations Stage

_____ 1. Tommy looks at his lunch plate and becomes angry because he wants another sandwich. His mother removes the plate and cuts the sandwich into four triangles. Tommy is perfectly satisfied.

_____ 2. Fred's mother has taken him to the doctor's office. He becomes bored with the waiting. She entertains him for a long time by letting him play with her keys. He drops them on the floor and she picks them up over and over again.

_____ 3. Jane is looking for a screwdriver to use in refastening a screw on her bicycle. She gets down the box of screwdrivers and tries one after another in random order.

_____ 4. Jane's brother comes along, and she asks his help in reattaching the screw. He notices that the screw has a Phillip's head. He pushes aside all the "slot" screwdrivers and begins to look for a Phillips screwdriver the same size as the head of the screw.

_____ 5. Allen is building a pinebox derby. He puts the weights on the front and measures the speed the derby travels. Then he conducts the same experiment with the weights in the middle and at the back.

_____ 6. Sue is watching a sad movie. A child dies. Sue starts crying and her mother asks, "What is wrong?" Sue does not know why she is crying.

_____ 7. You give Mary a box of buttons to occupy her time and tell her to sort them. Soon you return and discover that she has made neat piles of brown, black, white, red, yellow, and blue buttons.

_____ 8. Jack has lost his baseball cap. He remembers he had it when he came home from school. So, he goes back to check the kitchen where he got a snack, the homework desk and finally the bathroom, because he remembers that these are all places he has been since school was out.

_____ 9. You ask Ann what she is going to be when she grows up. She says that she is going to be a "daddy."

CHAPTER THREE

COGNITION, CULTURE, AND LANGUAGE

CHAPTER OBJECTIVES

Students mastering the content in Chapter Three will be able to:

- Modify instructional procedures based on different cognitive/learning styles of students.

- Develop culturally compatible classrooms.

- Enhance the language development of students.

FOCUS QUESTIONS

1. How can cognitive/learning style impact student learning?

   Cognitive style refers to consistent ways in which an individual responds to a wide range of perceptual and intellectual tasks. Cognitive styles tend to identify one element or dimension of learning with one of two polarities. Educators and psychologists became interested in the implications of cognitive style because they felt that students with a particular cognitive style might learn more efficiently in an instructional environment that was selected on the basis of these characteristics. In some cases they have used cognitive style instruments to assess learning style. The major focus of the research on learning styles is on an attempt to provide a specific instructional environment for a student that is based on the student's learning style.

2. Why do some divergent thinkers have difficulty in the classroom?

   Divergent thinking generates new ideas and solutions to problems that have more than one correct answer, whereas convergent thinking produces a well-determined answer to a routine problem. Students with excellent divergent thinking abilities often have difficulties in a classroom where the teacher emphasizes primarily convergent thinking activities. In addition, due to their learning styles divergent thinkers may be viewed by the teacher as troublemakers or difficult students because they approach learning tasks differently than other students.

   Teachers' cognitive styles may influence the way that they structure instructional tasks as well as how they motivate students. Students' cognitive styles, on the other hand, may influence how they learn most efficiently and how they can best be motivated.

3. What problems do students from different cultural backgrounds face when entering schools in the U.S.?

The typical North American classroom has certain distinct characteristics which may be incongruent with home experiences of students from different cultural backgrounds. Hilliard identified a number of possible problems that can arise from teachers not understanding cultural differences. The teacher can make mistakes in estimating a student's or a cultural group's academic potential which leads to a low expectation for success. Misunderstanding of cultural differences can lead teachers to misjudge their student's language abilities. The linguistic processes in a classroom which are related to instruction may differ from the oral discourse experienced at home by students from different cultural backgrounds. Misunderstanding of cultural differences can influence the quality of teacher-student interaction. Students' dominant cognitive styles may conflict with the cognitive style orientation of the teacher and/or classroom organization. Since most classrooms function according to field-independent cognitive style, culturally diverse groups which do not emphasize verbal/analytic problem solving may have some difficulty in school. Some students may have difficulty in the classroom, not because of their academic ability, but because the organization of the classroom environment is not consistent with their cultural experiences and styles of learning.

4. How can modifications in classroom organization, sociolinguistics, cognition, and motivation help culturally diverse students?

The KEEP program manipulated a number of instructional variables in an attempt to make the classroom more compatible with primary level Hawaiian students. It was discovered that the classroom needed to be organized into small groups which emphasize peer interaction. The children can work together in these groups on different language activities. Also, the wholistic/visual pattern is associated with certain aspect of cultural learning. This method emphasizes learning by doing rather than through verbal instructions. Third, an important linguistic process in the classroom is wait-time, or pauses in interaction. It appears that students from different cultures have different preferences for the way they respond. Finally, students seem to be more involved in academic tasks when teachers use school-based rather than individual praise and incentives.

5. What is the difference between Piaget's and Vygotsky's approach to cognitive development?

Piaget and Vygotsky differ in their perceptions of the relationship between development and learning. Piaget believes that development precedes learning whereas Vygotsky believes that learning precedes development. According to Piaget, an individual's developmental stage determines the quality of thinking. Instruction above this level will not produce learning. On the other hand, Vygotsky believes that developmental processes lag behind the learning processes. The zone of proximal development is the difference between an individual's current level of development and potential level of development.

6. According to Vygotsky, what role does social interaction have on language and cognitive development?

Vygotsky points out that children can often complete tasks with the help of peers or teachers that they can not accomplish working independently. Since Vygotsky believes that higher-level thinking develops best in social contexts, he encourages learning situations where teachers, parents, and more capable peers interact directly with students who are at lower levels of thinking.

7. How does Krashen's approach to language acquisition differ from traditional approaches?

The natural or interactional approach to second language acquisition proposed by Krashen emphasizes interesting and relevant subject matter in low-anxiety classroom environments. He believes that acquisition is subconscious and is developed through natural communication where the emphasis is on meaning. Learning occurs through conscious study of the formal aspect of the language. Krashen believes that the teacher does not have to focus on formal instruction in the target language. And, although Krashen believes that there is a role for error correction in language acquisition, he doesn't believe error correction is an important factor in learning a language.

8. What are the issues involved in developing bilingual rather than English-only language programs?

There is an increasing number of students entering school in the U.S. whose primary language is not English. Proponents of bilingual education feel that for schools to promote maximum student learning they must present instruction in the student's primary language. Many educators, however, are opposed to bilingual education because they believe students would learn English more rapidly if they spent more time exposed to the language. Other educators have concerns regarding the role of minority groups in society. They fear that cultural groups will retain their primary language and not assimilate into American culture. Also, there is concern that immigrants will be unwilling to speak the English language. Others believe that if individuals are allowed to speak their native language in school, it will interfere with their learning English and cause confusion in their thinking. There is no evidence, however, that bilingualism interferes with performance or thinking in either language. In fact, bilingual education increases achievement in areas other than the language studied.

CHAPTER OUTLINE

  I. ORIENTATION

   A. Focus Questions

 II. COGNITIVE/LEARNING STYLES

   A. Conceptual Tempo
   B. Field-Independent/Field-Dependent
   C. Hemisphericity: Left Brain Versus Right Brain Processing

KEY TERMS

cognition (p. 77)	field-independent (p. 83)
culture (p. 77)	field-dependent (p. 83)
cognitive style (p. 77)	hemisphericity (p. 86)
multicultural education (p. 77)	creativity (p. 87)
sociolinguistics (p. 77)	convergent thinking (p. 87)
learning style (p. 78)	divergent thinking (p. 87)
conceptual tempo (p. 81)	aptitude by treatment interaction (ATI) (p. 89)
impulsive (p. 81)	Nonstandard English (p. 94)
reflective (p. 81)	wait-time (p. 101)

imitation (p. 102)

reinforcement (p. 102)

zone of proximal development (p. 102)

i + 1 (p. 103)

motherese (p. 105)

bilingual education (p. 107)

CHAPTER GUIDELINES

Chapter Three discusses aspects of cognitive styles which can influence student learning. The controversy over whether or not educators should make sharp distinctions between the functioning of the two parts of the brain is discussed. The association between divergent thinking and creativity is discussed along with the tendency of teachers to emphasize convergent thinking. Using student preferences for determining methods of instruction is pointed out as a procedure which is not always appropriate.

The incongruity between school learning environments and the learning experiences in the homes of many cultural groups is presented. The impact of recent increases in immigration and the legal statutes mandating the education of illegal immigrants is discussed along with the effect of cultural factors on achievement and motivation patterns. Teachers are encouraged to consider cultural diversity and resist the tendency to misinterpret the academic potential, language ability, and classroom behavior of minority students. Finally, cultural patterns of strengths and weaknesses on various tests of mental ability are discussed.

The impact of socialization practices on cognitive style is discussed. Cognition, classroom organization, sociolinguistics, and motivation are presented as factors that need to be considered in developing culturally compatible classrooms.

The theories of Piaget, Vygotsky, and Krashen are summarized. The controversy over whether learning precedes development or development precedes learning is discussed. Also, discussed is Krashen's position on language acquisition, which emphasizes language comprehension over language fluency and grammatical accuracy. Finally, the lack of evidence that bilingual education interferes with language proficiency or thinking in either language is emphasized.

Supplementary Material

Instructors wishing to elaborate on the material in Chapter Three could provide more information on the models of ability groupings which are common in schools and how these school practices affect low socioeconomic and minority students. The interaction between ability grouping and segregation could be presented. Also of interest would be a discussion of grouping students according to their performance in other areas such as cognitive style.

Models of ability grouping

- **Between-class ability grouping.** Students are scheduled for different courses of study (i.e., algebra or general math) based on ability.

- **Regrouping.** Students within a grade level are grouped in only one or two subjects such as reading and math.

- **Joplin Plan.** Students are grouped in selected subject matter areas, but they are regrouped across grade levels depending on achievement test scores.

- **Within-class ability groupings.** Small homogeneous groups are formed within each classroom for selected subjects.

Research on ability grouping shows that between-class ability grouping is not justified. The high achievers do only slightly better and the lower group do considerably worse. Regrouping in the same grade levels and across different grade levels (Joplin Plan) is somewhat successful. Teachers must insure however, that grouping is based on performance ability rather than IQ and that appropriate instructional materials are available even if they need to be provided at a different grade level. Within-class grouping can only be justified by research results for the mathematics curriculum in upper elementary grades.

For more detailed information on ability groups consult the research contributions of Slavin.

Slavin, R. E. (1987). Grouping for instruction in the elementary school. Educational Psychology, 22, 109-127.

Slavin, R. E. (in press). Grouping for instruction: Equity and effectiveness. Equity and excellence.

Court cases which have shaped educational policy for minority students could also be presented as a means of elaborating on the material in Chapter Three.

SUMMARY OF LITIGATION AFFECTING MINORITY AND LOW SES STUDENTS

Date	Case	Major Effect
1954	Brown v. the Board of Education of Topeka	Decided that segregation violates the Fourteenth Ammendment to Constitution. Prohibits schools from blocking program access to minority students.

1972	Larry P. v. Riles	Ruled that intelligence tests discriminate against black learners and may not be used to classify them as mentally retarded.
1973	Diana v. California State Board of Education	Ruled that intelligence testing discriminates against non-English speaking children. Required that these children be tested in their native language using unbiased instruments.
1979	Mattie T. v. Halladay	Required that handicapped children be educated in the least restrictive learning environment. Reiterated that placements must be based on nonbiased testing.

Instructors who want to expand the text material on hemisphericity can refer students to Zenhausern's (1982) article, "Rights and Lefts and How They Learn." After reading the article students can be asked to discuss how this author's ideas could be used to change the curriculum for preschool and primary-aged students.

Zehausen, R. (1982). Rights and lefts and how they learn. Early Years, 57(2), 67.

An additional topic which instructors could present in Chapter Three is psychological type. Discussion could begin by introducing psychological type as a learning style variable. Tests for determining psychological type are available for both children and adults. The tests type individuals as one of four basic psychological types. A discussion could entertain possible implications for students and teachers who manifest the various psychological type. The psychological types covered on the type indicator tests are:

- introvert - extrovert
- intuitive - sensor
- thinking - perceiving
- judgmental - perceptive

Meyers, I. B., & Briggs, K. C. (1987). Myers-Briggs type indicator for children. Palo Alto, CA: Consulting Psychologist Press.

Murphy, E., & Meisgeier, C. (1987). Murphy-Meisgeier type indicator for children. Palo Alto, CA: Consulting Psychologists Press.

Discussion Questions

1. As a seventh grade math teacher you have three students who are rushing through the computation problems on their math tests. Working too quickly is causing these students to commit careless errors, and their working habits are affecting their grades. You think that these students fit Kagan's definition of having an impulsive conceptual tempo. What instructional and classroom management

strategies might you employ to slow them down and improve the accuracy of their responses?

2. According to the text, field-independent students are more inclined to internalize and create the structure needed for organizing and learning new material. Field dependent students are more likely to need the material structured for them. What would be the difference in the way students with these two cognitive styles would differ in their reaction to Discovery Learning?

3. Labov encourages educators to consider how much of our standard English is useful and functional before we impose our linguistic style on students who speak non-standard English. Consider then that you are a teacher of black high school students. Structure two different curricula for your ninth grade English classes. One curriculum has as its objective teaching basic standard English skills. The other seeks to teach the students to analyze, generalize, and communicate using non-standard English. What might some of the outcomes and results of these two programs be?

4. According to the text, some Indian cultures structure learning so that children practice tasks independently, then demonstrate these tasks for the adult when they feel they have practiced sufficiently for mastery. Because of this cultural phenomenon many of the Indian children are embarrassed by school practices that require students to respond orally to teacher questions before they feel they have mastered the skill. Knowing this, how could a seventh grade teacher structure and evaluate an objective for "having students recite the Declaration of Independence?"

5. Consider a cultural minority group that is prevalent in your geographic region. Do students in this group evidence any particular learning preferences or styles of which you are aware? Can you think of strategies for observing in these cultures which might provide cultural information that has implications for educational practices?

6. Typically kindergarten students are given a reading readiness test. How might Piaget and Vygotsky differ in the way they would interpret the results of these tests and in the way they would structure subsequent instructional activities.

7. Compare what Labor has to say about teaching students using non-standard English with what Krashen has to say about methods for second language acquisition. What are the similarities in their reasoning with regard to helping students use language for the purposes of communication and concept development?

8. Thus far, bilingual education has largely been confined to Spanish-speaking students. Some metropolitan school districts, however, have students who speak ten or fifteen different native languages. What are some of the educational implications for this linguistic diversity on the concept of bilingual education and ESL.

9. Schools have often been accused of teaching and perpetuating the middle-class culture. What do you see as the role of the school in helping students from different cultural backgrounds learn and appreciate their own cultures?

10. What are the differences in educational philosophy which underlie bilingual education as apposed to ESL programs?

Audiovisual Aids

Cultural Illiteracy (VC 25/26, Films for the Humanities and Sciences, 1988, 28 min.). E. D. Hirsch defines cultural literacy as familarity with the common knowledge literate Americans take for granted and ascribes teenage ignorance to reading instruction that has stressed skills over content.

What's the Difference Being Different? (Research Press, color, 19 min.). This film demonstrates how a multicultural program can be implemented in a school system.

Race, Intelligence and Education (Time-Life Films, color, 1975, 53 min.). Professor H. J. Eysenck presents his theory that heredity largely influences intelligence. Six other scientists discuss their controversial ideas as well as the oppositional views of other American psychologists.

Language Development (CRM/McGraw-Hill Films, color, 1975, 20 min.). Based on recent studies of language acquisition, this film notes that children worldwide progress through the same sequence of language stages at the same rate. The film includes a discussion of David Pumack's study of chimpanzees.

Cognition (Harper & Row, color, 1975, 24 min.). The development of perception, memory, evaluation, and reasoning from birth through adolescence is examined. The film describes each of Piaget's four cognitive stages of development.

FOLLOW-UP ACTIVITIES

1. Recognize Learning Styles

   Instructors can expand on Follow-up Activity 1 by reproducing and distributing several copies of the Teaching Styles Evaluation Form which is included in Follow-up Activity Sheet 3-1. The class can then evaluate each of their university instructors on the Field-Dependent Field-Independent variables. Subsequent class discussion could then center around individual preferences of class members for instructors who demonstrate one or the other of these learning styles.

2. Identify Differences in Learning Styles

   Instructors can adapt Follow-up Activity 2 to an out-of-class assignment by having the class observe in a classroom and complete the grid provided in Follow-up

Activity Sheet 3-2. Observations can be followed by a class discussion on how teachers are likely to respond to these behavior patterns.

3. Debate the Value of Bilingualism

    Instructors who have the class debate the value of bilingualism might expect some of the following responses:

    Pros

    -   A second language is a valuable asset and definitely should be encouraged by the schools.
    -   In many other societies people speak several languages; it is only in America that we encourage monolingualism.
    -   Preserving the native language helps the individual preserve a cultural referent and provides a healthy identity.

    Cons

    -   The student must be proficient in English to compete in the American economic sector.
    -   Despite multilingual citizens most countries have a native language which society uses in education and business.
    -   Trying to offer bilingual education is beyond the scope and ability of the school.

4. Debate the Best Approach to Cultural Literacy

    Instructors who have the class debate the best approach to cultural literacy might expect some of the following responses:

    Pros

    -   Cultural literacy is necessary to promote patriotism.
    -   Cultural literacy is a desirable condition for developing an appreciation of democracy and individual freedoms.
    -   It is the personal responsibility of individuals to learn about the culture in which they live.
    -   People who understand a culture can function more productively in that culture.
    -   By failing to learn the majority American culture, minority group members will make many of the mistakes in judging others which have been made toward them.

    Cons

    -   Being culturally literate doesn't mean being literate in the American culture.
    -   By maintaining pride and knowledge of cultural heritage, individuals develop self-respect and a sense of positive identity.
    -   Cultural literacy is an attempt to make everyone conform to white, middle-class standards.

- An overemphasis on the American culture devalues the individual heritage which all Americans have as a result of the fact that all except native American Indians were immigrants.

5. Evaluate the Benefits of Culturally Congruent Classrooms

In an evaluation of the benefits of culturally congruent classrooms, instructors might present the culturally congruent classroom as one in which the student is able to make a smooth transition from home to school. On the other hand these classrooms do not promote the concept of culturally diversity. They do not require students to adapt to the demands of a new environment. It is questionable whether or not culturally congruent classrooms prepare the student for future learning experiences and assimilation into the culture at large.

Additional Follow-up Activities

6. Administer the Embedded Figures Test

As an additional follow-up activity, instructors can administer the Embedded Figures Test (Witkin, Altman, Raskin, & Harp, 1971) to perspective teachers in their classroom. This is a pencil and paper test which can be independently completed by college-age students. The tests can be used for rating individuals on the field-dependent/field-independent variable. The test is available through the Consulting Psychologists Press in Palo Alto, California.

7. Evaluate Teaching Strategies for Culturally Diverse Classrooms

Follow-up Activity Sheet 3-7 presents several teaching strategies which might be used in a culturally diverse classroom. Have each student evaluate the value of each of the strategies as an out-of-class assignment. Then discuss responses during class time.

TEACHING STYLES RATING FORM

DIRECTIONS: During the next week observe the teaching styles of the teachers in each of your college classes. At the end of the rate each instructor on each of the variables of cognitive style listed below. Which of your instructors exhibit Field-Independent versus Field-Dependent teaching styles. Based on your experience with these instructors, which teaching style seems most suited to your individual learning style?

Field Independent	Never	Seldom	Sometimes	Often	Always
1. Prefers teaching situations that allow interaction and discussion with students.	X	X	X	X	X
2. Uses questions to check on student learning following instruction.	X	X	X	X	X
3. Uses student-centered activities	X	X	X	X	X
4. Viewed by students as one who teaches facts.	X	X	X	X	X
5. Provides less feedback; avoids negative evaluation.	X	X	X	X	X
6. Strong in establishing a warm and personal learning environment.	X	X	X	X	X

Follow-up Activity Sheet 3-1 (Cont.)

Field-Dependent	Never	Seldom	Sometimes	Often	Always
1. Prefers impersonal teaching situations such as lectures; emphasizes cognitive aspect of instruction.	X	X	X	X	X
2. Uses questions to introduce topics and following student answers.	X	X	X	X	X
3. Uses teacher-organized learning situation.	X	X	X	X	X
4. Viewed by students as encouraging them to teach principles.	X	X	X	X	X
5. Gives corrective feedback; uses negative evaluation.	X	X	X	X	X
6. Strong in organizing and guiding student learning.	X	X	X	X	X

Adapted from: Garger, S., & Guild, P. (1984). Learning styles: The crucial differences. Curriculum Review, 23.

Follow-up Activity Sheet 3-2

IDENTIFYING LEARNING STYLES

DIRECTIONS: Observe the students in a public school classroom. Identify a student who exhibits each of the following behavioral extremes. Report the student's behavior and the teacher's reaction to the behavior on the grid provided below.

Impulsive	Reflective
Student Behavior: _____ _____ _____	Student Behavior: _____ _____ _____
Short Attention Span Student Behavior: _____ _____ _____	**Long Attention Span** Student Behavior: _____ _____ _____
Resistance to Change Student Behavior: _____ _____ _____	**Flexibility** Student Behavior: _____ _____ _____

EVALUATE TEACHING STRATEGIES FOR
CULTURALLY DIVERSE CLASSROOMS

DIRECTIONS: Following are five teaching strategies which could hypothetically be used in a culturally diverse classroom. Read each strategy and respond as to whether or not you think that it would be an appropriate and effective strategy. Give your reasons.

1. Ms. Red teaches in a junior high that has students from a wide range of socioeconomic levels. In an effort to meet the needs of all the learners, ability groups are formed at each grade level, by each subject matter area. As students change classes, they may be in an advanced group for math and a lower group for English. Still, most of the lower groups seem to be filled by low SES students.

2. Mr. Green is a P.E. teacher in a high school that is controlled for racial balance. Half of his students are black and half are white. He never lets them choose sides for in-class competition because he is afraid all the blacks will end up on one team and all the whites will end up on the other.

3. Ms. Brown teaches art in a typical urban "melting pot" elementary school. She has students from oriental, black, caucasian and hispanic extraction. She has considered teaching a unit on "Art of the World," but she is afraid if she mentions various cultures or countries of origin that she will offend some students or make them self-conscious.

4. Mr. White teaches in a school which serves numerous oriental immigrants. In fact, 13 different oriental languages are spoken by children in the school. Some of the children have been here from birth and are completely bilingual. Others seem to know little English. He has decided to use a peer teaching strategy in which he pairs two children who speak the same language. One of the children is fluent in English. The other one he suspects is not, but the two children speak the same language at home.

5. Ms. Black teaches in a largely hispanic school. Some students are Mexican Americans whose parents have been here for several generations. Others have recently come from Mexico. Still others are from other countries in Central and South America. Some are from Puerto Rico and she even has two Cuban children. She is very conscientious in teaching Latin music, art, and folklore. She is relieved that her students are all from the hispanic culture and she does not have to worry about competing or conflicting cultural values or mores.

CHAPTER FOUR

PERSONAL AND SOCIAL DEVELOPMENT

CHAPTER OBJECTIVES

Students mastering the content in Chapter Four will be able to:

- Use Erikson's theory of personal and social development to explain students' identity formation.

- Reduce sex-role stereotyping in the classroom.

- Explain how different child-rearing practices influence students' behavior.

- Identify child abuse and neglect.

- Identify warning signs for possible suicide.

- Interact with students facing family transitions.

- Provide guidelines to parents who want to monitor their children's television viewing.

FOCUS QUESTIONS

1. How do parents, teachers, and friends contribute to the identity development of an individual?

   The critical question that adolescents must resolve is "Who am I?" Children enter adolescence in a diffuse state. They are not sure of their attitudes, beliefs, and values. During this period, they experience diverse situations, meet many people, experiment with various identities, and begin to integrate their previous and present identities into a meaningful sense of self. As adolescents develop and have greater interpersonal, work, and educational experiences through a network of parents, friends, and teachers, they may begin to reflect on the kinds of long-term commitments that can be made. Parents, teachers, and friends can also be helpful in decisionmaking about future careers and educational options.

2. How does the psychosocial development of a parent influence a child's or adolescent's development?

   In order for parents to influence their children positively it is important that they have achieved positive resolutions in their own psychosocial stages of development. Past experiences influence the ways in which they solve their current developmental crises. Parents of school-age children fall into the developmental stages of intimacy and generativity. Hopefully, they have become individuals who trust others, feel a sense of autonomy, are willing to take initiative and have a good sense of their abilities and beliefs. These emotional and attitudinal accomplishments will enhance their parenting skills and help them to serve as a positive influence on their children.

3. How do socialization experiences influence different behavior for males and females?

Most psychologists and sociologists view gender differences in terms of role training and social expectations. As children grow, they learn "appropriate" male and female behaviors from family members, teachers, friends, television, and books. This learning often emphasizes that the female-male relationship is not equal and that each sex has certain gender-related roles. A number of investigations identify differences in socialization experiences that may account for differences in achievement and behavior. Dowling traces the socialization pattern of boys and girls and suggests that girls are trained into dependency while boys are trained out of it. This form of psychological dependence is a major factor preventing women from achieving at the level of their potential. Research findings indicate that bright women have problems with self-confidence and that they consistently underestimate their own ability. In general, females are more likely than males to use lack of ability as an explanation for their failures. Also, research on the college level indicates that some women actually desire to avoid achievement. In regard to personality differences, girls are generally more dependent and have a higher degree of anxiety, whereas boys are more aggressive and have higher expectations of success.

4. How can teacher expectation and interaction with males and females influence their motivation and achievement?

Many educators believe that a combination of courses, materials, and student-teacher interactions make the majority of female students passive, shy and dependent but provide male students with learning experiences that help them become self-assured, competitive, and independent. Although teachers may not be the major source of sex-role stereotypes, they do not play an active role in changing them or providing boys and girls with the types of information that might lead them to change their sex-stereotyped beliefs. As a result, teachers passively reinforce the sex-typed academic and career decisions made by their students that contribute to the differences in the levels of educational attainment achieved by males and females. Teachers need to help children become more aware of sex-role stereotyping and of the variety of forces that influence attitudes, thinking, and behavior so that they increase motivation and achievement for both boys and girls.

5. Why do most attempts to change students' self-concepts fail?

As one ascends the self-concept hierarchy, self-concept depends increasingly on specific situations and thus becomes less stable. Many special programs have been developed by schools to improve students' self-concepts but have failed to demonstrate any change. Two of the major problems are the weak intervention programs and the poor relationship between the intended goals of the intervention and the specific dimensions of the self-concept being evaluated.

6. What factors in a school or classroom contribute to students' self-concepts?

One factor which contributes to students' self-concepts is teacher behavior. The teacher can exert considerable influence on the direction of a child's self-concept by establishing a positive learning environment and by communicating effectively with students in the classroom. An important point to remember is that a student's concept of ability develops mainly from performance on classroom tasks; the teacher can enhance the self-concept of ability by helping students to select learning objectives according to their abilities. Another important factor in school experience that can have a strong effect on self-esteem is the school setting. The impact of school transition is different for boys, who rely less on "looks" as a factor in their total evaluation of themselves.

7. How do parents' child-rearing styles influence their children's social behavior?

Baumrind demonstrated how different parenting styles influence the social/personality development of children. She identified three categories of parenting styles: 1) the authoritarian, 2) the permissive, and 3) the authoritative. Authoritarian parents attempt to control their children's behavior and attitudes to conform to strict rules of conduct. Their children are more discontented, withdrawn and distrustful. Permissive parents make few demands on their children, allowing them to regulate their own behavior. Their children are the least self-reliant, explorative, and self-controlled. Authoritative parents try to direct their childrens' activities by establishing firm rules and standards but are willing to discuss the reasons behind their regulations. These children are the most self-reliant, self-controlled, explorative, and contented.

8. What type of parent is likely to abuse his or her child?

No one type of parent is more likely than another type of parent to abuse his or her child. Many individuals incorrectly believe that child abusers come from some particular type of background. The fact is that child abusers come from all religious, ethnic, occupational, and socioeconomic groups. Furthermore, many child abusers were themselves abused as children. Researchers have found that certain family and/or personal problems of mothers and fathers can be an important determinant in child abuse.

9. How can a teacher deal with students exhibiting stress?

An important factor for teachers to consider is that children do not deal with stress as well as adults. One of the most common strategies for reducing stress is alleviating its symptoms. In this regard, relaxation techniques have been successful in decreasing certain measures of anxiety. If a student's stress reaches a point that it can't simply be alleviated by rest or relaxation, a teacher needs to be able to recognize these problems and seek additional help from parents, knowledgeable school staff, and student-centered programs.

10. How can divorce impact students of different developmental ages?

It is difficult to predict how a specific child or adolescent will respond to parental separation or divorce. It does not appear that there is a "good time" for a divorce since it affects children at all ages. Wallerstein and Kelly provided information on some common responses to divorce that are related to the developmental level of the child. It must be noted however that not all children responded in this manner:

- Preschool children are likely to regress in an area of recent achievement such as toilet training, dressing, and going to school. They fear routine separation and are irritable and demanding.

- Children between five and eight years of age cry a great deal and are preoccupied with feelings of rejection. The school performance of these children may decline.

- Children between 9 and 12 years of age tend to be angry, particularly at the parent they see as causing the divorce. They grieve, are anxious and lonely, and some also have some academic problems.

- Adolescents, who are already experiencing their own developmental difficulties, acquire additional problems with the separation. They become anxious as they realize their parents are not perfect and are concerned with their own futures, and their own sexual and marital failure. Finally, they tend to disengage from their families and seek support from peers and other significant adults.

11. How can a teacher help families of latchkey children?

Schools and communities are making attempts to help latchkey children and their families deal with this problem. Teachers can play an important role by listening to students' concerns and providing information about personal safety. In addition, teachers can advise parents about how to monitor students' homework and television viewing. These steps can be helpful in assuring that latchkey children attain normal academic progress.

CHAPTER OUTLINE

I. ORIENTATION

    A. Focus Questions

II. ERIKSON'S THEORY OF PERSONAL AND SOCIAL DEVELOPMENT

    A. Basic Trust versus Mistrust
    B. Autonomy versus Shame and Doubt
    C. Initiative versus Guilt
    D. Industry versus Inferiority
    E. Identity versus Identity Confusion

        1. Marcia's identity statuses

    F. Intimacy versus Isolation
    G. Generativity versus Stagnation
    H. Ego Identity versus Despair
    I. Gender Differences in Identity

III. IMPLICATIONS OF ERICKSON'S THEORY FOR EDUCATION

IV. GENDER DIFFERENCES

    A. The Development of Sex-role Stereotyping
    B. Androgyny
    C. Aptitude and Achievement Differences
    D. Mathematics Achievement
    E. Reading Achievement
    F. Personality and Social Differences
    G. The School's Response to Gender Differences

V. SELF-CONCEPT

    A. Self-concept and Achievement
    B. Physical Growth and Development

        1. The impact of others
        2. Rate of development

    C. School Experiences

VI. SOCIALIZATION AND THE FAMILY

    A. Child-rearing Practices
    B. Child Abuse and Neglect

        1. Child sexual abuse

    C. Student Stress

        1. Controlling stress through relaxation
        2. Suicide

    D. Maternal Employment
    E. Divorce

        1. Implications for teaching

    F. Latchkey Children

VII. TELEVISION AS A SOCIALIZATION AGENT

VIII. THINKING ABOUT THE TEACHING-LEARNING MODEL

KEY TERMS

psychosocial crises (p. 119)   identity diffusion (p. 123)

psychosocial moratorium (p. 122)   identity moratorium (p. 123) identity foreclosure (p. 124)

identity achievement (p. 124)

androgyny (p. 129)

self-concept (p. 138)

self-esteem (p. 138)

self-fulfilling prophecy (p. 142)

anorexia nervosa (p. 143)

puberty (p. 144)

authoritarian parenting style (p. 146)

permissive parenting style (p. 146)

authoritative parenting style (p. 146)

stress (p. 150)

anxiety (p. 150)

latchkey children (p. 157)

prosocial behavior (p. 158)

CHAPTER GUIDELINES

Chapter Eight begins with a summary of Erikson's eight major psychosocial crises. The teacher's role in helping children achieve initiative and industry is discussed. The need of the individual to resolve each of the crises is emphasized.

Research on gender differences is presented. The importance of socialization and classroom practices in developing gender differences and sex-role stereotypes is discussed.

Self-concept is presented as a multidimensional construct which embodies the ideas children have about themselves and the value they place on their behavior. Teachers are encouraged to refer to specific rather than general types of self-concepts and to resist the temptation to assume that children from poverty backgrounds have a poor self-concept. The poor results of programs designed to change self-concept are discussed along with the tendency toward underachievement and school failure of students with poor self-concepts. Finally, the relationship between physical development and self-concept is discussed.

The impact of differing parenting styles on social and personality development is presented. The implications of such diverse factors as child abuse and neglect, stress, maternal employment, and divorce on child development are considered. Teachers are alerted to the warning signs of suicide, as well as to situations in which they can be falsely accused of unprofessional conduct.

Supplementary Material

To expand on the textbook presentation of Erikson's theory of Psychosocial Development, instructors can introduce the principal of Epigenesis. The epigentic principle is central to Erickson's ideas concerning crisis resolution and the evolution of development from one developmental stage to another. The principal was borrowed from the biological concept that all growing things have a plan or growth pattern. From this wholistic pattern, specific parts emerge on a predetermined, hierarchical pattern. All are parts which are necessary to create a functioning whole.

The theory of Harry Stack Sullivan could also be used to supplement Erickson's theory. Sullivan's ideas are particularly relevant to Erickson's stages of Intimacy versus Isolation and Identity versus Identity Confusion. Sullivan believes that a prime human need is fulfilled by establishing secure interpersonal relationships. Adolescents not only need to establish intimate relationships but also need to attain sexual gratification. A major task of adolescence is to develop the interpersonal relationship and communication skills necessary to establish intimacy.

Erikson, E. (1968). Identity youth and crisis. New York: Norton.

Sullivan, H. S. (1953). Interpersonal theory of psychiatry. New York: Norton.

A more contemporary view of Erikson's ideas could be presented in a discussion of mid-life crisis and its relevance to the increasing emphasis placed on psychology and education across the individual's life span. Students who would like more information on this topic could be referred to Gail Sheehy's book Passages.

Sheehy, G. (1977). Passages. New York: Bantam.

The textbook section on gender differences can be supplemented by Maccoby and Jacklin's book, which reviews research on gender differences. According to their findings, there are only four areas of difference which cannot be explained by culture or socialization experiences. These are:

- Females demonstrate greater verbal aptitude than males.
- Males demonstrate greater visual-spatial aptitudes than females.
- Males demonstrate greater mathematical aptitude than females.
- Males evidence more physical and verbal aggression than females.

Maccoby, E. E., & Jacklin, C. N. (1974). The psychology of sex differences. Stanford, CA: Stanford University Press.

A recent article by Marsh could serve as the basis for expanding the textbook discussion of self-concept and self-esteem. This article maintains that bright students develop a healthier self-concept if they are "big-fish-in-little-ponds." Some of the research conclusions drawn are as follows:

- When researchers control for ability, students earn higher grades in lower-ability schools.
- When researchers control for ability, students in lower-ability groups have a more positive self-concept than students in higher-ability groups.
- Academic self-concept has an affect on subsequent performance in school that cannot be explained by either academic ability or previous school performance.

Marsh, H. W. (1987). The big-fish-little-pond effect on academic self-concept. Journal of Educational Psychology, 79, 280-295.

Another excellent source for expanding the textbook material on self-concept is a 1976 article by Klinger and McNelly. They divided a Boy Scout troop into competitive groups of four members each. Then they assigned captains to serve in the leadership role. Some of the leaders would have been chosen anyway, but a number of leaders were chosen from among boys who traditionally served in follower roles. Through subsequent interviews and observations, they determined that boys who were accustomed to leadership performed well as team captains. They were comfortable and enjoyed the competitive activities. The boys who had traditionally been followers were made uncomfortable and anxious by the leadership position. The authors concluded from the study that individuals develop a well-established self-concept with regard to their leader-follower status. Changing this status creates discomfort even when the leadership role is an attractive one.

Klinger, E., & McNelly, F. (1976). Self-status and performance of pre-adolescent boys carrying out leadership roles inconsistent with their social status. Child Development, 47, 126-137.

The textbook discussion of the eating disorder of anorexia nervosa can be elaborated by presenting information on bulimia and obesity. These are three increasingly common disorders which occur in adolescence. These disorders are the result of personal and social development not proceeding as it should. An excellent source for obtaining additional information regarding these disorders is provided by Maloney and Klykylo.

Maloney, M. J., & Klykylo, W. M. (1985). An overview of anorexia nervosa, bulimia and obesity in children and adolescents. In S. Chess & A. Thomas (Eds.), Annual progress in child psychology and child development (pp. 436-453). New York: Bruner Mazel.

Finally, instructors can expand on the textbook presentation on androgyny by administering the Bem Sex Role Inventory to each student in the class. Students' tests can be scored and returned. Test scores can then serve as the basis for a discussion on masculinity, feminity, and androgeny.

Bem, S. L. (1974). The measurement of psychological androgyny. Journal of Consulting and Clinical Psychology, 42, 155-162.

Discussion Questions

1. Consider each of Erikson's eight stages of psychosocial development. As a teacher what could you do to assist an individual who is experiencing a crisis at each level to reach a positive resolution.

2. Why do you think that Erikson chooses the term "crisis" to describe an individual's developmental progression from one stage to the next. Compare and contrast Erickson's concept of "crisis" with the Piagetian concept of "disequilibrium."

3. As a seventh grade teacher you notice that one of your children is a social isolate. The other students seldom pick on this child and aren't really mean to her, so you decide that the situation is best left alone. How do you think Erikson would respond to your decision. What are some strategies he might endorse for helping this child?

4. Consider each of the following experiences. At which developmental stage is this experience likely to produce a crisis resolution. Will the resolution be positive or negative?

- Joey's mom selects pullover shirts and pants with elastic waistbands so that Joey can dress himself independently.

- Mary's mom puts Mary on a feeding schedule suited to her appropriate level of physical development. She is flexible in that she will feed Mary a few minutes early if she starts to cry. She does, however, let her cry in her room while she prepares the food, because she doesn't want Mary to be spoiled.

- Tim has worked for hours preparing his book for creative writing. His book is very creative but the teacher grades his work a C because he left out the table of contents.

- Rather than selecting the ten best paintings every week, Anne's art teacher randomly chooses five children's work for display. Her principal feels that this procedure really doesn't reward the best artists.

- Ward decides to make popcorn for a family treat. Everyone enjoys the popcorn and praises him. The next morning his mother finds a terrible mess in the kitchen, but she decides to clean it up without comment.

5. Ms. X and Mr. Y team-teach a high school sociology class. They want to make their students aware of the "hidden curriculum" which sex-role sterotypes males and females in American schools. They want to involve their students and make it a productive learning experience for everyone. They are interested in knowing if sexism is present in their curriculum content, in the student-to-student interactions, and in their teacher-to-student interactions. How could they go about collecting the evidence they need to determine whether or not their school has a "hidden curriculum."

6. Helping individuals develop high self-esteem and a positive self-concept are constructs that are central to every theory of personality development. Consider the age and grade level of students you plan to teach. What are some strategies that you as a teacher could employ to assist in the development of these constructs?

7. Recent research indicates that divorce presents a serious adjustment problem to children of all ages. Based on the information in the book, what suggestions could you provide to a parent who is contemplating divorce which would make the adjustment easier for their children?

8. Consider that you have been appointed to the Suicide Prevention Committee at your high school. The charge of the committee is to devise an intervention program for students who are at risk for teenage suicide. Design the program that you think would be most effective.

Audiovisual Aids

Child's Play: Window on Development (Harcourt Brace Jovanovich, color, 1976, 20 min.). This film shows children at play from infancy through adolescence to illustrate how children acquire increasingly complex perceptions about themselves and establish and practice their relationships with others.

Coming of Age (New Day Films, color, 1983, 60 min.). This is a documentary of adults, gathering at a summer camp to discuss sexual, racial, and family relationships with their peers and counselors.

Everybody Rides the Carousel (Yale University Design Studio, color, 1983, 72 min.). This is a three-part animated film discussing the eight stages of life as described by Erikson.

Child Abuse and Neglect: The Hidden Hurt (VC 23954, Guidance Associates Media, 1985, 25 min.). This film encourages understanding and prevention with a sensitive program. Experts and victims speak candidly; psychological and social factors can make even loving parents abusive.

Asset: A Social Skills Program for Adolescents (Research Press, color). This film is specifically designed for teaching social skills to a wide range of adolescents. Included are those who are experiencing the typical problems of adolescence as well as those who are labeled delinquent. It contains an individual videocassette for each of the social skill areas: giving positive feedback, giving negative feedback, accepting negative feedback, resisting peer pressure, problem solving, negotiation, following instructions, conversation.

The Skillstreaming Video: How to Teach Students Prosocial Skills (Research Press, color, 26 min.). This film is designed for teachers of students who display aggression, immaturity, withdrawal, or other problem behaviors. It trains teachers in the use of modeling, role playing, performance feedback, and transfer training.

Token Economy: Behaviorism Applied (CRM, color, 1972, 20 min.)
The use of operant conditioning principles in establishing a token economy system is discussed in this film.

One Step at a Time: An Introduction to Behavior Modification (CRM/McGraw-Hill Films, color, 1973, 32 min.). This film shows positive reinforcement and schedules of reinforcement and how they shape classroom performance.

FOLLOW-UP ACTIVITIES

1. Debate Gender Differences in Behavior

   Instructors opening classroom debate to gender differences in behavior might expect some of the following reactions to the two positions presented in the book.

   a. Eliminating gender differences was one of the positive outcomes of the women's movement of the sixties and seventies. This is necessary if women are going to continue to occupy the work force in significant numbers. The right to equal treatment is guaranteed under the U.S. Constitution. Failure to provide equal treatment in the schools and elsewhere is a violation of legal as well as moral statutes.

b. There are basic biological differences between men and women which can never be ignored. Pretending these do not exist is to deny reality. The impact of developing women's intellectual potential on the family system and child-rearing practices should be examined. If androgeny inhibits sensitivity women may pay for fully developed intellectual potential with their sensitivity, nurturing, and child-rearing skills.

2. Analyze Texts for Sex Sterotyping

Another approach to Follow-up Activity 2 is to have the class select a contemporary basal reading series such as Scott Foresman, Houghton Mifflin, or Ginn. They can then compare a current reading text with the same text which was published prior to 1960. They can rate each of these books on the Textbook Evaluation Form contained in Follow-up Activity Sheet 4-2. The comparison will demonstrate that over the past thirty years, textbook publishers have responded not only to concern over sexism but to concern over racism as well.

3. Learn About Child-Rearing Methods

This Follow-up Activity could be adapted to an out-of-class assignment by requiring the class to adapt their summary of major ideas to a list of Do's and Don'ts recommendations which can be used to help parents in improving their child-rearing practices.

Additional Follow-up Activities

4. Observe Stages of Psychosocial Development

Have each class member observe in a classroom which is at the grade level they intend to teach. First they should determine the developmental crisis which is likely to be affecting students in that age range. Then they can record events which occur during their observation which might positively or negatively affect the resolution of this crisis. Of particular importance might be:

- instructional practices
- peer interactions
- teacher interactions
- behavior management strategies
- rules and class procedures

5. Construct a Sociogram

Have each class member construct a sociogram based on the directions provided in Follow-up Activity Sheet 4-5.

TEXTBOOK EVALUATION FORM

DIRECTIONS: Analyze a textbook published before 1960 and another published after 1985. Rate each book on the variables cited below.

Published Before 1960	Published After 1985
Number of white characters _____	Number of white characters _____
Number of minority characters _____	Number of minority characters _____
Diversity of minority characters _____	Diversity of minority characters _____
Number of male characters _____	Number of male characters _____
Number of female characters _____ Number of working women _____	Number of female characters _____ Number of working women _____

Number of women in traditional
    roles _____
	Number of women in traditional
	    roles _____

Number of men in traditional roles _____	Number of men in traditional roles _____

Number of women in non-tradititional
    roles _____
	Number of women in non-traditional
	    roles _____

Number of men in non-traditional
    roles _____
	Number of men in non-traditional
	    roles _____

Number of boys/men portrayed
    negatively _____
	Number of boys/men portrayed
	    negatively _____

Number of girls/women potrayed
    negatively _____
	Number of girls/women portrayed
	    negatively _____

Number of boys/men portrayed
    positively _____
	Number of boys/men portrayed
	    positively _____

Number of girls/women portrayed
    positively _____
	Number of girls/women portrayed
	    positively _____

DIRECTIONS FOR CONSTRUCTING A SOCIOGRAM

1. Make arrangements to observe in a classroom.

2. Call each child aside for a private conference.

3. Present each child with the following scenario:

   "Your mother has decided to let you have a party, but you can only invite two friends. You decide to invite your two favorite friends from this class. Who would you invite?"

4. Chart the data as in the example below.

Student		Choices	Times Chosen
Tom	-	Mark, Randy	Tom 5
Ann	-	Jane, Sue	Ann 3
Mark	-	Tom, Jake	Mark 1
Jane	-	Ann, Sue	Jane 4
Bill	-	Randy, Tom	Bill 2
Sue	-	Ann, Jane	Sue 2
Pete	-	Tom, Randy	Pete 0
Mary	-	Jane, Sara	Mary 0
Randy	-	Tom, Bill	Randy 4
Sara	-	Bill, Jane	Sara 2
Jake	-	Tom, Randy	Jake 1
Ellen	-	Ann, Sara	Ellen 0

5. Construct a diagram like the one presented on the next page.

6. Determine from your diagram who the stars, or most popular children, in your class are. Also, determine the social isolates.

7. Devise some strategies which are appropriate for your age group which might improve the sociability of the isolates.

SOCIOGRAM

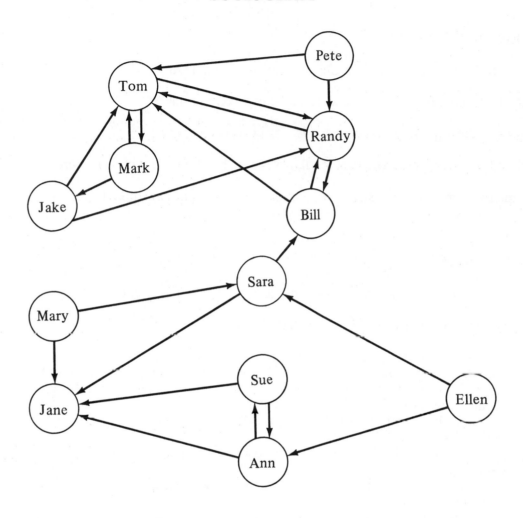

CHAPTER FIVE

EXCEPTIONAL CHILDREN

CHAPTER OBJECTIVES

Students mastering the content in Chapter Five will be able to:

- Identify students who may need special education assistance.

- Identify the legal requirements and issues in special education.

- Identify the teacher's role in referral, assessment, and placement procedures.

- Implement intervention strategies that can help exceptional students succeed in the regular classroom.

FOCUS QUESTIONS

1. What are the advantages and disadvantages of special education labels?

   Possible advantages of labeling are that:

   - Categories can relate diagnosis to specific treatment.
   - Labeling may lead to a "protective" response, in which nonlabeled children accept certain behaviors from their handicapped peers more fully than they would accept those same behaviors in "normal" children.
   - Labeling helps professionals to communicate with one another and to classify and assess research findings.
   - Funding of special education programs is often based on specific categories of exceptionality.
   - Labels allow special interest groups to promote specific programs and spur legislative action.
   - Labeling helps make the special needs of exceptional children more visible in the public eye.

   Possible disadvantages of labeling are that:

   - Labels usually focus on negative aspects of the child, causing others to think about the child only in terms of inadequacies or defects.
   - Labels may cause others to react to and hold expectations for a child based on the label, resulting in a self-fulfilling prophecy.
   - Labels that describe a child's performance deficit often mistakenly acquire the role of explanatory constructs.
   - Labels lead peers to reject or ridicule the labeled child.

- Special education labels have a certain permanency about them. Once labeled as "retarded" or "learning disabled," it is difficult for a child to ever again achieve the status of being "just like all the other kids."
- Labels used to classify children in special education emphasize that learning problems are primarily the result of something being wrong within the child, thereby reducing the likelihood of examining instructional variables as the cause of performance deficits.
- Labels often provide a basis for keeping children out of the regular classroom.
- A disproportionate number of children from minority culture groups have been inaccurately labeled handicapped, especially as educably mentally retarded.

In summary, many professionals maintain that the classification of exceptional children requires the expenditure of a great amount of time and money that could better be spent in planning and delivering instruction.

2. What are the issues involving the identification of learning disabled and mentally retarded children?

There is confusion concerning the criteria that must be met for a student to be identified as learning disabled or mentally retarded. One issue is the question of what constitutes a discrepancy between intellectual potential and academic achievement? Some students may not qualify for special education services if they do not meet the criteria for classification and often these criteria vary from state to state. That is, a student may be labeled learning disabled in one state but not in another. Also, in states where psychological processing dysfunction is used as a criterion, there is little consensus as to which psychological processes should be considered and few accurate instruments for measuring process dysfunctions. The identification of mentally retarded students often depends primarily on the performance of the student on individual IQ tests. Many professionals question the validity of these tests. Others point to the discriminatory nature of the tests and the fact that many retarded children perform satisfactorily outside of the academic demands of the classroom.

3. What factors differentiate a student who is a lowachiever from a student who is mentally retarded or learning disabled?

A low achiever is one whose academic performance is below his peers, but the student may also be achieving up to the level of his cognitive potential, which is in the normal range of cognitive ability. A mentally retarded child on the other hand has depressed cognitive ability. A child may be identified as having a learning disability if the child exhibits one or more of the following characteristics: hypteractivity, perceptual-motor impairments, emotional lability, general coordination deficits, attentional disorders, impulsivity, memory and thinking disorders, specific academic problems, speech and hearing disorders, and equivocal neurological signs that are difficult to interpret. The key determiner is whether or not he or she meets the specific criteria designated by the state or local school district. If a child possesses any of the identified characteristics but is achieving normally in school, the child would not be considered learning disabled, because the differential diagnosis of a learning disability most often rests on an aptitude/achievement discrepancy.

4. What are the behavioral characteristics indicating that a student should be assessed for possible special education in the following areas: behavior disorders, hearing impairment, visual impairment, and communication disorder?

There are many definitions and classification procedures used to identify behavior disordered individuals. P.L. 94-142 uses the following characteristics based on their degree and duration:

- An inability to learn which cannot be explained by intellectual, sensory, and health factors
- An inability to build or maintain satisfactory relationships with peers and teachers
- Inappropriate types of behaviors or feelings under normal circumstances
- A general pervasive mood of unhappiness or depression
- A tendency to develop physical symptoms or fears associated with personal or school problems (Federal Register, August 23, 1977, p. 42478)

Behavioral characteristics of hearing impairment are:

- Missing school frequently because of earaches or sinus congestion
- Suffering from allergies and head congestion severe enough to bring about reduced hearing acuity for a short time
- Appearing inattentive or daydreaming
- Being reluctant to participate in class activities
- Having difficulty speaking or understanding language
- Demonstrating unusual behavior in response to oral directions

Behavioral characteristics which might indicate a visual disability are:

- Rubbing eyes excessively
- Shutting or covering one eye
- Tilting head, or thrusting head forward
- Having difficulty in reading or in other work requiring close use of the eyes
- Blinking more than usual or being irritable when doing close work
- Holding books close to the eyes
- Being unable to see distant things clearly and/or squinting eyelids together or frowning
- Having crossed eyes; red-rimmed, encrusted, or swollen eyelids; inflamed or watery eyes, and/or recurring sties
- Complaining that eyes itch, burn, or feel scratchy and that he or she cannot see well
- Complaining of dizziness, headaches, or nausea following close eye work and/or having vision which is double or blurred

Behavioral characteristics of a child with communication disorders are:

- Talking little, failing to establish eye contact, and avoiding situations requiring talking
- Evidencing articulation problems such as omissions, distortions, and substitutions
- Using poor sentence structure and limited vocabulary
- Having difficulty explaining
- Having difficulty understanding word meaning, directions, or word problems
- Having difficulty responding in a timely and fluent manner

5. What are the advantages and disadvantages of educating exceptional students in and outside of the regular classroom?

The requirement for placement in the least restrictive educational environment attempts to reverse traditional procedures for dealing with handicapped children. The law states that, to the maximum extent appropriate, handicapped children are to be educated with children who are not handicapped. The emphasis has shifted to the regular classroom as the preferred instructional base for all children. Even with the least restrictive environment stipulation in the law, there are some who advocate the regular education initiative. The goal of this initiative is to restructure the regular classroom to be more responsive to students with special needs. The major argument for this approach is that the regular classroom is the best place to remediate academic deficiencies. Educating students in separate "pull-out" programs results in substantial reduction in classroom instruction. Also, procedures for classifying students for special education is flawed and, therefore, it is difficult to determine who should be "pulled out." A major concern of individuals opposed to the initiative is that today's general education teachers are not well prepared to meet the special needs of handicapped students, and as a result, the plan would lead to a less than adequate education for special needs students. Also, they argue that changes in the present program can be made to improve it without overhauling the total system of instruction.

6. What are the important issues and concerns of parents of special education students?

Many parents are concerned with mainstreaming issues, though there is disagreement about what constitutes the best educational environment. Other parents are concerned about vocational training and the implementation of a functional and normalized curriculum. Many parents want to make certain that the school prepares their children for future employment and independent living and that the school structures the transition phase into adult life. All parents of exceptional children can play an important role in helping to teach their handicapped children by being active in the assessment and decision-making process. When parents are involved in their children's education, the children tend to do better in school. Teacher-parent conferences are an important source of information for both the teacher and the parent.

7. In what ways can a teacher assist special education students to maximize both academic and social behavior in the classroom?

Classroom teachers play important roles in the identification, diagnosis, referral, and instruction of exceptional students. There are a number of teaching methods that have been successful in improving handicapped children's social acceptance and/or academic achievement in the regular classroom. Problems of social rejection of mainstreamed students can be remedied by providing social skills training. Another type of intervention used for improving both social acceptance and academic achievement is cooperative learning. This technique encourages handicapped and nonhandicapped students to work in teams on academic and class projects. Finally, individualized instruction is a widely used method for accommodating the needs of low-achieving and handicapped students in regular classes.

CHAPTER OUTLINE

I. ORIENTATION

    A. Focus Questions

II. EXCEPTIONAL CHILDREN - AN OVERVIEW

    A. Labeling: Pro or Con

        1. Possible benefits of labeling
        2. Possible disadvantages of labeling

III. CATEGORIES IN SPECIAL EDUCATION

    A. Mental Retardation
    B. Learning Disabilities
    C. Behavior Disorders
    D. Hearing Impairment
    E. Visual Impairment
    F. Communication Disorders
    G. Physical and Health Impairment
    H. Gifted and Talented

        1. Intelligence as an indicator of giftedness
        2. Creativity as an indicator of giftedness
        3. Special talents as an indicator of giftedness
        4. An integration perspective
        5. Programs for gifted and talented students

IV. LEGAL RIGHTS OF EXCEPTIONAL CHILDREN AND THEIR PARENTS

KEY TERMS

CHAPTER GUIDELINES

Chapter Five discusses the incidence of handicapping conditions within the school-age population. The concept of labeling along with its advantages and disadvantages is discussed.

Definitions and diagnostic criteria used in labeling children as mentally retarded, hearing impaired, visually impaired, speech impaired, and physically and other health impaired are presented. Gifted and talented students are discussed in terms of high intelligence as well as special talents.

The major legal requirements of Public Law 94-142, The Education for All Handicapped Children Act, are outlined. Students are introduced to the concepts of due process, the individualized education program, and the least restrictive educational environment. Mainstreaming is presented as an instructional model which allows handicapped students to be educated with their non-handicapped peers to the maximum extent possible.

The Regular Education Initiative is discussed as a model for delivering special education services in the regular classroom. The rationale for this approach is based on the lack of positive effects that the pull-out, or resource room, programs have had on student achievement.

The legal requirements of Public Law 99-457 are also discussed. This law is an ammendment to P.L. 94-142 and provides for the identification and intervention services for preschool children who are developmentally delayed.

Finally, this chapter explores the role of parents and regular class teachers in the education of exceptional learners. A collaborative effort between the home and school is encouraged.

Supplementary Material

Numerous techniques have been proposed for assisting regular class teachers in the mainstreaming process. A presentation of some of these techniques could be an effective way of enriching the material in Chapter Five for the regular class teachers. The work of Bauer and Shea and Johnson and Johnson are valuable resources to use in this effort. They recommend:

- Modifying material presented in the text.
- Modifying material required on tests.
- Utilizing cooperative learning experiences.
- Utilizing whole-class teaching strategies.

Students could be asked to entertain alternatives for implementing these recommendations in the various subject matter or content areas in which they intend to teach.

Bauer, A. M., & Shea, T. M. (1989). Teaching exceptional students in your classroom. Boston: Allyn and Bacon.

Johnson, D. W., & Johnson, R. T. (1980). Integrating handicapped students into the mainstream. Exceptional Children, 47, 90-99.

Management of problem behavior is a major concern in the regular education process. Long, Morse and Newman outline surface behavior management techniques which may be helpful to classroom teachers who are involved in the mainstream process. Instructors can present these strategies to students and have the students generate specific examples of each of their surface management techniques.

SURFACE MANAGEMENT TECHNIQUES

- **Planned Ignoring.** Do not acknowledge behaviors which do not interfere with the ongoing program.
- **Signal Interference.** Use non-verbal gestures such as eye contact or a frown to eliminate an undesirable behavior.
- **Proximity Control.** Interfere with a negative behavior by moving in close proximaty to the offending student.
- **Interest Boosting.** Use praise or a subtle suggestion to redirect the student's interest to appropriate activities.
- **Tension Decontamination Through Humor.** Use humor or a funny remark to ease tension and help students over a difficult time.
- **Hurdle Helping.** Create a hurdle lesson to help a student through a difficult time or to overcome an immediate problem.
- **Restructuring the Program.** Modify or change an activity which is not going well.
- **Support from the Routine.** Provide additional structure for acting-out students by implementing a stable routine.
- **Direct Appeal to Values.** Appeal to the child's values, sense of fairness, and respect for others.
- **Remove Seductive Objectives.** Put tempting objects out of reach and out of sight.
- **Antiseptic Bouncing.** Anticipate acting-out behavior and send the child to get a drink or on an errand to provide time to regain control.
- **Physical Restraint.** Hold the student who is trantruming or fighting.

Long, N. J., Morse, W. C., & Newman, R. G. (1980). Conflict in the classroom (4th ed.). Belmont, CA: Wadsworth.

Instructors can expand on the topic of children who are behavior disordered by having students identify the types of classroom behaviors which they think would warrant special education referrals for this disability. The discussion can be supplemented by information from Hutton, who conducted a study on the primary reasons classroom teachers make such referral. The reasons identified in the study are rank-ordered below. The list begins with the reason which is most often cited:

- Poor peer relationships
- Displays frustration
- Below academic expectations
- Disruptive
- Shy, withdrawn
- Fighting
- Refuses to work
- Short attention span
- Argues
- Distractible
- Hyperactive
- Does not participate
- Impulsive
- Immature
- Daydreams
- Lacks motivation
- Disorganized

Hutton, J. B. (1985). What reasons are given by teachers who refer problem behavior students? Psychology in the Schools, 22, 79-82.

Instructors can expand textbook material on the topic of giftedness by presenting the research finding in a recent article by Feldhusen. This research report synthesizes published research conclusions on educating gifted students. It makes observations in the following three areas:

Identification. Schools are not effective in their practices of identifying gifted students. This is especially true for poor, minority and underachieving students. Multiple criteria and data sources should be used in the identification process.

Acceleration. Acceleration is an effective technique which motivates gifted students. It does not have a negative effect on their social or emotional development.

Grouping. Grouping gifted students also serves as a motivator. This practice does not have a negative impact on students remaining in the regular class.

Feldhusen, J. F. (1989). Synthesis of research on gifted youth. Educational Leadership, 46(6), 6-12.

One of the major concerns in the mainstreaming movement has been the reaction of peers to the exceptional child and the impact that their reactions and disapproval might have on the self-esteem of the exceptional child. An excellent source of information on this subject is an article by Sutherland, Algozzine, Ysseldyke, and Freeman. The article explores the impact of labeling and provides numerous suggestions for assisting the regular class teacher in introducing a mild to moderately handicapped student into the regular classroom.

Sutherland, J., Algozzine, B., Ysseldyke, J., & Fruman, S. (1983). Changing peer perceptions: Effects of labels and assigned attributes. Journal of Learning Disabilities, 16(4), 217-220.

In an effort to assess preservice teachers' receptivity to working with mainstream students, the instructor could administer the Teacher Receptivity Questionnaire. Results of the questionnaire could serve as the basis for discussing teacher expectations and the critical role of the regular education teacher in the mainstream process.

Aloia, G. F., & Aloia, S. D. (1983). Teacher Receptivity Questionnaire. Journal of Special Education, 19(2), 11-20.

Discussion Questions

1. The rationale for mainstreaming is based on the civil rights of handicapped students. Little attention is given to the impact this process might have on "normal" students. Speculate about what this impact might be on the age-level student you plan to teach. What are some strategies you might employ to insure that the impact is socially and academically favorable for these learners?

2. Consider the bell-shaped, or normal, distribution of educational and psychological characteristics and the percentage of students that are likely to fall within the given ranges of one, two, and three standard deviations above and below the mean. Relate what we know about this distribution to the term "exceptionality," or "exceptional learners."

3. What are the social, developmental, educational, and vocational distinctions between students who are classified as mildly, moderately, and severely retarded? What are the characteristics of students in each category which have educational relevance.

4. Most states depend on some type of age/ability/achievement formula for diagnosing and labeling children as learning disabled. In other words a student must have normal ability and an achievement level at least two years below his chronological age. From this diagnosis we infer that the child has a condition which limits his functioning on learning tasks. Think of some other reasons that a student might have this type of performance pattern other than a true learning disability.

5. Ask students to reflect on the experiences that they had in public schools. Have them give specific examples in which they or others they knew experienced embarrassment or rejection because they could not meet the academic or social demands in an educational setting.

6. Consider that you are a ninth grade home economics teacher. You have 13 students in your various classes who have been identified and are receiving services under the label of "teenage pregnancy." What modification would you make in the curriculum to accommodate their specific needs? You might consider:

   - variations in learning rate
   - variations in learning style
   - variations in learning content

7. You are a 12th grade teacher at Sensitive N. Bright High School. Over the years tremendous tension has developed between the ideology of the special educators at your school versus the regular educators. The issue at variance is the type of diploma special education students receive. The regular education faction feels that all special education students should have a diploma and transcript that reflect a special education curriculum. Special educators, on the other hand, feel that this practice would lead to lifelong labeling and interfere with the life span integration of, particularly, the mildly handicapped. Affiliate yourself with one viewpoint and develop a rationale in support of your position.

8. Some authorities are calling for a Regular Education Initiative. This plan would provide special education services to special education students, but within the regular education setting. Other authorities feel that successful special education practices should be provided for normal children as well. For example, they would like to see IEP's developed for all children. How do you react to these suggestions?

9. The least restrictive educational environment (LRE) might not be the same for a moderately retarded student and a partially sighted student. Explain how the concept of the LRE is a relative term. What are some of the criteria you would use in determining what constitutes an LRE for a given student?

10. Two of the most common strategies for accommodating the needs of gifted children are acceleration and enrichment. As a classroom teacher, which strategy would you prefer and why?

Audiovisual Aids

Teaching Mildly Handicapped Students: Video Training in Effective Instruction (Research Press, color, 1987, 20 min. each). This training film instructs teachers on techniques for working with mildly handicapped students at elementary and secondary levels.

Learning Disabilities - First Hand (VC 24803, Journal Films, 1987, 16 min.). This film involves a thorough examination of learning disabilities, how they affect young people, and how they can be overcome.

Teaching People with Developmental Disabilities (Research Press, color, 88 min.). This video training series is designed to help teachers master the behavioral techniques of task analysis, prompting, reinforcement, and error correction. The series features four videotaped lessons that provide viewers with clear and simple teaching demonstrations of each of these techniques.

Education for All Children: The Challenge of the Eighties (Research Press, color, 28 min.). This film examines traditional attitudes toward individuals with developmental disabilities or physical handicaps. It reviews the legislative history that has led to changes in those attitudes over the last several decades, and talks about the Right to Education Movement in light of court decisions and government actions.

Education for All Children (Research Press, color, 1982, 28 min.). This film examines attitudes toward individuals with developmental disabilities or physical handicaps; reviews education laws affecting the handicapped, and discusses controversial issues such as allocation of scarce resources, potential backlash from parents, and new legislation.

Learning Disabilities (Films for the Humanities and Sciences, color, 1983, 19 min.). The nature of learning disabilities is described. A nine-year-old boy is profiled as he is diagnosed and schools and parents plan for his future education.

The Special Child: Maximizing Limited Potential (Films for the Humanities and Sciences, color, 1984, 26 min.). Physicians, psychologists, speech and physical therapists, and teachers are seen working together to measure a child's potential. The film covers Down Syndrome, autism, problems of neurological control, and speech problems.

FOLLOW-UP ACTIVITIES

1. Educate Exceptional Children

   Instructors wishing to adapt Follow-up Activity 1 to a group activity can do so by specifying a learning task such as "identifying the elements necessary to sustain and promote life." Then ask the class to formulate instructional objectives, daily lesson plans, and evaluation procedures for teaching this content in a regular third-grade science class. Finally ask the students to tell how they would adapt their objectives, lessons, and evaluation techniques to accommodate the following students:

   * a gifted 8-year-old
   * a mildly retarded 10-year-old
   * an 8-year-old learning disabled student who can't read
   * an "on-grade-level achiever" with a vision impairment

   Another option would be available to instructors who had students complete Follow-up Activity 5 in Chapter Six. They could refer to those lesson plans for making the prescribed adaptations.

2. Observe an Exceptional Child in the Classroom

   A variation of Follow-up Activity 2 is to have prospective teachers observe in a regular classroom, but **do not** identify the exceptional students beforehand. Have them try to determine through their observation which of the students receive special education. They can record specific characteristics they observe which led them to conclude that a child might have a handicapping condition. These potential characteristics can be recorded on copies of Follow-up Activity Sheet 5-2. After the observation is completed they can check with the classroom teacher to identify how many of the special education students they were able to identify during their observation. This type of record can serve as a basis of future discussion in which the following points are made:

   * Handicapped children are more like other children than they are different from them.
   * Stereotypical characteristics do not always accompany a handicap.
   * Most mild to moderately handicapped children look and act like normal children.

3. Interview a Handicapped Adult

   Instructors can adapt Follow-up Activity 3 to an in-class activity by inviting a panel of handicapped adults to attend a class discussion. Many campuses have an Office of Handicapped Student Services which might provide a tentative list of handicapped college students who would be willing to serve as panel members.

4. Report on a Current Issue in Special Education

   To adapt Follow-up Activity 4 to an in-class activity, the instructor could have individuals or small groups select opposing views on one of the current issues provided in the textbook. The written research reports could then serve as the basis for in-class debates. After each debate is concluded, the instructor can make an effort to establish group consensus on an appropriate regular education perspective on the issue.

5. Teach Students About Exceptional Children

One of the class who completes the lesson plans described in Follow-up Activity 5 could actually be videotaped teaching the lesson. The videotape could then be viewed in class. It would provide a basis for addressing personal fears and concerns that both children and adults are likely to have when they first begin to relate to exceptional populations.

Additional Follow-up Activities

6. Assess the Psychological Impact of Labeling

Ask your students to discuss whether or not the positive effects of individualized instruction and receiving special education services are justified in terms of the social stigma that is created by using labels. After the discussion proceeds for a while, tell students that you are going to entertain a special education model for conducting the rest of the semester of their class. Explain to them that you have an ability test and will be administering it at the end of class meeting. Let them know that you intend to group them on the basis of test results so that low scorers will be able to receive extra help. If their scores are high you will allow them to be peer tutors, group leaders and academic facilitators. Then pass out copies of any bogus ability measure. After you collect their test forms readdress the original question.

7. Visit a Community Agency for the Handicapped

Have students investigate community services which are provided in your area. These can be either local, state, or county agencies. Often some services are supported by the United Way campaign. After they complete each observation, have them evaluate their experience by filling out a copy of the Observational Rating Form, which is contained in Follow-up Activity Sheet 5-8.

8. Simulate Being a Handicapped Individual

Ask the class to assemble in small groups of two or three each. Then have each group member generate a short list of errands they need to attend to before the day is over. After the list is complete, pass out crutches, wheelchairs, glasses with the lenses painted black, or any other device that they might use to simulate a handicapping condition. Tell them to take turns doing their errands as handicapped persons. Then have them respond to the following issues during the next class meeting.

- difficulty of accomplishing objectives with a handicap
- interference of the handicap with mobility
- reactions of other people to a person they believe is handicapped

Follow-up Activity Sheet 5-2

Student Characteristics Observation Form

DIRECTIONS: As you observe the operations of a regular classroom note the things you see which indicate that a student might receive or need to receive special education. Classify each according to the type of characteristic it represents. Then write down the name of the student who exhibited the behavior.

Characteristics	Student
Behavioral Characteristics	
Academic Characteristics	
Appearance	
Other	

OBSERVATIONAL VISIT REPORTS

DIRECTIONS: Contact a local, state, or county agency which provides services to handicapped citizens. After your visit respond to each of the questions below.

1. What was the name of the service provider?

2. What was the purpose of the services delivered?

3. What type and age of clients were served?

4. What did you observe?

5. How do you evaluate what you saw?

6. What are your personal reactions to what you saw?

CHAPTER SIX

BEHAVIORAL APPROACHES TO LEARNING

CHAPTER OBJECTIVES

Students mastering the content in Chapter Six will be able to:

- Describe the procedures used in applied behavior analysis for modifying behavior.

- Use shaping to develop complex behaviors.

- Use behavioral principles in designing a lesson.

- Develop and implement a mastery learning program.

FOCUS QUESTIONS

1. How does Skinner's view of learning differ from other behaviorists?

    Skinner viewed reinforcement as the most important element in the learning process. He believed that the purpose of psychology is to predict and control behavior. Skinner thought that most human behavior takes the form of operant responses that the individual emits. Operant conditioning, although closer to Thorndike's theory than to Pavlov's, is different from Thorndike's explanation of learning. Thorndike felt that reward strengthened a bond that existed between a stimulus and a response, whereas Skinner felt that what is strengthened is not an S-R bond but the probability that the same response will occur again.

2. What is the difference between classical and operant conditioning?

    Skinner defined operant conditioning as a learning situation in which a response is made more probable or frequent as the result of immediate reinforcement. An important difference between Pavlov's classical and Skinner's operant conditioning is that in classical conditioning the consequences of a behavior carry no weight in the learning of that behavior. Reinforcement is unnecessary because the stimuli bring about the desired response.

3. What is the role of discrimination training in instruction?

    A discriminative stimulus is a cue that increases the probability of a response. People respond differently to different stimuli. The teacher wants students to learn certain responses under specific conditions. An important part of teaching, therefore, is presenting stimuli so specific that only one response is correct.

4. What is the difference between negative reinforcement and punishment?

Negative reinforcement is the removal of an unpleasant stimulus or condition. Because the negative situation is terminated, the operant behavior which was responsible for the removal is reinforced and, therefore, more likely to occur in the future. Punishment is the presentation of an unpleasant consequent stimulus, or the addition of an unpleasant condition. It decreases the probability that the operant behavior which preceeded it will occur again.

5. Why is shaping needed in behavior change programs?

Shaping applies reinforcement responses which successively approximate the desired behavior. This technique allows for reinforcement to occur before the terminally desired behavior is in evidence. Shaping is utilized in situations in which there would be no reinforcement opportunity if the reinforcement of successive approximations did not occur.

6. How are cognitive processes used in observational learning?

Bandura's work on observational learning helped modify the behavioral and cognitive perspectives and contributed greatly to the practice of cognitive-behavior therapy. Bandura identified four components of observational learning: 1) the learner must attend to and accurately perceive the behavior of the model, 2) the individual must remember what was seen, 3) the individual must convert symbolic representations into appropriate actions, and 4) reinforcement must follow the behavior and act as a source of information and an incentive.

7. What is the difference in the role of reinforcement in operant conditioning and Bandura's social learning theory?

According to Bandura, children learn social behaviors by observing the actions of important people in their lives. He rejected the unidirectional view of the effects of the environment on the individual, the major premise of the S-R perspective. Instead, his central theme is reciprocal determinism, a process whereby personal factors, environmental factors, and behavior all operate as "interlocking determinants of each other." In social learning theory, both behavior and the environment are changeable, and neither is the primary determinant of behavioral change. As a result of these views, Bandura believes that reinforcement is most impotant as a source of information and motivation. Skinner believes that reinforcement's most important property is that it strengthens the operant behavior.

8. When is social learning theory a more effective approach to instruction than operant conditioning?

Social learning is especially appropriate when the learning task is complex. Operant conditioning is more conducive to trial and error type learning situations. Also, social learning is useful when reliance on operant learning procedures would be less efficient or even dangerous. In teaching by modeling, the instructor demonstrates how to perform the task or skill and the student observes this behavior. The student then attempts to imitate the teacher or model. The student is often able to learn complete sequences of behavior in a much shorter time by modeling than by shaping.

9. How does cognitive behavior modification depart from the traditional behavioral approach to behavior change?

The theory behind the incorporation of various cognitive processes within the behavioral framework is that children and adolescents have deficient cognitive processes that guide or control their behavior. The rationale for this approach is that if the thought processes, or cognitions, that direct or control behavior can be changed, behavioral change will follow.

10. How does programmed instruction and computer-assisted instruction employ behavioral principles of learning?

Programmed instruction is a self-instructional package that presents a topic in a carefully planned sequence and requires the learner to solve a problem or to respond to questions by selecting from a series of answers. Immediate feedback occurs after each response and students can work at their own rate. Computer-assisted instruction (CAI) is an attempt to use behavioral principles in a more efficient way than traditional programmed instruction. The predominant use of CAI has been with drill and practice activities in the basic skills areas. Such programs are used with skills already learned in order to improve speed or accuracy. CAI also provides the student with additional practice in basic skills. This practice gives the student one or more chances to answer the question correctly. If the student fails to answer the problem correctly, the computer provides prompts that guide the student to the correct response. When the student successfully completes the assignment, the student is praised by the computer, and is moved to the next program or level of the program.

11. What are the similarities and differences between Bloom's Mastery Learning and Keller's Personalized System of Instruction?

In 1968, Bloom and Keller both published articles describing methods for increasing student mastery over content in a regular class or course. Bloom emphasized the importance of improving the achievement of students in elementary and secondary schools in his system of Mastery Learning. Bloom's system advocated the use of operant conditioning principles. Keller developed his Personalized System of Instruction (PSI), which was also based on operant conditioning principles, but was designed for use in college classrooms.

CHAPTER OUTLINE

I. ORIENTATION

A. Focus Questions

II. CLASSICAL CONDITIONING

A. Pavlov
B. Watson

III. APPLIED BEHAVIOR ANALYSIS

A. Early Developments - Thorndike
B. Skinner

　　1. From operant conditioning to applied behavior analysis

C. Discrimination, Stimulus Control, and Generalization
D. Consequent Stimuli
E. Schedules of Reinforcement
F. Extinction
G. Shaping - A Method for Developing New Behaviors

IV. SOCIAL LEARNING THEORY

A. Types of Modeling
B. Processes in Observational Learning

　　1. Attentional processes
　　2. Retention processes
　　3. Motor reproduction processes
　　4. Motivational processes

C. Social Learning in the Classroom

V. COGNITIVE BEHAVIOR MODIFICATION

A. Self-management
B. Self-verbalization

VI. INSTRUCTIONAL APPLICATIONS OF BEHAVIORAL LEARNING PRINCIPLES

A. Programmed Instruction
B. Computer-assisted Instruction (CAI)

　　1. Drill and practice activities
　　2. Simulations
　　3. Tutorials

C. Computer Competence
D. Research on CAI

E. Mastery Learning and Personalized System of Instruction

    1. Mastery Learning
    2. Personalized System of Instruction (PSI)

VII. THINKING ABOUT THE TEACHING-LEARNING MODEL

KEY TERMS

classical conditioning (p. 222)

applied behavior analysis (p. 222)

operant conditioning (p. 222)

social learning theory (p. 222)

cognitive behavior modification (p. 222)

unconditioned stimulus (p. 223)

unconditioned response (p. 223)

conditioned stimulus (p. 223)

conditioned response (p. 223)

stimulus generalization (p. 224)

extinction (p. 224)

connectionism (p. 224)

law of effect (p. 225)

reward (p. 225)

law of exercise (p. 225)

respondents (p. 226)

operants (p. 226)

baseline (p. 228)

behavior modification (p. 229)

discriminative stimulus (p. 229)

reinforcing stimulus (p. 229)

discrimination learning (p. 230)

response generalization (p. 230)

negative reinforcement (p. 231)

punishment (p. 231)

time-out (p. 231)

primary reinforcement (p. 231)

secondary reinforcement (p. 232)

Premack's principle (p. 232)

fixed-ratio schedule (p. 233)

variable ratio schedule (p.233)

fixed-interval schedule (p. 234)

variable-interval schedule (p. 234)

spontaneous recovery (p. 235)

shaping (p. 236)

successive approximations (p. 236)

prompting (p. 236)

fading (p. 236)

modeling (p. 237)

observational learning (p. 237)

reciprocal determinism (p. 237)

inhibitory-disinhibitory effect (p. 238)

eliciting effect (p. 238)

self-efficacy (p. 239)

vicarious reinforcement (p. 239)

self-reinforcement (p. 239)

programmed instruction (p. 244)

teaching machines (p. 244)

linear programs (p. 244)

branching programs (p. 245)

computer-assisted instruction (p. 247)

computer-managed instruction (p. 247)

mastery learning (p. 252)

Personalized System of Instruction (p.252)

formative test (p. 253)

summative test (p. 253)

CHAPTER GUIDELINES

This chapter presents four major perspectives of behavioral psychology: classical conditioning, applied behavioral analysis, social learning theory, and cognitive behavior modification.

Pavlov and Watson are presented as early behavioral psychologists who formulated the principles of behavioral psychology. They viewed learning as forming connections between a stimulus and a response. Skinner believed that all behavior is learned. His experiments in operant conditioning focused on the element of reinforcement. Learning is defined as a situation in which a response is made more probable as the result of immediate reinforcement. Applied behavior analysis is an extension of operant conditioning principles. It is the application of specific methodology and evaluation procedures in the changing of human behavior in natural settings. Four guidelines for utilizing applied behavior analysis in teaching are presented in this chapter. Also, the effects of reinforcement schedules, shaping, and modeling are illustrated.

The chapter discusses observational learning as occurring without any immediate reinforcement. Attentional, retention, motor reproduction, and motivational processes in observational learning are discussed.

Reinforcement in social learning is viewed as a source of information and an incentive rather than a consequent condition of behavior. Alternative systems of reinforcement (direct, vicarious, and self-reinforcement) are compared.

The chapter points out that cognitive processes can be incorporated in behavioral approaches to help individuals self-regulate their own behaviors. Programmed instruction and computer-assisted instruction are two teaching models based on the principles of cognitive behavior modification. Mastery learning programs can be developed to ensure higher levels of learning for most children. The chapter concludes with a discussion of the utility of computers and other technological advancements in education, and a challenge to the reader to become more proficient in their usage.

Supplementary Materials

One means of expanding the material in Chapter Six is to demonstrate some of the principles of behavioral psychology using the students in your college class as subjects. Numerous demonstration activities which are suitable for this purpose are provided in the Activities Handbook for the Teaching of Psychology. A typical activity and one which is well suited for use in a college classroom is described below:

> Fill a container with numerous pieces of paper cut into geometric shapes. Make half of them round and half square. Have a student volunteer select pieces of paper one at a time. Very casually and in an unobtrusive way, provide verbal reinforcement only when the student chooses round papers. Notice how the proportion of round papers increases with reinforcement.

> Benjamin, L. T., & Lowman, K. D. (1981). Activities handbook for the teaching of psychology. Washington, DC: American Psychological Association.

Textbook information on the schedules of reinforcement can be expanded using the following excerpt taken from Morris. It demonstrates the use of various schedules of reinforcement in reducing talking-out behavior in a mildly handicapped girl.

> Carmen is a ten-year-old mildly mentally retarded girl. The goal that the teacher established was to increase the percentage of times Carmen raised her hand to talk during the free group discussion time period, and to decrease the percentage of time she talked without raising her hand and being called on. The criterion for success was 100% hand raising to talk (and 0% talking without raising hand).

> Carmen's teacher decided to praise her each time she raised her hand to talk during the discussion period (continuous reinforcement), and to ignore her talking out of turn—saying nothing to her and not looking at her and continue talking to and listening to those children who raised their hand. This intervention resulted in an increase in the percentage of Carmen's hand-raising within the first week, and a noticeable decrease in her percentage of talking-out behavior. By the middle of the second week of the behavior program, Carmen's percentages had reached about 65% raising hand and 35% talking out. Her teacher then switched Carmen to a FR 2 schedule of reinforcement for the next week, and a FR 3 schedule the following week. By the end of the third week Carmen reached the success criterion for both target behaviors, and the teacher switched her to a VR 2 reinforcement schedule—deciding to maintain her on this schedule for three more weeks. At the end of this

period, her percentage of raising her hand to talk (and waiting to be called on) had stayed at 100%, and she no longer talked out without raising her hand (Morris, 1985, p. 71).

Morris, R. J. (1985). Behavior modification with exceptional children. Glenview, IL: Scott, Foresman.

The discussion on shaping techniques can be expanded to include other popular operant conditioning techniques such as chaining, prompting, and fading. These techniques have been utilized most often with severely handicapped populations but can be useful with normal populations as well. Alberto and Troutman provide an excellent description of these techniques. The following example taken from their book can be used to demonstrate chaining, prompting, and fading as well as behavior modeling.

Carole Learns to Go Through the Lunch Line

It was Carole's first day in a regular school. She had previously attended a center for moderately retarded students but was now placed in a self-contained class in a regular elementary school. Her teacher, Mr. Grist, knew that meals at the center were served family-style and that the self-service line in the school cafeteria might be confusing to Carole. He put her in line behind Linda and walked beside the girls, saying, "Look, Carole, Linda took a fork. Now you take a fork." If necessary, he added a gesture or a physical prompt. He repeated this strategy for each of the steps required. When Carole reached the table safely, he praised her. He repeated this strategy daily, waiting to see whether she needed prompting before he offered it. By the end of the week Carole was managing nicely (Alberto & Troutman, 1986, p. 293).

Alberto, P. A., & Troutman, A. C. (1986). Applied behavior analysis for teachers. Columbus, OH: Merrill Publishing.

The textbook material on modeling and vicarious learning can be supplemented by introducing the students to role theory. Role theorists maintain that each individual assumes a number of different roles which are viewed as being consistent with the group position or status that the individual occupies. Other significant persons respond to the individual's chosen roles in reciprocal ways. The roles of people tend to be relatively fixed and mutually dependent. If one of the roles is inappropriate it is likely to continue unless the person who reciprocates fails to play out the expected role. Often disturbing role relationships of this type can be observed between teachers and students. The following example by Blackman and Silberman will illustrate to students how role redefinition can be used to break the cycle.

Suppose a mother has the habit of constantly nagging her son each morning to get ready for school. The more mother nags, the more Johnny resists. To help deal with this situation, she is instructed to perform a different role. She is told to request only once that he get ready for school. She is instructed not to nag, criticize, or punish. If Johnny does not carry out the demand within ten minutes, she quietly goes to his room and indicates that she will help him get dressed. Johnny is allowed to assume as much of the responsibility as he wishes, and mother begins to reinforce these efforts. On each successive morning, the same procedure is followed, with reinforcement being given for each preparatory gesture. When Johny has gotten dressed by himself, a bonus reinforcement (or reinforcing event) is given. When independent getting-dressed behavior has increased to reasonable frequency, tokens or points may be given, and the reinforcement schedule may be changed.

It is apparent from the example that several things may be operative when role shift and positive reinforcement are used. The mother's behavior becomes more predictable, the child's old resistance and delay tactics are inappropriate, and he gets reinforced for behaving differently. Since the mother's verbal behavior is no longer likely to evoke negative counterreactions, Johnny's minirebellion is brought to a halt (Blackman & Silberman, 1980, pp. 112-113).

> Blackman, G. J., & Silberman, A. Modification of child and adolescent behavior (3rd ed.). Belmont, CA: Wadsworth.

An excellent source is available for expanding the textbook material presented for cognitive behavior modification. The book, Cognitive Behavior Therapy with Children in the Schools, provides excellent strategies for using this technique with special problem populations which the teacher is likely to encounter. Some of the particular problems addressed in the book are:

- social anxiety
- school phobia
- test anxiety
- depression
- hyperactivity

> Hughes, J. M. (1988). Cognitive behavior therapy with children in the schools. New York: Pergamon.

Coaching is a behavior-change strategy based on the concepts of modeling. Coaching is a helpful technique for teaching new behaviors to older children who are socially incompetent. Several studies (Ladd, 1981; Oden & Asher, 1977; Whitehead, Hersen & Bellach, 1980) have shown the coaching technique to be effective with children who are aggressive and/or rejected. Instructors can share with the class the following five steps for implementing a coaching program which have been adapted from the work of Ogden and Asher.

Step 1:	Coach proposes the concept which is crucial to enjoyable interaction with others.
Step 2:	Coach probes the child's understanding of the concept as it relates to the target activity.
Step 3:	Coach paraphrases the child's example if it is appropriate or provides another example.
Step 4:	Coach asks the child to provide opposite examples to those which are desired.

Step 5: Coach asks the child to evaluate each example in terms of the effect it has on others and the target activity.

Ladd, G. W. (1981). Effectiveness of a social learning model for enhancing children's social interaction and peer acceptance. Child Development, 52, 171-178.

Oden, S., & Asher, S. (1977). Coaching children in skills for friendship making. Child Development, 48, 495-506.

Whitehead, M., Hersen, M., & Bellack, A. S. (1980). Conversation skills training for socially isolated children. Behavior Research and Therapy, 18, 217-225.

Discussion Questions

1. Robert is a nine-year-old who plays Little League baseball. Last Saturday when he was up to bat he got hit in the ribs by a wild pitch. He was hurt and badly frightened. The next day even a discussion of baseball made him very nervous. Now every time he tries to bat he automatically and involuntarily steps out of the batter's box when the pitcher begins his release. He cannot even take batting practice with the pitching machine. It is all he can do to play pitch and catch with his dad. Review this experience and explain if and when Robert experienced each of these: 1) classical conditioning, 2) unconditioned response, 3) unconditioned stimulus, 4) conditioned response, 5) unconditioned stimulus, 6) stimulus generalization, 7) stimulus discrimination.

2. Consider an inappropriate social behavior such as "refusing to share." Describe how a traditional behaviorist might try to change this behavior. Then describe how a cognitive behaviorist might try to change the same behavior. Finally, design a strategy for encouraging "sharing" behavior which would combine these two approaches.

3. Lonnie, a high school junior, has been watching Jack Nicklaus' Golf My Way tapes. He enters a high school golf tournament and steps up to the number one tee. He picks up his seven iron and adjusts his stance exactly like Jack. He tugs at both batting gloves and sets his cleats in the dirt. He concentrates on each phase of the golf swing. He is determined to get the swing right because last time he made a perfect imitation, and it resulted in his reaching the green in one shot.

   Review Lonnie's experience from the social learning perspective. Tell if and when each of the following processes occurred: 1) attentional, 2) retention, 3) reproduction, 4) motivational.

4. Angela is a student in your third grade class. She really has some social problems. She becomes very aggressive in unstructured situations. She is likely to push, shove and call other students names any time the class is waiting in line or playing on the playground. Outline three different behavioristic strategies for eliminating Angela's aggressive behavior that do not involve punishment.

5. Many students who have had failure experiences attempting to learn to read become very anxious when required to read aloud. How could you use classical conditioning techniques to eliminate this fear?

6. Your text describes programmed instruction. Select an instructional content area suitable for the grade level you intend to teach. Use the information in the text to design a programmed instruction lesson for teaching this objective which includes several frames.

7. Programmed and computer-assisted instruction are techniques which have been recommended as methods of individualizing instruction. How might you utilize these techniques to accommodate the needs of students in your fifth grade classroom whose reading levels range from the third to the tenth grade levels.

8. Consider the principles of Mastery Learning and explain how a teacher might be able to determine whether or not a student has learned a particular task in the school curriculum.

9. Your textbook says that learning is a change in behavior that results from experiences. Yet, it is unlikely that all experiences engender the same learning in all students? Are there some experiences that don't produce any learning at all? Defend your answer.

10. Some teachers are inclined to nag and harp on students who are engaging in irritating behaviors such as talking out, acting silly, fussing, etc. The teachers continue with this punitive technique because it is very effective at stopping these behaviors immediately. This type of teacher response, however, suffers from all the shortcomings of punishment and soon the behaviors return as strong or stronger than before. Teachers are aware of this, but they continue nagging anyway. It has been said that nagging and punishment are operant behaviors which are very negatively reinforcing to teachers. Explain this phenomenon.

Audiovisual Aids

B. F. Skinner and Behavior Change (Research Press, color, 45 min.). This film provides an excellent introduction to the work of B. F. Skinner and to behavior modification. It features on-site interventions with students in a variety of settings.

Behavioral Principles for Parents (Research Press, color, 13 min.). This film shows examples of positive reinforcement, punishment, extinction, and effective use of time-out procedures. The importance of giving simple, clearly stated instructions is stressed throughout the film.

Reward and Punishment (CRM/McGraw-Hill Films, color, 1970, 31 min.). This film examines the use of reward and punishment in classrooms as well as other settings.

FOLLOW-UP ACTIVITIES

1. Evaluate the Impact of Operant Conditioning

   This Follow-up Activity is ideally suited to helping the class understand the distinction between pleasant consequences and reinforcing consequences. To accomplish this, the instructor could identify several items or activities which most of them will identify as positive. Some examples are money, movies, chocolate, etc. Instructors could then establish operant levels of behavior in which individuals are willing to engage in order to obtain one of these reinforcers. Several interesting factors will surface. For example, most will claim to desire money. Many would be willing to walk to the teacher's desk for a dollar, but few would walk across campus for a dollar. On the other hand most of them would walk across campus for $100. Positive reinforcement then becomes a function of the required operant. What reinforces one behavior will not necessarily reinforce another.

2. Identify Appropriate Reinforcers

   Follow-up Activity 2 could be adapted for use as an out-of-class assignment by having class members administer the survey which is included in Follow-up Activity Sheet 6-2 to a group of junior high school students. After students have completed the questionnaire, results can be consolidated to provide an indication of which reinforcing agents are likely to be most powerful in changing the behavior of students this age.

3. Use Shaping to Change Behavior

   This Follow-up Activity can be depersonalized by having class members consider a second grade classroom. There is a child in the classroom who has been diagnosed as having an Attention Deficit Disorder. About the longest she ever concentrates on a learning task is 6 or 7 minutes. The average attention span for a child her age is about 25 minutes. How could shaping techniques be employed to develop a normal attention span?

4. Discuss the Usefulness of Teaching Machines, Computers, and/or Programmed Textbooks

Instructors can adapt this Follow-up Activity to an out-of-class assignment by having each class member analyze a computer software game and determine what learning principles are applied in its design. Have them pay particular attention to sequencing, reinforcement strategies, and any discrimination variables which are in effect.

5. Plan a Lesson Using Applied Behavior Analysis

Use Follow-up Activity Sheet 6-5 to convert this activity to an assignment. Have the class individually record their lesson plans on the sheet, then determine which aspects of operant conditioning are applied at various points in the lesson.

Additional Follow-up Activities

6. Apply Reinforcement and Punishment Principles

Have the class complete Follow-up Activity Sheet 6-6. This sheet contains real-life situations which students can evaluate to determine whether the operating principle which shapes the behavior is reinforcement, punishment, or extinction. Examples on this sheet are especially useful for demonstrating that reinforcement and punishment are always a function of whether the operant behavior is increased or decreased.

7. Evaluate Computer Software

Have each student in the class obtain a computer software package appropriate for students of the age or grade level they plan to teach. Then have them evaluate an activity from the package in terms of the criteria provided in Follow-up Activity Sheet 6-7.

8. Define an Effective Peer Model

Discuss how different model characteristics or attributes affect the probability that viewers will imitate the observed behavior. Then entertain observational learning strategies as behavior-change techniques. After your discussion have the students complete the library assignment described in Follow-up Activity Sheet 6-8.

Follow-up Activity Sheet 6-2

RATE YOUR FAVORITE THINGS

DIRECTIONS: Read about the things or activities in each of the categories below. Rate your favorite thing in each category as number 1, your second favorite as number 2. Continue numbering each item. Add other things if you would like.

Treats
Chocolate Bar   _____
Pizza Party   _____
Fast Food Hamburgers   _____
Hot Dogs   _____
Soft Drinks   _____
Popcorn Party   _____

In-class Activities
Work Out in Gym   _____
Play Computer Games   _____
Listen to Music with Headphones   _____
Shoot Baskets   _____
Free Time   _____
Play Board Games/Cards/Dominos   _____

Out-of-Class Activities
Have a Friend Spend the Night   _____
Spend the Night with a Friend   _____
Go Skating   _____
Eat Out   _____
Attend a Sporting Event   _____

Things
Baseball Cards   _____
Athletic Poster   _____
Pocket Cars   _____
Ball   _____
Stickers   _____
Music Cassette   _____

Other

IDENTIFY LEARNING PRINCIPLES IN YOUR LESSON

DIRECTIONS: Write an instructional objective and daily lesson plan in the space
provided below.

Instructional
Objective

Monday: Outline of content
                Procedures
                Materials

Tuesday: Outline of content
                Procedures
                Materials

Wednesday: Outline of content
                Procedures
                Materials

Thursday: Outline of content
                Procedures
                Materials

Friday: Outline of content
                Procedures
                Materials

Follow-up Activity Sheet 6-5 (Cont.)

See how many of the learning principles listed below you can identify in your lessons.

- discriminative stimulus
- stimulus generalization
- operant
- operant rate
- reinforce stimulus
- schedule of reinforcement
- discriminative learning
- response generalization
- negative reinforcement
- positive reinforcement (primary and secondary)
- shaping
- prompting
- fading
- modeling
- observational learning

REINFORCEMENT VERSUS PUNISHMENT

DIRECTIONS: Read each of the vignettes below. Indicate whether the operant behavior was positively reinforced, negatively reinforced, punished, or extinguished.

1. Mary is not one for taking medicine. The last time she had a headache, however, she took an Extra Strength Militol. Her headache stopped immediately. Now she takes Militol at the slightest hint of a headache. Mary's aspirin taking behavior was _____.

2. Mark is an autistic boy who has difficulty establishing eye contact. Now his therapist delivers a mild electric shock to him when he looks away. Mark's inattentiveness was _____ by the electric shock.

3. Mr. Jones read somewhere that propping your feet up for 15 minutes will regenerate the system. He tried this technique during his coffee break. It made him feel much more rested. Now he does it every day. Mr. Jones' foot propping behavior was _____.

4. Coach Jones made the mistake of screaming at the umpire during a Little League game. He was immediately thrown out of the game and his team lost in the ninth inning after maintaining a lead all the way. You can bet he hasn't tried screaming at the umpire again. His screaming was _____.

5. Ms. Manners' husband was driving her crazy by chewing with his mouth open. Finally she decided to just let him have it and she really told him off. Since then he has been really careful to take small bites and not chew offensively. Ms. Manners' "telling him off" behavior was _____. Mr. Manners' chewing with his mouth open behavior was _____.

6. Susan's mother used to brag about her for keeping such a neat room. Lately, however, she's been busy and really hasn't had time to notice. Suddenly Susan's room is looking pretty sloppy. Susan's "room cleaning behavior" was _____.

7. One day Susan's mother noticed the room and immediately had a fit. She started in on Susan right away, announcing that something must be done. Susan had several other things on her agenda at that time, but she put them on hold and immediately started cleaning her room. Her mother was satisfied by this and went on to other things. Susan's room cleaning behavior was _____.

8. Susan's mother didn't want a hostile relationship to continue with Susan so she made her a proposition. If you keep your room clean all week, on Saturday I'll give you $20.00. Susan's room has been spic-and-span ever since. Susan's room cleaning behavior was _____.

Follow-up Activity Sheet 6-7

EVALUATE COMPUTER SOFTWARE

DIRECTIONS: Obtain a computer software package appropriate for use with students the age you intend to teach. Select a learning activity from the package and evaluate the activity on each of the variables listed below.

1. What prerequisite skills would a student need to utilize the software package format?

2. What prerequisite skills would a student need before this content is attempted?

3. How will mastery of the learning activity be ascertained?

4. How can this activity be correlated to curriculum presented in the textbook?

5. What stimulus and response generalization would be required for the student to apply computer activity content to an in-class group activity which will be covered by the text?

DEFINE AN EFFECTIVE PEER MODEL

DIRECTIONS: Social learning theorists believe that one determining factor which governs whether observed behavior is modeled or not involves the attributes of the model who is being observed. The following article examines the type of model attributes which foster behavior change in children:

Schunk, D. H. (1987). Peer models and children's behavioral change. Review of Educational Research, 57, 149-174.

Based on the content of the article, describe the characteristics of the model who would be most effective in changing behavior of the children in the grade level you teach.

CHAPTER SEVEN

COGNITIVE APPROACHES TO LEARNING

CHAPTER OBJECTIVES

Students mastering the content in Chapter Seven will be able to:

• Identify how the information-processing system influences learning.

• Plan and implement lessons based on declarative and procedural learning tasks.

• Teach student learning strategies to make them more effective learners.

FOCUS QUESTIONS

1. Why is it important to develop students' metacognitive abilities?

   From the cognitive perspective, one of the major goals of teaching is to help students to manage and control their own learning. If students do not have the strategies needed to master academic content, the teaching goal must be to help them to acquire these strategies. When compared to poor learners, good learners have been shown to have better metacognitive skills. These include more effective strategies for selecting and attending to important information in texts and lectures, and the ability to organize material in a more efficient manner. There is also evidence that students can be taught to use learning strategies to improve their classroom learning.

2. What are some methods that students can learn to increase their memory of factual material?

   Mnemonics are elaboration techniques that impose a useful linkage between new data and visual images or semantic knowledge. These techniques are often recommended for helping students increase their memory of factual information. For example, a useful mnemonic for learning foreign language vocabulary is the key-word method, which involves the creation of an image that relates the English to the foreign word. Acronyms use the first letter in each word to form a mnemonic. The peg-word method uses visual imagery and semantic associations in remembering serial data.

3. How can the use of learning strategies improve student achievement?

   For the most part, teachers deal with meaningful knowledge that is connected or interrelated, such as information from textbooks and lectures. Such knowledge obtains its meaning from one's ability to connect the ideas of the text or lecture with knowledge that is stored in long-term memory. When new information about something is stored, the meaning or main ideas contained in the text are stored. Teachers can use four strategies to facilitate the storage of their ideas in long-term memory and, therefore, improve student achievement. They are: 1) rehearsal, 2) elaboration, 3) organization, and 4) comprehension monitoring.

4. What advice would you give students about underlining?

First, students must determine what is important in a passage, such as the topic sentence. The next step is to underline sparingly, perhaps only one or two sentences in a paragraph. Finally, students should review and paraphrase those passages underlined.

5. How can you improve students' note-taking?

Students should be taught to make brief notes in their own words that organize and summarize the important points of the lecture so that the notes make sense to them. Students should also be encouraged to make conceptual notes that stress the main ideas of the lecture. Detailed notes are related to performance and should be taken to supplement the lecture's main ideas. Kiewra identifies certain teacher behaviors which he believes can improve students' note-taking and review behaviors. These include:

- Lecturing at a slower rate
- Repeating complex subject material
- Presenting cues for note-taking
- Writing important information on the board
- Providing students with a complete set of notes to review
- Providing structural support for note-taking such as skeletal outline or matrix framework

6. How can a teacher help students improve their reading comprehension?

Devine suggests that teachers practice several strategies for monitoring and improving student comprehension of textbook material. He suggests that teachers have students:

- Ignore small or minor parts of the text that are difficult to understand, and read ahead to make sense of these sections.
- Change the rate of reading to accommodate differences in the comprehensibility of the text. Speed up for easier sections to quickly get an idea of the author's overall plan, but slow down for more difficult sections.
- Suspend judgment. If something is not clear, continue to read; the author will probably fill in the gaps, add more information, or clarify points in the text.
- Hypothesize when something being read is not clear. Make it a habit to hypothesize about the meaning of the unclear passage and read along to see if your guess makes sense.
- Reread difficult passages. This strategy can often be particularly effective when information appears contradictory or ambiguous.

Another way in which schemata have proven useful in promoting comprehension is through the use of advance organizers. Advance organizers present information before a lesson to make the lesson content more meaningful and easier to understand. The information in an advance organizer is presented at a higher level of abstraction and generality than the lesson content to aid the learner in subsuming or integrating the new material.

7. How can you help students improve their attentiveness to academic tasks?

Students can use self-verbalization to monitor and control their behavior in eliminating distractions while they are attempting to learn. Knowledge of the information-processing system also can be helpful to the teacher concerned with student attention.

8. What are differences in teaching pattern-recognition knowledge and action sequences?

One type of procedural knowledge is pattern recognition. Pattern-recognition knowledge pertains to the student's ability to recognize and classify patterns of stimuli. One important example of pattern recognition is the ability to identify new incidents of a concept, or concept learning. A concept represents a group of ideas or things that share some common characteristics and have the same name. The second type of procedural knowledge refers to knowledge of action sequences. An action sequence is simply a sequence of behaviors or cognitive actions to be taken to reach some goal. When teaching pattern recognition teachers must be careful to provide true examples of the concept that will promote accurate generalization. They must also provide non-examples so that students can make accurate generalizations. To teach action sequences, teachers must first be sure that students know the steps. If more than nine are required, the steps should be written. Practice then makes the steps automatic and the teacher must help students guard against the set effect.

9. Can students be taught critical thinking skills?

Most teachers believe that critical thinking skills can be taught. There is, however, considerable disagreement over how these skills should be taught. To date, research on programs designed to teach these types of skills has shown that they are only moderately successful.

CHAPTER OUTLINE

I. ORIENTATION

A. Focus Questions

II. THE INFORMATION-PROCESSING SYSTEM (IPS)

A. Short-Term Sensory Store (STSs)

B. Short-Term Memory (STM)
C. Long-Term Memory (LTM)
D. Executive Control

    1. Learning Strategies

III. DECLARATIVE KNOWLEDGE

IV. ROTE LEARNING

A. Types of Rote Learning
B. Using Learning Strategies for Improving Rote Learning

    1. Rehearsal
    2. Elaboration
    3. Organization

V. MEANINGFUL LEARNING

A. Using Learning Strategies to Improve Meaningful Learning

    1. Rehearsal
    2. Elaboration
    3. Organization
    4. Comprehension monitoring
    5. Affective strategies

VI. PROCEDURAL KNOWLEDGE

A. Pattern-Recognition Knowledge
B. Action-Sequence Knowledge

    1. Transfer characteristics of procedural and declarative knowledge

C. Problem-Solving Strategies/Critical Thinking Skills

VII. THINKING ABOUT THE TEACHING-LEARNING MODEL

KEY TERMS

information-processing system (p. 268)   chunking (p. 270)

short-term sensory store (p. 268)   rehearsal strategies (p. 270)

short-term memory (p. 269)   long-term memory (p. 270)

working memory (p. 269)   automaticity (p. 271)

decoding (p. 271)

encoding (p. 271)

episodic memory (p. 271)

semantic memory (p. 271)

declarative knowledge (p. 271)

procedural knowledge (p. 271)

executive processes (p. 271)

metacognition (p. 272)

learning strategies (p. 273)

elaboration strategies (p. 273)

organizational strategies (p. 273)

comprehension-monitoring strategies (p. 273)

affective strategies (p. 273)

meaningful learning (p. 276)

rote learning (p. 276)

free recall (p. 277)

serial recall (p. 277)

paired-associate learning (p. 277)

distributed practice (p. 278)

massed practice (p. 278)

serial position effect (p. 278)

part learning (p. 278)

positive transfer (p. 278)

negative transfer (p. 278)

proactive inhibition (p. 279)

retroactive inhibition (p. 279)

overlearning (p. 279)

mnemonics (p. 279)

loci method (p. 280)

acronyms (p. 280)

peg-word method (p. 280)

key-word method (p. 280)

matrix notes (p. 285)

adjunct questions (288)

SQR3 System (289)

schemata (p. 289)

advance organizer (p. 291)

pattern-recognition knowledge (295)

concept learning (p. 295)

action sequence (p. 296)

set effect (p. 297)

task analysis (p. 297)

CHAPTER GUIDELINES

Chapter Seven presents three cognitive approaches to learning. The information-processing system (IPS) is described as a cyclical procedure for perceiving, storing, and retrieving information. The flow of information through this model is monitored by executive processes called metacognitive knowledge. The chapter utilizes this model to identify how successful learners acquire metacognitive skills to control these processes and become independent learners. Rehearsal, elaboration, organization, comprehension-monitoring, affective, and problem-solving strategies are each described.

Declarative and procedural knowledge are defined. Both rote and meaningful forms of declarative knowledge are described. Massed practice is compared to distributed practice in rote learning. Rehearsal, organization, mnemonics, acronyms, peg words, and key words are presented as instructional strategies provided for increasing rote memory. As meaningful learning connects new information to pre-existing, long-term memory knowledge, the implementation of comprehension strategies are emphasized. Sample lesson plans illustrate note-taking procedures, outlining of text or lecture material, comprehension monitoring, adjunct questioning, schemata organizers, and advance organizers. Affective strategies to motivate students, focus their attention, and help to reduce their anxiety are described. Instructional objectives and advance warning of possible test questions are specifically suggested to help focus student attention. The ability of teachers to develop metacognitive strategies in helping students monitor and control their attention is stressed.

The two types of procedural knowledge, pattern-recognition and action-sequence knowledge, are discussed. Problem-solving strategies are identified to demonstrate the interaction of declarative and procedural knowledge. Teachers are guided toward objectives which show students how to use different learning strategies in completing assignments and preparing for examinations.

This chapter concludes with a comparison of the effectiveness of various thinking skills programs and a caution to teachers for careful evaluation of available programs prior to their implementation.

Supplementary Material

One source for expanding the material in Chapter Seven is a research article recently published in the Educational Psychologist. The article reports results of a survey that was conducted with teachers in the elementary school grades. The teachers were asked to report the strategies which they used to teach memory skills. The strategies teachers named most often are listed below in descending order beginning with the strategy most often cited as being used:

- **Specific Aids for Problem Solving and Memory.** Students are encouraged to use familiar items (i.e., food or clothing), objects (i.e., blocks for math), or reading content to enhance memory or problem solving ability.

- **Attention.** Students are prompted frequently to gain or maintain their attention.

- **Deduction.** Students are encouraged to combine their knowledge with context clues to obtain problem solutions or deduce correct answers.

- **Rote Learning.** Rehearsal strategies such as "go over" the work, reread, and repeat are used in various combinations.

- **Elaboration.** Students are instructed to assign meaning to meaningless work by creating analogies or creating meaningful relationships.

- **Self-Checking.** Students are advised to go over their work and check for erros. Also, study with a friend might be suggested to determine that content is mastered before a test.

- **Specific Attentional Aids.** Students are presented with strategies for using items, things, or body parts to maintain attention systematically.

- **Transformation.** Difficult or unfamiliar problems are reformulated into a simpler form which can be mastered.

- **General Aids.** Students are taught to use a variety of aids such as a dictionary which can be generalized to a variety of problem-solving situations.

- **Metamemory.** Teachers provide skills and explanations that help students understand and improve their memory processes.

- **Imagery.** Students are instructed to visualize items or characters and take a mental picture of them.

- **Exclusion.** Students are taught to rule out or eliminate incorrect responses first.

Molly, B. E., Hart, S. S., Santilli, K., Leal, L., Johnston, T., Rao, N., & Burney, L. (1986). How do teachers teach memory skills? Educational Psychologist, 21, 55-72.

Instructors can expand on the content in Chapter Seven by including the work of Mayer. This author describes a model for facilitating recall which stresses the importance of providing examples, creating associative images, and making practical applications.

Moyer, K. (1984). Aids to text and comprehension. Educational Psychologist, 19, 30-42.

In an effort to expand on the concepts in the text related to adjunct questions, instructors can have students read an article by White which addresses the topic of prepassage questions. Specially tell students to use the SQ3R system and document each step in the process when they are reading the article. When class reconvenes discuss first what declarative knowledge they gained from the article that will assist them in using prepassage questions to enhance student learning. Then ask them what procedural knowledge they gained from using the SQ3R technique.

White, S. (1983). Prepassage questions: The influence of structural importance. Journal of Educational Psychology, 75, 234-244.

Instructors can expand on the information in Chapter Seven by having the students engage in some memory tasks during class. For example, the following series of 12 numers could be flashed on the screen for 30 seconds.

| 8 | 2 | 8 | 7 | 6 | 4 | 5 | 8 | 9 | 3 | 2 | 8 |

After viewing the numbers, students could be asked to rewrite them in the original order. After this exercise has been completed, the instructor can discuss the value of the chunking technique. This discussion could easily be related to the way most people remember their telephone and social security numbers. After the discussion, a second series of numbers can be attempted.

| 6 | 5 | 6 | 4 | 2 | 4 | 5 | 9 | 8 | 5 | 6 | 5 |

A comparison of individual performance on the first and second attempts should show that class performed significantly better on the second trial.

Numerous activities of this type are provided for instructors who want to demonstrate the power of mnemonic as well as other learning strategies endorsed by information-processing psychologists.

Benjamin, L. T., & Lowman, K. D. (1981). Activities handbook for the teaching of psychology. Washington, DC: American Psychological Association.

Discussion Questions

1. Reflect on the operation of your long term memory by trying to remember some routine aspects of your daily lives as they have occurred over time. For example, try to remember:

   • What you wore yesterday
   • What you wore a week ago
   • What you wore last June 29
   • What you wore last Thanksgiving

Relate the speed, certainty, and accuracy of your responses to search and retrieval mechanisms of the memory system.

2. Mr. Bones is a high school biology teacher. Explain how he could use each of the following mnemonic strategies in teaching a unit on the skeletal system of the human body:

   • loci method

- acronyms
- peg-word method
- key words

3. Consider that you are a high school English teacher. You are responsible for teaching a study skills unit. Combine what you have learned about note-taking and outling in Chapter Seven with what you have learned about metacognition. Use this information to develop the instructional objectives for your study skills unit. What criteria will you use to determine whether your unit has been effective in improving your students' study skills? Consider generalization in your response.

4. Take a story from an elementary school reading series. Describe how you would use comprehension monitoring to improve the students' reading comprehension and to determine if they were understanding the material they read?

5. Matthew was a high school football player. In college he couldn't make the varsity team so he decided to join an intermural rugby team. The basic idea of the two games is the same, but many of the rules and regulations are different. Which of the following aspects of learning/forgetting could be causing Matthew difficulty in learning the new game?

- proactive inhibition
- retroactive inhibition
- positive transfer
- negative transfer

6. Ms. Hunter is a fifth grade social studies teacher. She has just finished a unit on American Indians. She focused on several topics. These included dwellings and food collecting practices of Indians in different geographic regions. She covered the material several times. Also, it was presented in the text. Still, the highest grade made by any student was 84. Almost no one answered all the ''home'' and ''food'' questions correctly. Propose some strategies she could use to improve the recall of her fifth graders.

Audiovisual Aids

A Search for Learning (McGraw-Hill Films, b&w, 1967,13 min.). Scenes show the use of the "discovery approach" in actual classroom situations. The teachers and narrator comment on the advantages and objectives of this teaching approach.

Choosing to Learn (Educational Development Center, color, 1969, 26 min.). The World of Inquiry School is an experimental school that follows cognitive principles. This film shows children of various backgrounds following their own interests in learning.

Memory: Fabric of the Mind (CC-1738, Films for the Humanities and Sciences, color, 30 min.). This video presents research on the physiology of the brain as it relates to memory and the process of forgetting.

<u>Teaching Reading as Thinking</u> (VC #614-143Vs, Association for Supervision and Curriculum Development color, 30 min.). This video shows a master teacher demonstrating three steps to teaching critical thinking skills through reading.

FOLLOW-UP ACTIVITIES

1. Teach Students to Think

   Three possible perspectives on this issue which might be generated by an in-class discussion are as follows.

   Piagetian. Piaget would tend to see this problem as failure of the student to create appropriate mental schemata through the processes of assimilation and accommodation. This pattern could emerge if developmental processes were rushed, or if the instruction relied too heavily on didactic teaching strategies rather than exploratory and discovery learning.

   Skinnerian. A Skinnerian or traditional behaviorist might view the problem as motivational. Either the student has been reinforced for the wrong thing, or not reinforced at all. Maintenance, generalization, and transfer would also need to be enhanced to improve the student's tendency to apply information in new situations and over time.

   Information Processing. These psychologists would believe that this student needs to be taught metacognitive and critical thinking skills. They would see the problem as faulty teaching/learning. They might also think that previous learning and interference variables are causing difficulty in the student's performance.

2. Think about Learning Strategies

   This Follow-up Activity could be personalized by having class members reflect upon the last exam they took in your class (or possibly their most difficult class). Ask them how they prepared for the exam. Then have them compare the way they studied for the exam with the recommendations of the information processing psychologists provided in Chapter Seven. Finally, have them plan a strategy that they can use in preparing for their next exam.

   Revisit these issues during a future class session. Determine whether the class carried out their plan and whether or not the plan enhanced test performance.

3. Plan a Lesson Using Learning Strategies

   Instructors who previously had class members complete Follow-up Activity 6-5 can use that exercise as the basis for this Follow-up Activity. They can ask students to take the lessons that they previously designed and specify ten ways that the lesson could be improved by including suggestions from Table 7-4.

4. Lead a Discussion Exploring Students' Thinking

    To include Follow-up Activity 4 as an in-class activity divide the class into five small groups. Tell the groups that they will each be responsible for designing a daily lesson plan for teaching third grade students the concept and process of multiplication. Each group should focus on demonstrating the following learning strategies as they design the content to be taught over the course of a week.

    Monday, Group 1 -   Provide Advance Organizers (Ausubel) and Introduce the Concept.

    Tuesday, Group 2 -   Structure Group Problem Solving (Schoenfeld)

    Wednesday, Group 3 - Process Monitoring (Lester & Garofalo)

    Thursday, Group 4 -   Devise Mnemonic Strategies

    Friday, Group 5 -   Establish Overlearning, Generalization

5. Help Students Improve Their Metacognitive Skills

    Distribute a copy of Follow-up Activity Sheet 7-5 to each class member. Have them reproduce several copies of the form and construct packets of five of these sheets to distribute to each student in their class. They can ask the students to maintain the Daily Learning Logs in their science or social studies class for the period of a week. Class members should review the logs daily and clarify any misunderstanding their students may have.

    After the activity is completed, they can bring the completed logs to class and let the student responses provide the basis for a subsequent discussion on how teachers can help students improve metacognitive skills.

Additional Follow-up Activities

6. Using Imagery to Improve Memory

    To impress upon the class the value of using visual imagery to improve memory, conduct the following in-class experiment.

    Tell the class to have a pencil and paper ready, but not to write until instructed to do so. Then read the following list of six unrelated word pairs. Pause three seconds between each pair.

    1. flower   -   elephant
    2. spoon   -   box
    3. chest   -   foot
    4. door   -   grass

5. book - tray
6. lamp - nail

Immediately after the list has been read, ask the class to write as many word pairs as they can remember. Check to see how many individuals were able to recall and write as many as five or six.

Next tell the class that you are going to give a second list. This time you want them to construct a visual picture which associates the pair. For example, if the two words you give are "apple-shirt," have them imagine a shirt with an apple logo. Then proceed to call out the second list of pairs.

1. rug   - lipstick
2. arm   - bowl
3. skirt   - car
4. earring - glass
5. pencil - boy
6. banana - shoe

After the second reading check and see how many were able to remember five or six pairs. You will find the number greatly increased. You can even try asking the class to construct the two lists during the following class period. The difference in their ability to remember the two lists will be dramatic.

7. Evaluating Short-Term Memory

The textbook discusses the work of Miller who has determined that the short-term memory store of adults can only hold nine chunks of information at one time. For children the capacity is less. Have your class members evaluate the STM of children the age they plan to teach by completing the assignment contained in Follow-up Activity Sheet 7-7. After all class members have concluded the activity have them compare results and compile them by age. Can the relationship between age and increased STM be seen from the data? What are the implications of short-term memory capacity for the various aspects of teaching? This activity can also be related to previous textbook information on measuring intelligence and the Digit Span Subtest on the WISC-R and WAIS.

DAILY LEARNING LOG

DIRECTIONS: During science (social studies) class listen to or read the lesson. During
the last five minutes of class complete the Daily Learning Log below:

Name _____   Date _____

Today I Learned

_____

Things I Didn't Understand

_____

Questions I Would Like to Ask

_____

EVALUATING SHORT-TERM MEMORY

DIRECTIONS: Following are six sets of unrelated numbers which you can use to test the short-term memory of school-age students. Administer this test individually to five different students. Say to the student:

"Listen to the following numbers which I will call out to you. See how many you can remember."

Set   1. 4, 7, 3, 5
Set   2. 9, 4, 6, 8, 3
Set   3. 2, 9, 5, 8, 6, 7
Set   4. 7, 1, 8, 6, 9, 4, 3
Set   5. 3, 7, 1, 9, 10, 2, 6, 4
Set   6. 5, 8, 3, 10, 7, 6, 4, 2, 1

Call out the numbers from the first set. Then say:

"Can you tell me the numbers."

Circle each set the student correctly repeats on the form below. Continue through the list until the student is unable to reproduce two sets in a row.

Student #1,   Age _____;   Set   1   2   3   4   5   6

Student #2,   Age _____;   Set   1   2   3   4   5   6

Student #3,   Age _____;   Set   1   2   3   4   5   6

Student #4,   Age _____;   Set   1   2   3   4   5   6

Student #5,   Age _____;   Set   1   2   3   4   5   6

CHAPTER EIGHT

THE HUMANISTIC PERSPECTIVE

CHAPTER OBJECTIVES

Students mastering the content in Chapter Eight will be able to:

- Use humanistic principles to facilitate learning and human development.

- Lead a class discussion on a moral dilemma.

- Use values clarification exercises to help students better understand their own values.

- Develop an open classroom.

- Prepare students for cooperative learning.

FOCUS QUESTIONS

1. How do humanistic psychologists view learning?

   Humanists conceptualize two parts in the learning process. These are the acquisition of new information and the individual's personalization of this information. Teachers make the mistake of assuming that students will learn if subject matter is properly organized and presented. Meaning, however, is not inherent in the subject matter. It is the individual who instills subject matter with meaning. The dilemma in teaching is not how to present subject matter but how to help students derive personal meaning from the subject matter. If they can relate it in some way to their lives, the teacher will have succeeded.

2. What classroom practices would humanistic psychologists encourage?

   Carl Rogers was a humanistic psychologist whose ideas have strongly influenced educational thought and practice. He has adapted many of his strategies for classroom use. Foremost among Rogers' beliefs is that human beings have a natural desire to learn. In the humanistic classroom, children are given the freedom to satisfy their curiosity, to pursue their interests unabated, and to discover for themselves what is important and meaningful about the world around them. The second humanistic learning principle that Rogers identified is that significant, or meaningful, learning occurs when it is perceived by students as being relevant to their own needs and purposes. A third principle identified by Rogers is that learning is best acquired and retained in an environment free from threat. Also, for the humanists, learning is most significant and pervasive when it is self-initiated and when it involves both the feelings and the mind of the learner. They believe that being able to choose the direction of one's own learning is highly motivating and gives students the opportunity to learn how to learn. Rogers believed that the most socially useful learning is learning about the process of learning in order to learn in a changing environment. In support of this principle, Rogers suggested that teachers provide students with a variety of resources that can support and guide their learning experiences. Another strategy suggested by Rogers is peer tutoring. Finally, Rogers was a strong proponent of discovery and inquiry learning. These strategies allow students to seek answers to real questions, make autonomous discoveries, and become engaged in self-directed learning. Humanistic education is only as successful as the teacher who implements it. Success is largely dependent upon certain human qualities which the teacher brings to the classroom. According to Rogers, the teacher in a humanistic classroom is primarily a facilitator of learning. Humanists also believe that being real with students encourages open communication in the classroom and helps students to become more connected with their own feelings. Final qualities that enhance the teacher's role as a facilitator are trust and empathic understanding.

3. What factors do humanistic psychologists see as interfering with learning?

The traditional classroom is in sharp contrast to the educational approach that tries to make learning and teaching more humanistic. Some of the principles advocated in traditional classrooms may interfere with learning. One of these is having the teacher or the curriculum determine what children should learn. The value of curricular planning, the scholarly expertise of the teacher, or the use of technology may not be as important for the facilitation of learning as responsiveness to the student's feelings or the quality of the interaction between students and teachers.

4. What is the difference between values clarification and Kohlberg's approach to moral education?

Sidney Simon developed a program called values clarification that is based on the premise that many young people do not know clearly what their values are. He contends that values clarification does not focus on the content of a person's values but on the process of valuing itself. Kohlberg's theory is based on the belief that morality is a set of rational principles for making judgments about how to behave. His basic principles are based on justice and the regard for the dignity and worth of all persons.

5. What is the controversy concerning direct and indirect approaches to moral character development?

A number of educators are critical with the indirect approaches to moral education because these approaches emphasize how students think about moral issues rather than how they behave. The critics indicate the ineffectiveness of these approaches by pointing out that they have done little to deal with the moral problems in schools and society. The indirect approaches encourage teachers to present critical situations and serve as group facilitators but never to give their opinion concerning right and wrong in what students say. Today, there appears to be more concern that the teachers and the schools play a more direct role in developing standards and teaching moral behavior.

6. How are humanistic principles and Piaget's theory of cognitive development used in the open classroom?

Advocates of open education claim that it is both a philosophy and strongly influenced by Piaget's theory of cognitive development. Walberg and Thomas reviewed relevant literature on open education. They have constructed a list of eight themes which are listed below. They are a combination of humanistic and Piagetian principles.

- Provisions for Learning. Manipulative materials are supplied in great diversity and range. Children move freely around the room. Talking is encouraged. No grouping by ability using test scores is used.
- Humaneness, Respect, Openness, and Warmth. Student-made materials are used. Teachers deal with behavior problems by communicating with the child, without involving the group.
- Diagnosis of Learning Events. Students correct their own work. Teachers observe and ask questions.
- Instruction. Individualized instruction with no tests or workbooks is recommended.
- Evaluation. Teachers take notes. Few formal tests are given.
- Search for Opportunities for Professional Growth. Teachers use assistance of someone else. Teachers work with colleagues.
- Self-Perception of Teacher. Teachers try to keep all children within sight to monitor their work.
- Assumptions about Children and the Learning Process. Classroom climate is warm and accepting. Children are involved in their work.

7. How do individual differences influence group functioning?

Investigations on cooperative learning have found that in most cases individual differences have a positive effect on group functioning. There is some evidence to indicate, for example, that academic achievement is increased in heterogeneous groupings. Webb reviewed the research on helping behaviors that contribute to successful learning in cooperative groups. A few of Webb's findings concerning individual differences are as follows:

- High-ability students are most likely to give explanations to others.
- Extroverted students are more successful than introverted students in obtaining explanations when they ask questions.
- Boys may be more successful than girls in obtaining help.
- Groups with only students of medium ability spend more time explaining, and all students participate in group discussions.
- Heterogeneous groups with a moderate range of ability demonstrate a high level of explaining.
- Groups with only low-ability or high-ability students do little explaining.

- In groups with a wide range of ability, the high-ability students often explain to the low-ability students while ignoring the middle-ability students.
- In groups with an equal number of boys and girls, all students are able to obtain help when asked.
- In groups where boys outnumber girls or when girls outnumber boys, the boys are more successful than girls in obtaining help.
- In groups of mostly girls, the girls direct many of their questions to the boy who is not likely to answer all their questions.
- White students tend to be more active and influential in groups than minority students.

CHAPTER OUTLINE

I. ORIENTATION

    A. Focus Questions

II. HUMANISTIC PSYCHOLOGY

    A. Combs
    B. Maslow

        1. Instructional implications of Maslow's views

    C. Rogers

        1. The desire to learn
        2. Significant learning
        3. Learning without threat
        4. Self-initiated learning
        5. Learning and change
        6. Instructional implications of Rogers' views

III. INSTRUCTIONAL APPLICATIONS OF HUMANISTIC PSYCHOLOGY

    A. Moral/Character Education

        1. Character education and clinical intervention
        2. Indirect approaches to moral education
        3. Direct approaches to moral education
        4. A possible reconciliation

    B. Open Education

        1. Research on open education

    C. Cooperative Learning

1. Teams - Games - Tournaments (TGT)
2. Student Teams - Achievement Divisions (STAD)
3. Jigsaw
4. Group Investigation
5. Team-Assisted Individualization (TAI)
6. Research on Cooperative Learning

IV. CRITICISMS OF HUMANISTIC EDUCATION

V. THINKING ABOUT THE TEACHING-LEARNING MODEL

KEY TERMS

hierarchy of needs (p. 325)   values clarification (p. 333)

self-actualization (p. 326)   Kohlberg's stages of moral reasoning (p. 335)

person-centered education (p. 328)   Moral dilemmas (p. 336)

empathetic understanding (p. 330)   jigsaw method (p. 348)

CHAPTER GUIDELINES

This chapter investigates humanistic psychology and its influence on educational thought and practice. Several student-centered learning situations utilized by humanistic educators to help students learn more about themselves, relate to others, and make independent decisions are presented.

The principles of humanistic psychology are identified through an examination of the views of Combs, Maslow, and Rogers. The humanistic concern for an individual's feelings, perceptions, beliefs, and purposes is related through an account of Comb's work. In defining motivation, Maslow's Hierarchy of Needs is explained in depth followed by implications for instructional use. The learning principles of Carl Rogers are examined, with implications for a person-centered education and a description of the "humanistic teacher."

Because of recent changes in society requiring that the school assume more responsibility for character development, the chapter focuses on moral education by presenting direct and indirect instructional approaches. Simon's values clarification program and Kohlberg's stages of moral reasoning are indirect approaches which are discussed. Criticisms from educators are related for each approach. Open education and cooperative learning are two direct approaches to moral development presented in this chapter.

Criteria for establishing an open classroom are presented and research on its effectiveness is examined along with other teaching strategies which are compatible with humanistic education. One of these is cooperative learning. Cooperative learning has been shown to have a positive effect on student achievement and interpersonal relationships. Several other strategies are also described. These include Teams - Games - Tournaments, Student Teams - Achievement Divisions, Jigsaw, Group Investigation, and Team-Assisted Individualization. Guidelines for preparing students to work in cooperative groups are provided, along with considerations which need to be made for individual differences during group formation.

The conclusion of this chapter addresses criticisms of humanistic education and relates principles of humanistic education to the teaching-learning model.

Supplementary Material

Instructors can use Milgram's classic study of obedience as a means of expanding the material in Chapter Eight. This study provides an excellent example of the moral reasoning and decision-making processes that individuals employ as they are deciding whether or not to administer electric shock.

Milgram, S. (1963). Behavioral study of obedience. Journal of Abnormal Social Psychology, 67, 371-378.

The discussion on affective education could be expanded to include the work of Brown (1971), a pioneer in this area. His term "confluent education" was used to reflect the integration of affective objectives into subject matter content.

Brown, G. (1971). Human teaching for human learning. New York: Viking.

Another possibility for elaborating on the topic of affective education is to provide class members with some specific activites that they can adapt for use with children of varying ages. Simpson and Grey describe activities of this type in their book, Humanistic Education: An Interpretation. Two activities recommended by Simpson and Grey are the Magic Circle and the Trumpet March.

Magic Circle (elementary level). This activity is based on students coming together for regularly scheduled group meetings which are referred to as a Magic Circle. During this time the teacher directs peers to exchange perceptions and opinions about each other. The focus of the discussion can be on what students like about themselves as well as what they like about each other. Magic Circle time can be utilized to help students understand their own behavior, and other children's behaviors and also for group problem solving.

Trumpet March (secondary). In this activity students are asked to observe, record, and evaluate data on their own behavior and the behavior of their peers. The activity is structured on a seven-step program.

Simpson, E., & Grey, M. (1976). Humanistic education: An interpretation. Cambridge, MA: Ballenger.

Instructors can use Piaget's theory of moral development as background information before introducing Kohlberg's work. Piaget theorized two stages in moral development.

Heteronomous Morality. This moral structure is characteristic of young children. It tends to be rigid and arbitrary. There is an attitude of moral realism in which right is defined by obedience to adults and adherence to rules. Wrong is viewed in terms of the consequences of the behavior, and severe punishment is accepted as the consequence of events.

Autonomous Mortality. As children mature they develop more rational moral attitudes. The emphasis is on cooperation and equality among individuals. Peers are seen as a byproduct of mutual agreement. Wrong becomes a relative term which varies with an individual's intentions and sense of fair play. Punishment must be appropriate to be acceptable.

Piaget's theories of cognitive and moral development served as a basis for Kohlberg's contributions in the latter area. As a result his work provides an interesting source for comparing and contrasting. For a more detailed account of Piaget's work in this area instructors can consult Hogan and Emler.

Hogan, R., & Emler, N. P. (1978). Moral development. In M. E. Lamb (Ed.), Social and personality development (pp. 200-233). New York: Holt, Rinehart and Winston.

Instructors can also present the class with techniques for increasing students' moral reasoning. One such technique for accomplishing this is the One Plus Matching Principle. This technique utilizes moral dilemmas which require moral judgment at one level above the students' present level of moral reasoning. It is theorized that the discrepancy between the level required by the dilemma and the students' current reasoning ability will cause cognitive dissonance and will ultimately result in more sophisticated thinking and a higher level of moral reasoning.

Several studies have successfully used the One-Plus Matching Principle. Each contains a description of the technique, as well as a summary of the results obtained by utilizing the procedure.

Enright, R., Lapsley, D., Harris, D., & Shawver, D. (1983). Moral development interventions in early adolescence. Theory Into Practice, 22, 134-144.

Norcini, J., & Snyder, S. (1983). The effects of modeling and cognitive induction on the moral reasoning of adolescents. Journal of Youth and Adolescence, 12, 101-115.

Walker, L. (1983). Sources of cognitive conflict for stage transition in moral development. Developmental Psychology, 19, 103-110.

Instructors can refer students who are interested in humanistic education to the classic book Summerhill. The focus of the book is on a residential school in England. This school was operated on a very permissive basis with the students being in charge of their own learning. It was developed on the premise that children are innately wise and provided a realistic and consistent environment, they will utlimately make wise decisions. This book which was very influencial in the 60s set the standard for many of the principles of humanistic education.

Neill, A. S. (1960). Summerhill: A radical approach to child rearing. New York: Hart.

Discussion Questions

1. Humanists contend that affective goals are just as important as cognitive goals. What are the affective goals you might have when you are teaching objectives on the following topics?

   - Proper nutrition, basic food groups
   - The American Revolution
   - First manned space flight
   - Rules and procedures for playing golf
   - World economics, hunger

2. Kohlberg's theory of moral development is based largely on a measure of the individual's ability to make moral judgments. We know, however, that moral judgment does not necessarily lead to moral behavior. So a person can have moral judgment without moral behavior. Is the reverse true? Can a person have moral behavior without having moral judgment?

3. Consider that you are updating the curriculum for your school district. You have been asked to include instructional units on values clarification and resolving moral dilemmas. At what level of the curriculum (elementary versus middle school versus high school) do you think units in each of these categories would be most effective. Relate your decision to what you know about cognitive development.

4. As a fifth grade teacher you are very concerned at the lack of sensitivity your children have for each other. They often try to gain attention by making fun of other class members. How could you combine the work of Bandura on observational learning and modeling with character education to resolve this problem?

5. As a sixth grade teacher you have an over-zealous student in your class. She is always pushing and shoving to be first in line. Often she uses mild physical contact to attract the attention of other students. She is quick to make a comment on every subject, and usually her remarks are loud enough to be heard over everyone else. It is obvious to you as the teacher that she engages in these behaviors to gain much needed peer attention. The behaviors, however, are self-defeating. Others notice her, but they don't like what what they see. As a result she is lonely and isolated. How could you as the teacher utilize cooperative group work to improve this girl's relationships with others in the class?

Audiovisual Aids

Carl Rogers on Education: Part I (American Personnel and Guidance Association, color, 30 min.). This film describes how people acquire significant learning. Optimal learning situations are discussed.

Carl Rogers on Education: Part II (American Personnel and Guidance Association, color, 30 min.). In Part II of the Rogers film, the role of student expectations and the educational system itself are described.

Be an Effective Teacher (American Personnel and Guidance Association, color, 55 min.). This film demonstrates the underlying philosophy of teacher effectiveness training by providing film clips of actual training sessions.

Why Is It Always Me? (VC/MP Research Press, color, 1986, 14 min.). This film demonstrates a five-step, humanistic problem-solving method as it applies to everyday life situations of a thirteen-year-old girl.

FOLLOW-UP ACTIVITIES

1. Remember Your Teachers

   This Follow-up Activity could be converted to in-class use by having the class make a notation of the characteristics of teachers who they perceive as humanistic and non-humanistic. A frequency count could be recorded for characteristics of teachers who were assigned to each of the categories. These characteristics could then be rank-ordered and discussed. Through this activity, class members could obtain an idea of how their future students will perceive their behaviors.

2. Think about the School's Role in Teaching Values

   To adapt this Follow-up Activity to an in-class debate, instructors can divide the class into two large groups and assign one point of view to each of the groups. The groups could then defend the assigned point of view. Another alternative is to have four or five students volunteer to defend what they perceive to be the morally responsible position. As the debate unfolds some of the following points are likely to surface:

   a. For Indirect Values Training

      • The school has no right to determine moral behavior.
      • Legislating what is moral is a violation of civil liberties.
      • Students need to be taught critical thinking in this as well as in other areas.
      • Individuals won't incorporate the values into their behavior repertoire unless they reach the independent conclusion that the value is right.

   b. For Direct Values Training

- We have a standard moral code. It should be transmitted to students via the school curriculum.
- Training needs to focus on behavior rather than judgment.
- Students should be taught applicable skills.
- Students should be held accountable for an acceptable moral code.

3. Use a Method of Cooperative Learning

Instructors who had students complete Follow-up Activity 5 in Chapter Six could use the lesson plans called for in that activity as the basis for Follow-up Activity 3 in the present chapter. To do so, instruct students to take the lesson plans which they formerly completed and design a cooperative learning experience which would either teach or reinforce the content specified in that set of lesson plans.

Additional Follow-up Activities

4. Labeling Stages in Moral Development

Follow-up Activity Sheet 8-4 describes a moral dilemma which a schoolteacher might face. Reproduce and distribute the work sheet to all members of the class. Have them complete the activity by reading the moral dilemma and classifying each of the following responses according to its level of moral development.

This activity could be modified by having class members administer only the dilemma and response choices to a group of secondary students. The students could choose the most appropriate response. Class members could then classify students according to their levels of moral development.

Key: 1. <u>Stage 5</u> 2. <u>Stage 1</u> 3. <u>Stage 3</u> 4. <u>Stage 4</u> 5. <u>Stage 6</u> 6. <u>Stage 2</u>

5. Clarifying Your Values

Have students read the story "Sharks in the Sea" in Follow-up Activity Sheet 8-5. Then have them rank-order the characters beginning with the character whom they feel is the most objectionable.

After the exercise is completed, the instructor can pose a number of questions which focus on the many issues in values clarification.

- Can class members agree on a rank order for these characters?
- Would they like to be told how the characters should be ranked?
- Is there a right and wrong way to rank-order the characters?
- What criteria did they apply when deciding who was the most/least objectionable?

MORAL DILEMMA

DIRECTIONS: Read the moral dilemma below and the response choices which follow. Classify each response according to one of Kohlberg's six stages of moral development.

Marvin is a high school senior. He is the quarterback on the high school football team. It is likely that he will earn a slot on the All State Team, and it is almost certain that if things progress as expected he will receive a scholarship to a "big ten" college. Marvin, however, has one serious problem. He is about to fail senior English, which is a course required for high school graduation. According to the "no pass - no play" laws in his state, all athletes must maintain a C average to remain eligible to play. His coach and the other players are devastated. They have been predicted to win the District Title, which they couldn't possibly do without Marvin. His parents are upset because they cannot afford to send him to college, and they feel his scholarship is in jeopardy. Marvin has his six weeks' test on Monday. His girlfriend, who is a straight A student, has agreed to help him during the test. Should he cheat on the exam?

_____   1.   Regardless of the rule against cheating, Marvin should do whatever must be done to pass that test. It is more important for everyone concerned that he pass.

_____   2.   Marvin definitely should not cheat. He would probably be caught, and he would be humiliated on top of being punished.

_____   3.   Marvin should cheat because as a responsible team member he owes it to the other members of the team.

_____   4.   Marvin should not cheat. Cheating is against the rules and the rules must be maintained even if it causes Marvin hardship.

_____   5.   Marvin should cheat because benefiting all the other people and himself is more important than maintaining an arbitrary rule which does not have particular value to anyone.

_____   6.   Marvin should cheat and get it over with. He has been worried to death over this. If he passes the test by cheating he will at least have a chance to start over and do better the next six weeks.

CLARIFYING YOUR VALUES

DIRECTIONS: Read the story below. Following the story, each character is listed in the order he or she appeared in the story. Rank-order the characters, beginning with the individual you believe to be the most objectionable.

Sea of Sharks Story

Ursula is a beautiful island maiden. She and Hector are in love. They live on two Carribean islands which are very close together, but separated by a sea which is full of sharks. Hector rows over in his dingy to visit Ursula every day. One day he does not come. He sends a message that he is deathly ill. His message implores Ursula to come and visit him and bring medicine, but she has no way to cross the shark-infested sea that separates their islands.

Ursula gets the medicine and asks Captain Hook the ferry boat driver to take her over to Hector. Captain Hook says that he will be glad to, but he wants Ursula to exchange her "favors" for the ride. She refuses.

Ursula then goes to Fisherman Fred, who she knows has a boat. Fred refuses to get involved, so Ursula, having exhausted all other possibilities, returns to the captain and meets the conditions of passage.

She delivers the medicine to Hector and tells him the saga of her trip. Hector recovers in due haste, but can no longer love Ursula because of her indiscretion with the captain. Heartbroken Ursula cries on the shoulder of Bluto. Bluto is enraged at the unfairness. He has a fisticuffs with Hector. Hector was definitely on the losing end of the fight. He loses a mouthful of teeth and sustains a black eye. News of Hector's woes reaches Ursula. She is delighted at Hector's bad luck. She thinks he got what he deserves and has a good laugh at his expense.

Characters: Ursula _____

                       Hector _____

                       Captain Hook _____

                       Fisherman Fred _____

                       Bluto _____

CHAPTER NINE

PLANNING FOR INSTRUCTION

CHAPTER OBJECTIVES

Students mastering the content in Chapter Nine will be able to:

- Write behavioral objectives using the Taxonomy of Educational Objectives.

- Construct a task analysis.

- Develop unit lesson plans.

- Develop daily lesson plans for direct instruction, cooperative learning, and discovery learning.

- Establish homework policy.

FOCUS QUESTIONS

1. How does a teacher decide what should be taught?

   Instructional goals come from several sources. These include the student, society, and the academic discipline. One crucial issue in instructional planning is the specificity of educational objectives or the teacher's determination of precise goals for a lesson, unit, or course of study. Many educators support explicit instructional objectives because such objectives aid in teaching, learning, and evaluation. One approach to writing instructional objectives recommended by Mager uses three major components:

   - The behavioral term expressing the type of task required by the student
   - The situation or condition under which the behavior is to be performed
   - The criterion, or level of performance, that will be used to evaluate the success of the performance or product.

2. What are the alternative approaches in writing objectives?

   Gronlund recommends that teachers should first state the general instructional objective and then clarify the objective by listing a sample of the specific types of student performance that they are willing to accept as evidence of the attainment of the objective. If objectives are to help teachers plan for instruction, then any system that helps teachers while reducing the amount of work needed to write objectives should be carefully considered.

3. What are the advantages and disadvantages of using behavioral objectives?

Proponents of instructional objectives believe that they enable teachers to know exactly what student behavior is desired upon the completion of a lesson. Teachers are then in a better position to select appropriate teaching methods and materials for achieving the designated student outcome. Knowing the type of expected outcome is important in making decisions that will help to direct students to that outcome. They believe that instructional objectives help teachers during evaluation because the teachers can then construct test questions directly from their objectives. Constructing tests in this manner takes the guesswork out of the evaluation process. Finally, there is evidence to suggest that if teachers initially give students the objectives of a lesson or course, the students will spend more time focusing on the designated outcomes. In rethinking the role of objectives, some educators have raised questions about the need for precision in stating every objective. It is a time-consuming process and may not be necessary for improving instruction.

4. What is the difference between the organization of the cognitive and affective domains in the Taxonomy of Educational Objectives.

In the cognitive domain, the categories are arranged along a continuum from simple to more complex. They range from knowledge to comprehension, application, analysis, synthesis, and evaluation. In the affective domain, the continuum is based on the degree of internalization that each behavior exhibits. That is, the classification begins with an attitude or value from the level of awareness, proceeding to the point at which it guides or directs a person's actions in receiving, responding, valuing, organizing, and characterizing that value or value complex.

5. How do a unit and daily lesson plan relate to each other?

A daily lesson plan is a detailed outline of the objectives, content, procedures, and evaluation of a single instructional period. A unit plan is a detailed outline for a series of interrelated lesson plans on a particular topic of study lasting from two to four weeks. A good unit plan organizes the individual lesson plans into a meaningful experience. There is some evidence that unit planning is more important than daily lesson planning. Unit planning provides a broad framework for the activities in which the teacher and students will be involved over a longer period.

6. When and for what purpose would you use direct instruction, discovery, and cooperative learning lessons?

Instruction in which students are taught with a structured curriculum using direct or active involvement by the teacher has been called direct instruction, explicit instruction, or active teaching. This type of instruction appears to be most successful in highly structured academic areas where there is a specific body of knowledge to learn. It seems to be less relevant in more subjective areas such as identifying the moral positions of world leaders, analyzing literature, or discussing political views of senatorial candidates. In these areas, instructional objectives are less clear, the material is less structured, and the skills or knowledge do not follow in any particular order.

The essential criterion for discovery learning is that the learner organizes into final form the material to be learned. The discovery of the relevant concept or abstraction occurs during the student's involvement in a learning activity. Both Piaget and Bruner are advocates of this type of learning. Bruner believes that discovery learning helps students take responsibility for their own learning, emphasizes high-level thinking, focuses on intrinsic rather than extrinsic motivation, and helps students remember important information.

The evaluation of discovery learning methods is not as effective as direct instruction in teaching basic skills. Although it is not suggested that discovery learning be used on a regular basis as the primary method of instruction, it can be used as a supplementary procedure to teach problem-solving skills, stimulate curiosity, and encourage more self-directed learning. Discovery learning techniques are most useful when students have the necessary skills and motivation to succeed.

There are different types of cooperative learning situations as well as factors that need to be considered when formulating groups and preparing students to work cooperatively. It takes time to prepare students to work cooperatively and for the teacher to feel comfortable with this instructional method. Cooperative learning, however, can be an effective approach to dealing with the diversity of students in the classroom.

7. What factors should a teacher or school consider in devising guidelines for a homework policy.

Cooper completed a comprehensive review of research on homework. His findings regarding recommendations for establishing a homework policy suggest that first, homework does have positive effects on achievement. The impact of homework is related to students' grade level. Second, homework appears to have a greater effect on learning simple rather than complex tasks. Third, there are no consistent positive effects associated with the individualization of homework assignments. Fourth, the effects of homework tend to be similar for different types of students. Finally, research results are mixed on parents' participation in homework. Cooper stresses that homework can serve many purposes. In the early grades, the purpose of homework often is to develop positive attitudes and study habits needed to excel in school. In the upper grades, teachers often use homework to develop interest in a topic. More challenging assignments requiring higher-level thinking skills might best meet this purpose. Finally, Cooper finds no evidence that any particular type or form of grading or evaluative comments on homework assignments has an impact on achievement. The frequency and duration of homework assignments should be further specified to reflect local school and community circumstances. In schools where different subjects are taught by different teachers, teachers should know what days of the week are available to them for assignments, and how much daily homework time should be spent on their subject.

Administrators should communicate the district and school homework policy to parents, monitor the implementation of the policy, and coordinate the scheduling of homework among different subjects, if needed. Teachers should state clearly how the assignment is related to the topic under study, the purpose of the assignment, how the assignment might best be carried out, and what the student needs to do to demonstrate that the assignment has been completed.

CHAPTER OUTLINE

I. ORIENTATION

    A. Focus Questions

II. WHAT SHOULD STUDENTS LEARN IN SCHOOL?

III. SPECIFICITY OF EDUCATIONAL OBJECTIVES

IV. THE VALUE OF INSTRUCTIONAL OBJECTIVES

    A. Can Teachers Plan for Instruction without Using Objectives?

V. DEVELOPING OBJECTIVES FOR INSTRUCTION

    A. Academic Content

        1. Type of learning
        2. Level of difficulty
        3. A Taxonomy of Educational Objectives

VI. PLANNING FOR INSTRUCTION

VII. DEVELOPING A LESSON PLAN

    A. Direct Instruction
    B. Discovery Learning
    C. Cooperative Learning

IV. THINKING ABOUT THE TEACHING-LEARNING MODEL

KEY TERMS

behavioral objectives (p. 368)

expressive objectives (p. 374)

Taxonomony of Educational Objectives (p. 379)

cognitive domain (p. 379)

affective domain (p. 379)

psychomotor domain (p. 382)

lesson plan (p. 383)

unit plan (p. 383)

CHAPTER GUIDELINES

Making instructional decisions is the focus of Chapter Nine. It addresses the determination of what should be learned and how to communicate this information to students.

Sources of instructional goals are attributed to the student, society, and the academic discipline. Learning goals are expressed in terms of educational objectives, and directions for writing explicit goals are provided. The necessity for explicit goals, however, is debated. The dehumanization of the educational process is of concern, as is the effect of teachers emphasizing those experiences which are easiest to measure in behavioral terms.

In planning for instruction, elements for good unit plans and daily lesson plans are described. Adaptations for individual students while planning lessons are considered. The importance of including an evaluation component in a lesson plan is stressed.

The utility of direct instruction in highly structured subjects is discussed. Several teaching functions are illustrated in the application of direct instruction. These include the presentation of new material, guided practice, feedback and corrections, independent practice, and weekly and monthly reviews.

Discovery learning is presented as an alternate approach which can be used to change the format of classroom instruction, motivate students, and focus on higher-level thinking skills. Cooperative learning is discussed as another alternative, effective in achieving both cognitive and affective objectives.

Homework issues are analyzed. Recommendations are made for increasing the effectiveness of homework. The impact of homework on academic achievement and the student's attitude toward learning are both considered.

Supplementary Material

Information in the textbook on Bloom's taxonomy can be supplemented by the work of Simpson. Simpson designed a taxonomy of psychomotor objectives. These objectives are particularly useful for teachers of art, music, and physical education as well as for teachers of young children. The levels in Simpson's Taxonomy of Psychomotor Objectives are:

- Preparedness
- Imitation
- Proficiency
- Automaticity
- Adaptation

Simpson, E. J. (1966). <u>The classification of educational objectives: Psychomotor domain</u>. Urbana: University of Illinois Press.

Instructors can also use the content in <u>Reach Who You Teach</u> to relate the textbook content on Bloom's taxonomy to the actual writing of instructional objectives. This book provides a matrix for matching subject matter content to objectives at the different levels of the taxonomy. It is very helpful in providing a pragmatic orientation to Bloom's work, which is often viewed by teachers as being difficult to interpret and apply.

Treffinger, D., Hahn, R., & Feldheusen, J. (1989). <u>Reach who you teach</u>. Buffalo, NY: United Educational Services.

The book cites the Missouri Mathematics Program (MMP) as being an example of a teaching program which is based on the principles of direct instruction. A program based on similar principles is the Direct Instruction System for Teaching and Remediation (DISTAR). DISTAR is a highly structured program in the areas of reading and math. Procedures as well as actual teaching materials and activities are available for the teacher. Instructors wishing to expand on the content in Chapter Nine could do so demonstrating the use of DISTAR materials to the class. The demonstration could be used to provide examples of actual teaching activities that address the procedures recommended by proponents of the direct instruction method. Materials referred to by the DISTAR acronym are listed below.

<u>Reading Mastery</u>. Chicago: Science Research Associates
<u>Corrective Reading</u>. Chicago: Science Research Associates
<u>DISTAR Arithmetic</u>. Chicago: Science Research Associates

Work by Lyn Corno is also closely related to material presented in Chapter Nine. She advocates a series of teaching procedures designed to make students more responsible for their own learning. This approach, called Self-Regulated Learning, provides an interesting comparison to the direct instruction procedures discussed in the text. Also, Corno's material can be related to the metacognitive strategies discussed earlier and the motivational strategies which will be addressed in Chapter Ten.

Corno, L. (1988). Teaching and learning. In D. Berlinger & B. Rosenshine (Eds.), <u>Talks to teachers</u> (pp. 249-266). New York: Random House.

Discussion Questions

1. Advocates of direct teaching, discovery learning, cooperative learning and social inquiry all maintain that their method is the best. Research, however, has generally not shown one method to be vastly superior to the others. Which method would you prefer? Would any of the following variables affect your decision to select one of the instructional methods over another? If so, what would be the rationale underlying your decision?

- class size
- age level of students
- ability level of students
- heterogeneity of group
- content of subject matter
- engaged time available for lesson

2. The writing of instructional objectives has been a controversial topic for teachers for some time. The controversy has been intensified by P.L. 94-142, which requires that all special education students have instructional objectives as part of their IEP's. What value do you see in objectives? Do they really help teachers teach and children learn? Are they more trouble than they are worth? Would they be better left to the "ivory towers" and textbooks? What planning strategy might teachers use to substitute for instructional objectives?

3. You hear instructors talk about long-term goals, instructional objectives, short-term goals, annual goals, and behavioral objectives. What do each of these terms mean? Is there any fundamental difference between these concepts?

4. React to this statement:

"Proponents of task analysis claim that this technique can be used to teach anything to anybody. Actually, it completely misses some of the most crucial aspects of teaching. For example, you can task analyze the Blue Danube and teach anyone to sequence those keys on a piano. That does not mean that the student plays like Van Cliburn. How do you task analyze the really important aspects of creativity and understanding?"

5. Consider that you are teaching American government to a class of ninth grade students. Generate a list of topics that you believe could be most successfully taught using a lecture format for instruction. Then generate another list of topics which you feel could most effectively be taught using a group discussion format for instruction. How do you justify your choices for each teaching methodology?

6. Some authorities believe that teaching is an "art," or an innate skill that individuals either have or do not have. Others believe that teaching is a science. As such, individuals can be trained in the procedures for teaching. Consider these two positions as they relate to methods of direct instruction and discovery learning. Which facets of each of these models could best be executed as an art form? Which could best be executed as a science.

7. Chapter Nine provides numerous strategies for assisting teachers with their most important function, teaching. Should the teachers use of these and other effective strategies serve as the basis for teacher evaluation? If so, how could the evaluation process be structured to monitor and rate effectiveness in these areas? Should students participate in teacher evaluation?

Audiovisual Aids

Learning with Film and Video (VC 24335, Barr Films, 1985, 15 min.)
Teachers show how media enriches all subject areas by bringing the outside world into the classroom, and by providing learning experiences not otherwise available to the student. This program makes a persuasive presentation at budget time on this cost-effective teaching tool.

Study Skills: Part 1-6 (UDI, 1988)
Part 1 - Overview (VC25248, 48 min.)
Part 2 - Pup Study/Reading System (VC25285, 44 min.)
Part 3 - Building the Main Idea (VC25286, 42 min.)
Part 4 - Note Taking (VC25287, 42 min.)
Part 5 - Mapping (VC25288, 45 min.)
Part 6 - Scheduling Time/Taking Tests (VC25289, 31 min.)
This series of six films shows strategies for developing effective study skills. Each videotape is divided into two segments, with a break for activities and discussion. These skills can be implemented in a K-12 study skills program.

Study Strategies: Assignments (University of Illinois Film Center, color, 1981,15 min.). This film analyzes studying as a task and lists procedures for accomplishing it with minimum difficulty including careful recording of assignments, purposeful question asking and information gathering, and the formulation of study plans and time management.

FOLLOW-UP ACTIVITIES

1. Rank the Goals of Education

    Follow-up Activity 1 can be expanded by having the class share the rank ordering of their goals in class. This information could be used as the basis for a debate, or it could be related to the issues on values clarification, which were previously discussed in Chapter Eight.

2. Justify Your Own Subject Matter

    The discussion of the importance of various aspects of the subject matter which is proposed in Follow-up Activity 2 could serve as the basis for having the class examine the traditional liberal arts and science curriculum which is in place in most contemporary high schools. Using this curriculum as a measure, they could predict the kinds of skills people will need as society moves into the 21st century. They could then be asked to design a non-traditional curriculum which might be more meaningful to at least some of these students.

3. Interview Teachers Regarding Their Use of Objectives

Instructors could adapt this follow-up activity to a survey format. Have the class design the survey instruments as a group activity. Individual class members can then administer the survey to teachers in the school where they are observing. Survey results can be compiled in class and serve as the basis of a class discussion on teachers' perceptions of the value of instructional goals and objectives.

4. Write Behavioral Objectives

Instructors can adapt Follow-up Activity 4 to an out-of-class assignment by having the class complete Follow-up Activities Sheet 9-4. This assignment requires that class members select a content area and formulate appropriate instructional objectives for each of the levels of Bloom's Taxonomy of Educational Objectives.

5. Complete a Task Analysis

Follow-up Activity 5 can be adapted to an out-of-class assignment by having students complete the task analysis project specified in Follow-up Activity Sheet 9-5.

6. Develop a Lesson Plan

To adapt Follow-up Activity 6 to an out-of-class assignment, direct student attention to Follow-up Activity Sheet 9-6. Ask students to choose a concept and design two sets of lesson plans for teaching the concept. One set will conform to the specifications of direct instruction. The other will conform to the specifications of discovery learning.

If Follow-up Activity 5 for Chapter Six was completed, the instructor can have the class adapt the lesson content previously designed to a direct instruction or discovery learning format.

Additional Follow-up Activities

7. Establish a Homework Policy

Cooper conducted an extensive review of the research on the effectiveness of homework. Review his finding along with the Box Material, "Establishing Homework Policy Guidelines," which is included in the textbook. Based on the information you obtain write a policy statement that you could send to the parents and students you intend to teach. Tell them exactly what the homework requirements will be and why you have selected these requirements.

8. Evaluating Behavioral Objectives

Follow-up Activity Sheet 9-8 contains a list of behavioral objectives. Each objective is incorrectly written. Have the student evaluate each objective to determine the error and rewrite the objective correctly in the space provided.

WRITING BEHAVIORAL OBJECTIVES

DIRECTIONS: Choose one of the topics listed below. Using this topic, write a behavioral objective for each level of Bloom's Taxonomy of Educational Objectives in both the cognitive and affective domain.

- burning the American flag
- drug abuse
- apartheid
- genetic engineering

COGNITIVE DOMAIN
Knowledge:
Comprehension:
Application:
Analysis:
Synthesis:
Evaluation

AFFECTIVE DOMAIN

Receiving:

Responding:

Valuing:

Organization:

Characterization by Value:

TASK ANALYSIS

DIRECTIONS: Isolate a topic you would like to teach or choose one of the topics below. Write a behavioral objective which addresses the topic. Then complete the various aspects of task-analyzing the behavior called for in your objective.

- tooth brushing
- writing a check
- associating auditory sounds with alphabet letters
- crossing a street

TASK ANALYSIS

Task: _____

Grade Level: _____

Behavioral Objective: _____

Prerequisite Skills: _____

_____

_____

_____

Component Skills: _____

_____

_____

_____

Steps in Task: _____

_____

_____

_____

_____

_____

Integration of
Component
Skills: _____

_____

_____

Follow-up Activity Sheet 9-6

WRITING LESSON PLANS

DIRECTIONS: Using the forms shown below and on the following page, detail how you would teach the same concept using direct instruction and discovery learning.

DIRECT INSTRUCTION			
1. State Behavioral objective	2. Establish Anticipatory Set	3. List Procedures	4. Monitor Understanding
5. Provide Guided Practice	6. Execute Final Understanding Check	7. Assign Independent Practice	8. Evaluate Lesson

DISCOVERY LEARNING			
1. Write Behavioral Objective	2. Formulate Hypothesis	3. Organize Materials	4. Plan Question Sequence
5. Collect Data	6. Analyze Data Inductively	7. Draw Conclusions	8. Evaluate Lesson

EVALUATING BEHAVIORAL OBJECTIVES

DIRECTIONS: Below is a list of behavioral objectives. Each objective has an error in
either the condition, the behavior, or the criterion level. Locate the error
and rewrite the objective correctly in the space provided below it.

1. Following a unit of study on mammals, each student will know how to identify
mammals. _____

_____

_____

2. After six weeks of social reinforcement, student X will raise his hand before speaking
with 90% accuracy. _____

_____

_____

3. Student Y will pass 5 out of 6 questions on the algebra tests this six weeks with a grade
of 90 or above. _____

_____

_____

4. Given a road map and a calculator, student Z will calculate the distance from Boston to
Atlanta. _____

_____

_____

5. Each member of the basketball team will make three out of four free throws. _____

_____

_____

6. Students in Music 101 will learn to appreciate the complexity and variety of classical
music. _____

_____

_____

CHAPTER TEN

MOTIVATION

CHAPTER OBJECTIVES

Students mastering the content in Chapter Ten will be able to:

- Identify how student characteristics, teacher behavior, instructional procedures, and evaluation interact to affect motivation for learning.

- Make modifications in the teaching-learning process to enhance student motivation for learning.

FOCUS QUESTIONS

1. Why do students interpret success and failure differently?

   Success-oriented students tend to believe that they can handle most academic challenges. As a result, their ability is not viewed as an important issue in learning. These students view success and failure as a function of the quality of their efforts. The research clearly points out that success-oriented students tend to attribute success to ability and effort. They attribute failure to lack of proper effort. These explanations are helpful to the individual because success inspires further confidence as a sign of one's ability to do well, whereas failure signals the need to try harder. The success-oriented individual is not threatened by failure when it does occur, because it doesn't reflect on the individual's ability. This explanation also helps to explain why failure can be used to motivate already successful students.

   Failure-avoiding students generally have a different set of attributions. They tend to attribute their failures to a lack of ability and their successes to external factors such as luck or an easy task. They feel that they have little control over their academic destiny so they minimize pain by trying to avoid failure. Teachers need to spend more time learning about their students' beliefs about the causes of their success and failure. One important goal is to establish classroom conditions in which students learn that proper effort leads to success. Another goal must be to provide students with short-term goals and strategies so that they acquire the skills to reach the goals.

2. How do reinforcement and cognitive theories of motivation differ?

   Reinforcement theorists place greater emphasis on the external factors which inspire motivation. They would interpret lack of motivation in terms of inadequate consequential stimuli. Cognitive theorists place greater emphasis on intrinsic factors such as developmental readiness and metacognition.

3. How are emotions related to causal explanations of success and failure?

Covington and Omelich found that students experienced the greatest shame with a combination of high effort and failure and the least shame with low effort and failure. Expending effort and still failing poses a serious threat to one's self-esteem. If students don't try but fail, they can always rationalize that success could have been achieved through proper effort, thus maintaining a reasonable level of self-esteem.

4. How can causal attributions of students and teachers conflict?

If we examine the role of effort from both teachers' and students' perspectives, we find that in some cases teachers and students operate at cross purposes. Although teachers highly value achievement, they often reward (or punish) some students more than others for exactly the same level of performance. Students who are perceived as having expended effort (regardless of their ability) tend to be rewarded more and punished less than students who do not try.

5. Why are some students motivated to avoid failure?

One factor that determines whether children develop the need to achieve or the need to avoid failure is the type of experiences they have had at home. Parents of failure-avoiding children punish their children's failures but say little when they are successful.

6. How can teacher expectations influence student behavior?

Teachers don't treat all students the same and certain treatment may limit students' opportunities in the classroom. The result may be lowered academic performance. Teachers often have different interactions with different types of students. In some instances, these differences affect teacher expectations (i.e., beliefs about students' present and future achievement and behavior). These expectations can lead to self-fulfilling prophecies, a process in which teacher expectations determine the ways students are treated. Over time, the expectations influence how the students behave in the classroom and how much they learn. Race, social class, and personality are most likely to be related to teacher expectancies. That is to say, some teachers tend to have greater expectancies of success for white rather than black and other minority students. Also they expect more from high rather than low socioeconomic status students. Finally, they may prefer more conforming and docile students over independent and assertive students.

7. How can the improper use of praise have a negative impact on students?

Teachers need to reconsider the common strategy of finding opportunities to constantly praise students for all types of behavior and academic performance. Brophy has pointed that the incorrect use of praise can undermine achievement behavior. First, when teachers try to find something good in the work of low-achieving students to encourage them, the praise is often for some irrelevant or unimportant aspect of completing the task. The students then discount the praise. They often determine that the praise is not related to effort or performance, but they accept it as evidence that they lack ability. The result is a negative effect on self-confidence.

8. How can teacher efficacy impact student behavior?

It appears that high expectations for student achievement are related to a pattern of attitudes, beliefs, and behaviors that identify teachers and schools. High expectations can maximize gains in student achievement. Recently, researchers have been interested in the construct of teacher efficacy, or the teachers' beliefs in their own ability to affect student learning. A number of investigations have indicated that teachers who have a greater sense of efficacy produce higher achievement gains in their students.

9. How does the classroom climate influence student motivation?

Classroom climates that stress performance goals can be debilitating for individuals who are lacking in confidence or in perceived ability. Mastery oriented environments tend to reduce such debilitating effects. Students in mastery environments tend to take more risks in attempting problems and tasks that are unfamiliar or appear difficult whereas performance goals appear to induce a more careful or safe approach to learning. Students in this environment are more interested in avoiding failure. Environments that stress mastery goals tend to reduce such debilitating effects. Also, environments that place different stress on mastery or performance goals are likely to stir the development of different learning strategies in students. Students are more likely to seek out challenges and be open to novel experiences when mastery goals are stressed. Performance goals seem to induce a conservative approach to learning. Students do not wish to risk failure.

10. What are the consequences of the development of intrinsic or extrinsic motivation?

Teachers' beliefs regarding how motivation should be viewed can influence their classroom organization. A teacher who believes that students have little inclination to learn in school and need to be encouraged to learn through external incentives is more likely to be influenced by procedures which emphasize more teacher control over learning activities. A teacher who believes that children are naturally curious and that learning is a process of self-discovery such that motivation comes from within the person is likely to establish a different type of classroom situation. It is not necessary to take a position at either extreme. Some educators believe that intrinsic motivation can be used to guide much of classroom learning and that students may need some external incentives to learn material they are less interested in.

An important issue regarding intrinsic versus extrinsic motivation is how teachers can maintain student involvement in learning activities that are not very interesting or exciting. Often boring school activities alienate them from learning, or create a negative effect on their self-concepts or independence. This issue is especially important because there appears to be a steady decrease in students' intrinsic motivation for learning as they progress through school.

Researchers also have found that teachers can undermine intrinsic motivation and learning by too much emphasis on external rewards or incentives. It appears that when students already enjoy an activity and receive rewards for participating in the activity, they will be less likely to return to the activity than students with the same interest who didn't receive any rewards for participation.

11. How do different goal structures influence self-perceptions of ability?

A goal structure determines the way in which students will relate to one another and to the teacher while working toward instructional goals. There are three types of goal structures:

- Cooperative. Students work together to accomplish shared goals
- Competitive. Students work against each other to achieve goals that only a few students can attain
- Individualistic. One student's achievement of the goal is unrelated to other students' achievement of the goal

An example of each of these goal structures is students working together to survey political attitudes in the community (cooperative), students completing individual projects in science that will be graded on a curve (competitive), and students working individually on specific areas of weakness in mathematics with their grade being based on their own progress (individualistic).

Each type of goal structure promotes a different pattern of interaction among students, thus creating a different learning climate. In addition, different types of motivation are elicited under each learning condition. A cooperative goal structure promotes positive interpersonal relations such as trust, acceptance, sharing, and helping. A competitive goal structure promotes little trust and acceptance and often generates more attempts to mislead and obstruct others. An individualistic goal structure promotes interaction with the teacher rather than with peers and minimizes positive affective outcomes.

All three goal structures are effective under certain conditions and can be relevant to specific goals and objectives of a lesson. Knowing when to use cooperative, competitive, and individualistic learning is an important instructional decision that the teacher must make.

A competitive setting promotes a situation in which personal satisfaction depends on whether a student has won or lost. Self-assessment of ability based on social comparison information is the major attributional focus. Students evaluate their ability high after success and low after failure. If one is a low achiever, it is difficult to feel good about oneself or one's performance if the basis of comparison is the performance of others in the class.

A cooperative setting elicits a concern for responsibility to the group with a focus on group performance information and the degree to which effort was related to both individual and group performance. Although success and failure are still important factors influencing personal satisfaction and perception of ability, an important finding is that successful cooperative groups can alleviate the negative self-evaluation that many low achievers exhibit. The implication is that the teacher by using cooperative groups may be able to insulate the low-achieving students from the negative effects of failure on self-esteem. This condition is likely to occur because of the focus on effort and group outcomes in addition to personal achievement.

Finally, a noncompetitive-individualistic structure elicits a mastery orientation in which effort attributions prevail and personal performance over a series of assignments becomes salient. When low-achieving students can judge their progress according to individual improvement rather than by the performance of others, the students are more likely to believe that trying can pay off and the students will feel better about their performance. If individuals work independently, but their performance is compared to others in the class, the situation is similar to interpersonal competition.

12. How does anxiety influence student achievement?

Researchers have indicated that for some students small amounts of anxiety can facilitate learning. The type and degree of anxiety differ widely among students. For some, anxiety is a generalized fear of the total school situation. Others have a fear of specific aspects of the school environment such as teachers, peers, particular subject areas, or tests. In extreme cases (as in school phobias), the fear is so great that the child may refuse to go to school.

Several behaviors of highly anxious students in learning situations account for their low performance. First, highly anxious students have a tendency to avoid failure because they fear negative evaluation. As a result, they will attempt to avoid evaluative situations and choose, persist, and perform more successfully on easy tasks in which success is more certain. They also are likely to become involved in failure-avoiding strategies. Second, highly anxious students do not attend to tasks in sufficient detail because they are preoccupied with negative self-references or worry. As the teacher is presenting information on a topic, the highly anxious student is likely to be thinking about inadequacies that may make it hard to attempt to learn the material. Third, highly anxious students have difficulty when instructional methods require them to rely on short-term memory or when they are asked to perform quickly. Finally, highly anxious students have difficulty learning material that is not well organized. They tend to perform better when the teacher structures the material for them. Instructional methods such as independent study or inquiry techniques and other nondirective procedures often are less successful for highly anxious students.

13. What can teachers do to reduce anxiety in the classroom?

Children want to succeed in school, but sometimes stress and anxiety are so intense that they interfere with academic performance. If students respect their teachers highly and want to be liked by them, they must be reassured that they are capable and that a teacher will still like and accept them regardless of their academic performance. Sometimes teachers find this a burden because they have negative reactions to highly anxious students. Teachers should not compare such students to other students who are succeeding or question them rigorously in front of the class to find out the nature of their difficulties. The teacher should help these students to improve. Ignoring students' performance is not the answer, because anxious students' dependency needs are great. Perhaps the worst thing teachers can do is simply to neglect these students. Such behavior reinforces their ideas that their poor performance affects teachers' attitudes toward them.

Anxious students perform better in more structured learning situations. Certain students who prefer and excel in highly structured classrooms tend to be personally insecure and fear failure. If they know exactly what is expected of them, they can control their anxiety to some degree. This precludes independent study, discussion groups, and other types of student-directed learning activities as wise learning strategies for anxious students.

Anxious students have trouble memorizing information as well as retrieving information that has been previously learned. Therefore, diagrams, outlines, and other methods for organizing information can be helpful to these students. An occasional open-book test can also help to reduce anxiety. As anxious persons experience success in the less threatening open-book situation, they become better able to handle evaluation of other kinds with less anxiety.

CHAPTER OUTLINE

I. ORIENTATION

    A. Focus Questions

II. STUDENT CHARACTERISTICS

    A. Locus of Control
    B. Weiner's Theory of Attribution
    C. Covington's Self-Worth Theory

        1. Strategies for avoiding failure

    D. Self-Efficacy

III. TEACHER BEHAVIOR

    A. Teachers' Expectations as Self-Fulfilling Prophecies

B. Appropriate Teacher Expectations
C. Teachers' Sense of Efficacy

IV. INSTRUCTIONAL PROCEDURES

A. Classroom Climate
B. Task
C. Intrinsic Versus Extrinsic Motivation
D. Continuing Motivation
E. Goal Structure

1. Altering motivation through changes in methods of instruction

V. EVALUATION AND ACHIEVEMENT ANXIETY

A. Anxiety

1. Classroom behavior of anxious students
2. Causes of anxiety

B. Identifying Anxious Children
C. Dealing with Anxious Children in the Classroom

1. Test anxiety
2. Dealing with test anxiety

VI. THINKING ABOUT THE TEACHING-LEARNING MODEL

KEY TERMS

CHAPTER GUIDELINES

Motivation for learning is the topic of Chapter Ten. The interaction of student characteristics, teacher behavior, instructional procedures, and evaluation is shown to affect motivation. The types and causes of student anxiety are identified.

The cognitive approach to learning is used to illustrate how teachers can enhance student motivation through instructional decisions. The first decision involves an identification of student characteristics. Locus of control determines whether students see internal or external variables as being responsible for the various events in their lives. A discussion of Weiner's theory of attribution helps teachers understand the differences in the ways that various students account for their academic successes and failures. Strategies children employ to avoid failure are identified by Covington's self-worth theory.

The effect of teacher expectations on student achievement is explained. The decision to develop appropriate, realistic expectations can determine how much students learn. Teachers vary in their own sense of efficacy, or perception of their ability to influence student learning. Factors contributing to the development of a high sense of efficacy are related to the environment.

Instructional procedures which are shown to influence students' choices to use effective learning strategies include classroom climate, their perception of the task, the manner in which teachers introduce an assignment, teachers' classroom practices, and certain control measures. The implementation of different goal structures are shown to produce different motivational systems.

The debilitating effect of high anxiety on academic performance is discussed. The relationship of low self-concept, low academic performance, and high anxiety is examined. Ways to identify anxious children and deal with their anxiety are presented. The chapter concludes by recommending the consideration of these variables in the instructional planning for low-achieving students.

Supplementary Material

Instructors can expand on the material in Chapter Ten by demonstrating to the class the use of Student Teams-Achievement Divisions (STAD). This system combines many of the Cooperative Learning Strategies described in Chapter Nine with the motivational principles in Chapter Ten. The system provides specific guidelines for assigning students to five-member groups so that various abilities, ethnicities, and sexes are represented. It then requires that the teacher calculate an individual learning expectation (ILE) score for each group member. Students work and study with group mates, but are required to perform individually on tests. Students' performance scores are compared to ILE scores to determine how well the group performed.

Slavin, R. (1978). Student teams and achievement divisions. Journal of Research in Development in Education, 12, 38-48.

Slavin, R. (1983). Cooperative learning. White Plains, NY: Longman.

The early work of Murray is a useful source for introducing the general foundation for need theories as they relate to motivation. It also provides a smooth introduction to Maslow's theory, which came later. Murray sees needs emerging from an internal force combined with an external press. As these two come together they create discomfort in the individual, which eventually results in the motivation for goal setting and achievement related behaviors, which Murray refers to as themes. He identified 20 needs which he feels make up the psychogenic need system.

1. Need for abasement
2. Need for achievement
3. Need for affiliation
4. Need for aggression
5. Need for autonomy
6. Need for counteraction
7. Need for deference
8. Need for defendance
9. Need for dominance
10. Need for exhibition
11. Need for harm avoidance
12. Need for infavoidance (avoiding shame or humiliation)
13. Need for nurturance
14. Need for order
15. Need for play
16. Need for rejection of others
17. Need for sentence (sensory pleasure)
18. Need for sex
19. Need for succorance
20. Need for understanding

Murray, H. A. (1966). Explorations in personality. London: Oxford University Press.

Keller provides another source of elaboration on the material in Chapter Ten. He proposes four principles to increase the motivational design of instruction. This model is excellent for providing practical suggestions for helping teachers increase motivation in the classroom. The four basic principles in the model are:

- Generate student interest in task.
- Increase personal relevance of the task.
- Create expectancy for successful task completion.
- Insure rewarding outcomes that will foster future motivation for similar tasks.

Keller, J. (1983). Motivational design of instruction. In C. Reigeluth (Ed.). Instructional design theories and models: An overview or their current status. Hillsdale, NJ: Erlbaum.

Another addition to the textbook material presented in Chapter Ten is Festinger's Theory of Cognitive Dissonance. This theory offers an excellent opportunity to relate the material presented in Chapter Six on self-esteem with the principles of motivation discussed in this chapter. According to the Theory of Cognitive Dissonance, people become extremely uncomfortable when they are confronted with circumstances which violate their value system or belief structure. When these situations occur the individual makes every effort to resolve the dissonance without sacrificing self-esteem. For example, an animal rights activitist may violently oppose wearing fur coats because of the slaughter of animals. This same individual may, however, eat meat. When confronted with this violation of his value system, the individual must either change his diet or rationalize some reason to justify killing animals for food but not for clothing. Otherwise his self-esteem will suffer. Another example of cognitive dissonance occurred after the Orson Welles' "War of the Worlds" broadcast. Some people who heard the broadcast made elaborate plans to prepare for the invasion. When confronted with the fact that the broadcast was a fake, many of these people fabricated excuses to justify their behavior. Some even refused to admit that the broadcast was not real.

In a classic cognitive dissonance study, Festinger hired college students to perform a very boring task. He paid one group of students $1.00 per hour for doing the job. A second group he paid $20.00 for doing the identical job. Later he questioned both groups about their perceptions of the job. The group paid $20.00 reported that the job was boring while those paid $1.00 reported that it was not boring. Festinger interpreted from these data that the $1.00 per hour group would have sacrificed too much self-esteem if they had admitted that the job was boring after they had continued to work for such a small amount of money.

> Festinger, L. A. (1957). A theory of cognitive dissonance. Evanston, IL: Ron Peterson.

Finally, instructors can expand on the textbook material in Chapter Ten by administering the Rotter Internal Versus External Locus of Control Inventory to the class. After the tests are scored, students can be asked to interpret their results in terms of attribution theory.

> Rotter, J. B. (1966). Generalized expectancies for internal versus external control of reinforcement. Psychological Monographs, 80, 1-28.

Discussion Questions

1. During the course of the last 20 years, schools have assumed more and more responsibilities that were previously assumed by the family. Some examples of this phenonemon are free lunch and breakfast programs for low SES children and extended day programs for the children of working mothers. Relate these problems to Maslow's needs hierarchy and speculate on how he might feel about them.

2. Teachers often complain that the parents who need to come to school are never there. They say that the only ones who come are the parents of children who are doing okay anyway. Frequently the parents who fail to show up are either single parents or low SES parents or maybe they are both single and low SES. Analyze these parental behaviors in terms of Maslow's Theory of Self-Actualization. Where in the needs hierarchy would parents be functioning if they come to school and participated as expected. What are some of the lower-order needs that might interfere with parents participating in their children's school programs?

3. Teachers are generally provided with their students cumulative record folders at the beginning of each school year. These folders include detailed and specific information about the child's ability and past school performance. Interpret this school practice in light of what research has shown about teacher expectations becoming self-fulfilling prophecies. Do you think cumulative records should be shared with teachers? What might be some reasons for this practice? What might be some disadvantages of eliminating this practice?

4. Proponents of Mastery Learning claim that emphasizing successful completion of tasks and mastery of content promotes student motivation. They feel that grades and other comparative performance standards are a detriment to motivation. Some people would like to see grades eliminated entirely. What impact do you think the elimination of grades would have on motivation? If you were going to eliminate the grading system in a school district, what systematic steps might you take to accomplish this change in policy?

5. Describe how a teacher's expectation of low student achievement could combine with a low sense of teacher efficacy to insure the lack of achievement of almost any student.

Audiovisual Aids

Motivating Underachievers (VC 25125, Films for the Humanities and Sciences, 1988, 28 min.). This video explores the problem of underachieving children and examines why so many schools fail to deal with the problem effectively.

Motivation Theory for Teachers - Part II (MP403, Campus Film Distributors, 1971, 30 min.). This firm shows teachers how to get Johnny's intellectual motor started by controlling the six variables that influence his motivation to learn.

A New Look at Motivation (CRM/McGraw-Hill, color, 1980, 20 min.). This film is set in several business environments and examines achievement motivation, affiliation, and power motivation. It shows how the social environment influences individual motivation. Principles demonstrated can easily be generalized to the classroom.

FOLLOW-UP ACTIVITIES

1. Remember Your Teacher

   This follow-up activity could be expanded by shifting its focus to motivation. Many students exhibit different achievement profiles based on the personality characteristics of the teacher. It is not unusual for student grades to show wide fluctuations because the students like or dislike a particular teacher. Sometimes this occurs in the same subject matter area. For example a student may do very well in freshman English and very poorly in sophomore English, or vice versa. Have the class discuss what particular teacher characteristics were very motivating to them.

2. Consider Factors That Influence Student Motivation

Instructors can adapt Follow-up Activity 2 to an in-class activity by having the class take the motivation variables provided and create an ideal motivation paradigm in which the teacher, student lesson, and classroom environment all are designed to foster maximum achievement motivation.

3. Thinking About Student Characteristics

Follow-up Activity 3 can be used with the class as either an in-class or out-of-class activity. To make this adaptation have the class complete the Student Characteristics Rating Form which is presented in Follow-up Activity Sheet 10-3. The sheet was adapted from the work of Torrance (1970).

4. Observe a Classroom

Instructors can reproduce and distribute copies of the grid contained in Follow-up Activity Sheet 10-4. This grid provides a marking system to facilitate the observation of low- and high-achieving students. Group results can be compiled during class time to determine whether significant differences seem to emerge between the behaviors and interaction of low versus high achievers.

5. Explore Anxiety-Producing Situations in School

After students have checked the sources of anxiety which were presented in Follow-up Activity 5, the instructor can determine which are the most common sources of anxiety for the class members and have them generate alternative methods of alleviating these sources in a classroom learning situation.

Additional Follow-up Activities

6. Anxiety, Motivation, and High School Dropouts

Have class members consider the textbook discussion on factors of motivation and anxiety which contribute to low student achievement. Then have them speculate on how these factors could contribute to the high dropout rates that are characteristic of many low SES high schools. Finally, have the class outline some intervention strategies for use at the high school level which might result in increased student motivation and decreased student anxiety.

Follow-up Activity Sheet 10-3

STUDENT CHARACTERISTICS RATING FORM

DIRECTIONS: Following is a list of characteristics of students which you may encounter in your classroom. Read each characteristic carefully. Place a check by each characteristic that you would encourage. Place two checks by each behavior that you would strongly encourage. Place an X by each characteristic that you would discourage.

STUDENT CHARACTERISTICS	RATING
1. Adventurous, testing limits	
2. Affectionate, loving	
3. Preoccupied with tasks	
4. Competitive, trying to win	
5. Conforming	
6. Critical of others	
7. Energetic	
8. Careful	
9. Obedient	
10. Persistent	
11. Quiet, not talkative	
12. Assertive	
13. Sense of humor	
14. Talkative	
15. Timid	
16. Willing to take risks	

Adapted from Torrance, 1970.

COMPARE LOW-ACHIEVING AND HIGH-ACHIEVING STUDENTS

DIRECTIONS: Have the teacher in whose classroom you will be observing identify two students who are high achievers and two students who are low achievers. Monitor and record their interactions and participation on the form below.

	Low-achieving Student #1	Low-achieving Student #2	High-achieving Student #1	High achieving Student #2
1. How often did the students raise their hands?				
2. How often did the students contact the teacher for help?				
3. How long did the students' reading groups last?				
4. How long did the students work independently?				
5. How often were the students praised or encouraged?				

CHAPTER ELEVEN

CLASSROOM MANAGEMENT AND DISCIPLINE

CHAPTER OBJECTIVES

Students mastering the content in Chapter Eleven will be able to:

- Establish a management system for a classroom.

- Use teacher behaviors that lead to greater student involvement in tasks.

- Use behavioral techniques to modify behavior.

- Teach students appropriate social skills.

- Use I-messages and active listening responses to improve communication.

- Conduct classroom meetings.

FOCUS QUESTIONS

1. What are the major planning, managing, and implementation behaviors involved in a management plan?

   Evertson and Emmer recommend three major phases in the development of a management plan:

   - Plan before the year begins by determining expected student behaviors, translating expectations into procedures and rules, and identifying consequences of misbehavior.

   - Manage the class during the first few weeks by setting aside some time during the first class meeting for a discussion of rules, teaching classroom procedures as sytematically as any other learning objective, teaching procedures as they are needed by students to help them deal with specific aspects of the classroom routine, involving children in easy tasks and promoting a high rate of success for the first few days of school. Also recommended is using only those activities and formats that have a whole-group focus or that require simple procedures, at least for the first several days. Teachers should not assume that students know how to perform a procedure after one trial.

- Implement the system by monitoring student behavior to determine whether the rules and procedures are being followed, managing inappropriate behavior if it occurs, and developing student accountability.

2. How can teachers develop credibility for the importance of the rules and procedures they establish?

Teachers can develop credibility for the importance of the rules and procedures they establish by communicating to the students that they really mean what they say and by following through with guidelines set for monitoring student compliance and non-compliance.

3. How does assertive discipline differ from Evertson and Emmer's recommendations for classroom management?

Assertive Discipline is a more "take charge" approach than the approach recommended by Evertson and Emmer. Assertive Discipline emphasizes teachers' rights to an orderly classroom, and it identifies procedures that they can take to insure these rights. Assertive Discipline encourages teachers to expect students to behave appropriately, use an assertive response style, set limits, and learn to follow through on those limits. Evertson and Emmer emphasize controlling behavior through advanced planning, careful organization and monitoring and improved instruction. Assertive Discipline focuses largely on defining and responding to misbehavior. Evertson and Emmer, on the other hand, focus on creating a classroom climate that eliminates misbehavior before it occurs.

4. What type of instructional behaviors lead to effective classroom management?

Major instructional behaviors used by effective classroom managers include:

- Withitness, which refers to the teacher's ability to communicate by their actual behavior that they know what the students are doing.
- Overlapping, which refers to the teacher's ability to deal with two matters at the same time and to make transitions between different kinds of activities smoothly without having to stop and break the pace of classroom learning.
- Wasting little time moving from one activity to another, and giving students a signal as to what they should attend to.
- Providing seatwork that is challenging and varied.

5. Why is time-on-task an important component of effective management?

Time-on-task is important because researchers have identified that the more time a student actually spends engaged in an academic task the higher the student's achievement. This time is called time-on-task, or engaged time. Academic learning time, a subset of engaged time, is the amount of time a student spends on academic tasks while performing at a high rate of success.

6. How can teachers make seatwork more productive?

   Some ways teachers can make seatwork more productive include selecting content that is at the correct level of difficulty, diagnosing the assignments to determine possible problems that students may have in completing the work, and reminding students before they start the assignment why they are doing it and what strategy they should use to solve the task. Circulating around the room to see how students are doing before beginning a lesson with another group and developing routines for checking seatwork also help to make seatwork more productive.

7. What factors should be considered in determining the use of contingency contracting, group-based contingencies, and home-based contingencies?

   Contingency contracting is useful when the teacher wishes to focus on the behavior of an individual student. Using this technique allows the teacher to involve the student in developing the contract, including the reinforcers. The contract should be clear and fair for both the student and the teacher. It should emphasize and reinforce accomplishments rather than obedience. Finally, contingency contracting should reinforce the desired behavior soon after it occurs.

   Group-based contingencies are most appropriate when peer reinforcement is a factor in maintaining misbehavior. The use of peer influence in maintaining discipline in the classroom can have powerful effects.

   Home-based contingencies enable the teacher to meet with the student's parents and discuss the nature of the misbehavior and establish guidelines for the programs. School-home notes can provide information to the parents concerning the student's behavior. This technique is useful when the teacher wishes to involve the parents in a comprehensive program. Sometimes it can include the use of reinforcers which are too expensive or time consuming to be offered by the teacher.

8. How are different learning principles used in teaching social skills?

   A number of strategies for training students in social skills have been developed. These strategies are designed to teach students appropriate interpersonal behavior and skills for functioning more successfully in the classroom. Several of these are based on learning principles which have been found to be effective in teaching academic components of the curriculum. For example, students are asked to model such exemplary behavior of others as self-control, sharing, and cooperation. Then they are given the opportunity to practice, or role-play, appropriate behaviors. Operant conditioning principles such as using positive reinforcement to teach new social skills and/or to maintain the frequency of previously acquired skills has also been found effective. Cognitive behavior modification techniques such as self-instructional training to emphasize the development of specific thinking skills have also been adapted to social skills training.

9. What are the advantages and disadvantages in the use of punishment to control or modify classroom behavior?

One of the disadvantages of punishment includes the fact that the psychologists have found that it does not eliminate behavior; it merely suppresses it. Also punishment does not indicate to the student what behaviors are appropriate in the situation nor does it direct the student to alternative behavior. The person undergoing constant punishment learns to avoid situations. Punishment can produce fear or anxiety so that the teacher, the classroom, or the educational materials can become aversive stimuli because of their association with unpleasant consequences. An advantage of punishment is that it stops misbehavior quickly, for at least a little while. As a result it is negatively reinforcing to the teacher.

10. When should a teacher use I-messages and active listening?

I-messages and active listening are used when a teacher and student wish to achieve cooperatively a solution to their problem without the use of power or threat. It increases student motivation to carry out solutions. It enhances feelings of mutual respect, caring, and trust. Greater student responsibility and maturity are fostered using this technique. I-messages are most suited to situations in which the teacher owns the problem. Active listening is most suited to situations in which the student owns the problem

11. How does Reality Therapy incorporate both behavioral and humanistic principles?

The basic principle of Reality Therapy is that human problems arise when the primary needs of love and worth go unfulfilled. This need deficiency results in disruptive behaviors that tend to alienate individuals from the reality of the world around them. The primary goal of Reality Therapy is to help individuals meet their needs within the context of the real world in ways that are responsible and sensitive to the needs of others. In this respect Reality Therapy is based on humanistic principles. On the other hand Reality Therapy depends heavily on helping the student to determine what the consequences of misbehaviors are and letting the student experience the natural consequences of irresponsible behavior. In this sense it incorporates behavioral principles.

KEY TERMS

classroom management (p. 452)	signal continuity (p. 463)
discipline (p. 452)	time-on-task (p. 464)
assertive discipline (p. 460)	allocated time (p. 464)
with-it-ness (p. 462)	academic learning time (p. 464)
overlapping (p. 462)	token economy (p. 470)

CHAPTER OUTLINE

I. ORIENTATION

    A. Focus questions

II. DEVELOPING A MANAGEMENT PLAN

    A. Planning Before the Year Begins

        1. The physical environment

    B. Activities at the Beginning of the School Year
    C. Maintaining an Effective Management System Throughout the Year
    D. Assertive Discipline

III. KEY INSTRUCTIONAL STRATEGIES

    A. With-it-ness
    B. Overlapping
    C. Signal Continuity and Momentum in Lessons
    D. Variety and Challenge in Seatwork

IV. INSTRUCTIONAL ORGANIZATION

    A. Use of Time
    B. Seatwork

V. DEALING WITH MANAGEMENT PROBLEMS

    A. Behavioral Approaches to Classroom Management: Arranging Consequences That Increase Behavior

        1. Token economy
        2. Contingency contracting
        3. Group-based contingencies
        4. Home-based contingencies
        5. Social skills training

    B. Behavioral Approaches to Classroom Management: Arranging Consequences That Decrease Behavior

      1. Reinforcing incompatible behaviors
      2. Changing the stimulus environment
      3. Using Punishment
      4. Criticisms of behavioral approaches

  C. A Humanistic Approach - Teacher Effectiveness Training (T.E.T.)

      1. Active listening
      2. Problem solving
      3. Who owns the problem?
      4. What teachers can do to help students with problems
      5. What teachers can do to help themselves
      6. Resolving conflict

  D. An Interactionist Approach - Glasser's Reality Therapy
  E. Reality Therapy in the Classroom

      1. Agreeing on rules
      2. Focusing on current behavior
      3. Commitment directive
      4. Using directive statements
      5. Accept no excuses
      6. Evaluating behavior
      7. Providing consequences
      8. No punishment

VI. THINKING ABOUT THE TEACHING-LEARNING MODEL

LECTURE GUIDELINES

Chapter Eleven presents the reader with a wide variety of classroom management strategies. The research presented in this chapter emphasizes that effective classroom managers are also effective instructors. One of the keys to effective classroom management is preventing misbehavior from occurring. Effective managers prevent misbehavior from occurring by teaching students appropriate behavior and specific rules during the first few weeks of school. They hold students accountable for following classroom rules, and they monitor their students' behavior carefully. To increase their effectiveness in this area, they employ such strategies as withitness, overlapping, signal continuity and momentum in lessons, and variety and challenge in seatwork.

Time utilization is presented as a key to increasing student achievement. Increasing the amount of time a student is engaged in learning increases achievement. The relationship between increased seatwork and decreased engaged time is demonstrated.

Assertive Discipline is presented as a "take charge" approach which emphasizes the teachers' right to an orderly classroom. The controversial nature of this approach is discussed. Also, conflicting research findings on this technique are presented.

Behavioral approaches to classroom management are discussed within the context of a variety of strategies for increasing and decreasing student behaviors. Specific strategies such as a token economy, contingency contracting, social skills training, differential reinforcement of other behaviors, satiation, changing the stimulus environment and time-out are discussed. The criticisms of behaviorism along with a rebuttal are outlined.

Teacher Effectiveness Training is discussed as a humanistic approach to classroom management. Improving student-teacher communication through the use of active listening, I-messages, problem solving, and conflict resolution is emphasized.

Reality Therapy is presented as an interactionist model of classroom management. Guidelines for using Reality Therapy in the classroom are provided. Glasser's more recent work in Control Theory is presented and discussed. Control Theory is recommended as a method of meeting student needs in such a way that students ultimately become responsible for managing their own behavior.

Supplementary Material

Instructors wishing to elaborate on the material included in Chapter Eleven might include negative teacher behaviors which have been isolated by Kounin. Two examples of these are "dangling" and "fragmentation." Other ecological strategies would also interface smoothly with Kounins' material. A recent source for this approach is provided by Macht.

> Kounin, J. S. (1970). Discipline and group management in classrooms. New York: Holt, Rinehart & Winston.

> Macht, J. (1990). Managing classroom behavior: An ecological approach to academic and social learning. White Plains, NY: Longman.

Principles of operant conditioning could be expanded to include many of the techniques of applied behavior analysis recommended by Alberto and Troutman. With this source, techniques for increasing and decreasing behavior could be presented in more detail. Other concepts such as collecting and graphing data, single-subject designs, extinction, and generalization could be introduced.

> Alberto, P. A., & Troutman, A. C. (1986). Applied behavior analysis for teachers (2nd ed.). Columbus, OH: Merrill.

A discussion of Reality Therapy might include the steps for implementing Reality Therapy recommended by Glasser, or some of Glasser's suggestions for using behavioral contracts. The work of DeRisi and Butz (1975) on contracting could be used to supplement Reality Therapy or the Behavioral Approach. It could also be used to tie the two approaches together during lecture time.

DeRisi, W. J., & Butz, G. (1975). <u>Writing behavioral contracts</u>. Champaign, IL: Research Press.

Glasser, W. G. (1969). <u>Schools without failure</u>. New York: Harper & Row.

Glasser, W. G. (1975). <u>Reality Therapy: A new approach to psychiatry</u>. New York: Harper & Row.

Glasser, W. G. (1985). <u>Control theory</u>. New York: Harper & Row.

Instructors who would like a source for comparing and contrasting models of classroom management might wish to consult Wolfgang and Glickman. Their book includes chapters on nine models of classroom management, including Glasser's Reality Therapy. Gordon's Teacher Effectiveness Training, and Canter's Assertive Discipline. Strategies in each model are compared on a Teacher Behavior Continuum which rates teacher intervention behaviors on a scale ranging from more covert to more overt. A less elaborate strategy would be to list the major interventions provided in the text on Wolfgang and Glickman's continuum:

Teacher Behavior Continuum (TCB)

More covert

More Overt

Silently Looking On
Nondirective Statements
Questions
Directive Statement
Modeling
Reinforcement
Physical Intervention and
   Isolation

Adapted from: Wolfgang and Glickman (1986, p. 22)

Wolfgang, C. H., & Glickman, C. D. (1980). <u>Solving discipline problems: Strategies for classroom teachers</u>. Newton, MA: Allyn & Bacon.

Instructors wishing to provide additional information related to classroom management might present Doyle's work on the six characteristics of classrooms: 1) multidimensional, 2) simultaneity, 3) immediacy, 4) unpredictability, 5) public and 6) history. Another alternative would be to include a discussion of leadership and parenting styles which have been researched. These styles are based on the original work of Levin, Lippit, and White and were later investigated by Baumrind. They include the 1) authoritative/democratic, 2) authoritarian, and 3) laissez-faire styles.

Doyle, W. (1986). Classroom organization and Management. In M. Wittrock (ed.), <u>Handbook of research on teaching</u>. (3rd ed., pp. 392-431). New York: Macmillan.

Baumrind, D. (1971). Current patterns of parental authority. Developmental Psychology Monograph, 4 (no. 1, Part 7).

Levin, K., Lippitt, R., & White, R. (1939). Patterns of aggressive behavior in experimentally treated social climates. Journal of Social Psychology, 10, 271-291.

Techniques for helping teachers relate and communicate more effecitvely with students would also interface well with material presented in Chapter Eleven. Long and Wood's life-space intervention techniques could be used as a source for communicating with children using a psychoeducational approach.

Long, N., & Wood, M. (1990). Life space intervention: Talking with children and youth in crisis. Austin, TX: Pro-Ed.

Discussion Questions

1. What are the principles upon which you would base a classroom management strategy for setting and monitoring classroom rules? Synthesize the material presented in Chapter Eleven as a basis for developing your principles.

2. How would the methods of Assertive Discipline and Teacher Effectiveness Training differ in their response to a common misbehavior such as "talking out"?

3. Based on the information in Chapter Eleven, can you develop a profile of an effective behavior/classroom manager. Describe the teacher. Tell what organizational, rule-setting, monitoring, instructional, and problem-solving skills the teacher would have?

4. Consider that you are a teacher in an eighth grade math class. You are conducting your management system according to Gordon's Teacher Effectiveness Model. You have a child in your class who is a low achiever. You suspect that he is embarrassed about his poor performance because recently he has developed a very beligerent attitude towards you and absolutely refuses to do school work. You have tried active listening, but he refuses to talk. He is also unresponsive to I-messages. Your efforts at resolving conflict have fallen on deaf ears. What will you do Monday morning if he refuses to take his math test?

5. As a high school science teacher, you have difficulty with discipline on Thursdays when students are doing lab work. The problems are not serious but they are disruptive. The talking is too loud, several of the students are joking with one another, etc. You decide to introduce a group-based contingency management system. You tell them that if they maintain criteria on behavior during Thursday's lab work, they can have a popcorn party after their test on Friday. Most of the classes respond beautifully, but your fifth period class develops a serious problem. One boy, who does not have many friends, begins to act out. His behavior is much worse than before the program started. The boys in the class think it is funny and begin to encourage the behavior with their attention. The girls are

furious. Several of them begin to make rude and rejecting remarks. As the teacher, what do you do?

6. Occasionally, a student is sufficiently disruptive in the classroom to threaten the learning environment for the entire classroom. What is the extent of the teacher's responsibility in trying a variety of approaches to manage the student's behavior when the student presents no real danger to himself or anyone else in the learning environment? How would you merge the teacher's right to an orderly classroom which is proposed by Assertive Discipline with the student's right to a free and appropriate education in the least restrictive educational environment?

7. The variety of behavior and discipline problems which teachers encounter in the classroom is on a continuum. It ranges from those behaviors which are merely irritating to those which could be classified as delinquent. As a teacher, what are the criteria you would employ in deciding that a student's behavior is sufficiently inappropriate that a referral to special education is justified?

8. Allocated time, engaged time, and academic learning time are concepts related to the amount of instructional time that is devoted to subject matter learning. Can you distinguish between these three concepts and design a strategy for monitoring how much time is devoted to each during a six-week unit in health in a typical sixth grade classroom?

9. Often students respond more favorably to classroom rules if they feel some "ownership" of the rules and feel that the rules are important. Specify a grade level then outline some techniques you might utilize in the classroom to assist students in participating in the development and acceptance of reasonable and appropriate classroom rules.

10. As a third grade teacher, you are perplexed by a student who is constantly moving around the room to talk to other students during the time she is supposed to be working independently on seatwork. Based on the material in Chapter Eleven, what techniques could you employ to decrease this behavior? How would you apply such strategies as making the seatwork more meaningful, reinforcing incompatible behavior, satiation, changing the stimulus environment, and punishment. Which strategies are likely to be most effective?

Audiovisual Aids

Reinforcement Theory for Teacher - Part III (MP 404, Campus Film Distributors, 1971, 30 min.). This film shows how to manage the number-one cause of teacher frustration: children's behavior. It helps encourage behavior that advances learning and eliminates undesirable behavior.

Classroom Management: Alternative Curriculum (VC25041, Kentucky Educational Television, 1985, 30 min.). An elementary language arts teacher demonstrates how to use puppetry, ventriloquism, and a variety of other story-telling techniques to motivate students in a wide range of ability levels.

Classroom Management: Physical Intervention (VC 25037, Kentucky Educational Television, 1982, 30 min.). A physical intervention specialist discusses his views on when and how to make effective use of physical means to control student behavior. Using a teacher inservice workshop setting, he demonstrates a number of widely used techniques: body language and positions, verbal behavior, limited control walk, therapeutic hold and therapeutic walk, cradle hold, and passive restraint.

Classroom Management: Social-Cultural Difference (VC25040, Kentucky Educational Television, 1983, 29 min.). This film includes information teachers can use in adapting classroom procedures to accommodate culturally based behavioral differences among students. Also, it shows how teachers can use curriculum materials that will reflect a variety of cultural backgrounds and lifestyles.

Classroom Management: The Negotiation Process (VC 25042, Kentucky Educational Television, 1982, 30 min.). Practical negotiation techniques and strategies teachers may use are given in working with students under stress.

Classroom Management: Working with Parents - 1 (VC 25038, Kentucky Educational Television, 1984, 29 min.). This film gives strategies on how to work with parents in a variety of settings, including parent-teacher conferences, group meetings, and letters. Also, it demonstrates techniques to deal with typical problems that may arise between parents and teachers.

Classroom Management: Working with Parents - 2 (VC 25039, Kentucky Educational Television, 1984, 30 min.). The teacher/principal relationship and how to make it work effectively in dealing with parents and students is shown in this film.

Discipline Strategies That Work-Parts 1 & 2 (VC 22327, Educational Consulting Associates, 90 min.). This two-tape series provides an impressive step-by-step approach for effectively dealing with all types of discipline problems. Part 1 focuses on "preventive approaches." Part 2 focuses on "corrective approaches" to implement.

Discipline: Winning at Teaching (VC 22324, Educational Consulting Associates, 22 min.). Complete guidelines for an effective and equitable discipline structure that teachers, administrators, and kids can live with are presented.

FOLLOW-UP ACTIVITIES

1. To elaborate on Follow-up Activity 1, instructors could utilize one of the following two assignments. Ask class members to:

   a. Make a list of the misbehaviors you remember teachers experiencing when you were a school-age student. After the list is complete write beside each behavior problem the grade level at which you remember it occurring.

   b. Write the misbehaviors you witness occurring during your next school observation period. Make a note of the grade level of the classroom in which you are observing.

After they have completed their assignments have them share the misbehaviors on their list with other members of the class. By analyzing the differences in misbehaviors that occur among students at different age/grade levels, a developmental perspective on misbehavior can be established.

2. Instructors can adapt Follow-up Activity 2 for use in class by requiring the class to establish classroom rules based on the following list of commonly encountered misbehaviors:

   - failing to attend school or class
   - failing to complete assignments on time
   - fighting with other students
   - showing disrespect for other students
   - annoying others after their own work is completed

   After the rules are specified, students can be asked to design a token economy to be used in the implementation of these rules. Included should be:

   - schedules of reinforcement
   - a reinforcement menu of items and activities
   - values for each menu entry
   - methods of responding to noncompliance
   - a system for monitoring the frequency with which rule compliance/ noncompliance occurs.

3. Activity 3 could be debated in class by dividing the class members into two equal groups. Each group could be responsible for defending a position relative to the use of reinforcement systems in the schools. The two positions along with issues which might be raised in their defense are listed below:

Position 1

Students should not be "paid off" for something that they should do naturally. The problem with society today is that individuals are not developing self-initiative because they expect someone to give them something for acting responsibly.

   - Reinforcement interferes with the development of intrinsic motivation.
   - Reinforcement interferes with the development of creativity and independent thinking.
   - Reinforcement procedures encourage individuals to surrender their freedom of choice and be led rather than becoming leaders.

Position 2

Bribery is an incentive for someone to participate in illegal or immoral behavior. Reinforcement in school is used to encourage positive, not negative, behavior. Also, bribery offers an incentive at the time a student is not performing to get her to perform. Reinforcement programs specify the rules for earning tokens and obtaining privileges before the program starts. Thus, reinforcement is not bribery.

- The alternative to a reinforcement system is to let the student continue on the failure pattern which is currently in place.
- Most adults work on a monetary reinforcement system anyway, so this type of training is good preparation for later life.
- Reinforcement systems provide excellent training in goal-setting skills and actually encourage students to be in control of their own behavior.

4. Instructors wishing to convert Follow-up Activity 4 for use with the entire class may do so by distributing the Instructional Organization Rating Scale provided on Follow-up Activity Sheet 11-4. Completed rating scales can then serve as the basis for future class discussion.

5. Instructors wishing to use Follow-up Activity 5 as an in-class activity or an assignment may do so by reproducing and distributing the worksheet contained in Follow-up Activity Sheet 11-5.

6. Instructors could use Follow-up Activity 6 as an assignment to be developed for either a hypothetical behavior problem or one which would be implemented with an actual student. Follow-up Activity Sheet 11-6 provides a Sample Behavior Modification Plan which could be used as a teaching example for this activity.

Additional Follow-up Activities

7. Research findings presented in the textbook indicate that establishing and monitoring appropriate rules is an important aspect of effective classroom management. Generate a tentative list of appropriate rules for an elementary classroom. Then generate a list of appropriate classroom rules for a secondary classroom. What are the points of similarity and difference in the two lists?

8. Consider that you are a high school history teacher who wishes to implement a group contingency management system. The behavior you wish to increase is "rule following." The reinforcer you think will be effective is a Godfather Pizza Party. Design the program in detail. Explain what the rules are, how they will be established and how they will be enforced. How will you acknowledge appropriate behavior? What system will you utilize to distribute reinforcement? Be specific.

9. In pre-adolescence, students become very aware of appearances and place exaggerated importance on physical characteristics, athletic ability, clothing, hair styles, and the like. At the same time the students in this age group are often insensitive and unkind to one another. Consider that this is the case in your fifth grade classroom. Suddenly the more mature, attractive, and well-dressed students are beginning to single out several of their classmates as scapegoats. Some of the remarks that have been made are really cruel. As a result you decide to conduct a

classroom meeting as recommended by Glasser. First decide which type of meeting you want to conduct; then role-play the interactions which might take place between the teacher and students. Discuss how this same problem could be approached with a different type of classroom meeting.

10. Entertain the following situations which are likely to occur in a school setting. First, assign ownership of the problem to either the student, the teacher, or both. Then develop an appropriate response based on either active listening or formulating an I-message.

    a. You return to your classroom after your planning period and discover that the balloons on the bulletin board you constructed last evening have been removed, and the entire bulletin board is in a state of disarray.

    b. You find that you are completely exhausted after your first period class even though it is not yet ten in the morning. The problem is one of the girls who will not keep quiet. She is constantly asking one question after another. Even though most questions are appropriate, you find that the sheer volume of them has you on edge.

    c. One of the students in your physical education class absolutely cannot tolerate being "called down." Any time you try to enforce the limits, she claims that you are unfair and are always picking on her. From your perspective, you feel that you seldom need to call her down, but that when you do, you are only requiring of her the same behavior that you expect from everyone else.

    d. You are assigned to teach reading to the high-achieving fourth graders. One boy is too lazy to write complete and thorough answers to the essay items. His multiple-choice and short-answer items are almost perfect, but he rushes through the essay items and turns them in without ever even checking his work. As a result, he is making low B's and C's. You are sure he could be making A's, but when you discuss it with him he just shrugs his shoulders and walks away.

Follow-up Activity Sheet 11-4

INSTRUCTIONAL ORGANIZATION RATING SCALE

DIRECTIONS: After your observation is finished, respond to your overall impression of the teacher's behavior on the following variables:

1.   To what extent were students engaged in academic instruction?

2.   How was the teacher behavior related to students' engagement rates?

3.   What were the teacher's strengths and weaknesses?

4.   Write an overall description of the teacher's behavior.

Follow-up Activity Sheet 11-5

Following is a list of some areas in which you might want to implement a social skills training program:

- waiting your turn
- making friends
- asking for help
- interviewing for a part-time job

Choose one of these areas which is appropriate for the students you intend to teach and design a skill-streaming program based on the recommendations of McGinnis. Include the daily lesson plans you will use to teach the skill to your students. Make sure your plans provide instruction in each of these five steps:

- modeling
- role playing
- performance feedback
- practice
- reinforcement

SAMPLE BEHAVIOR MODIFICATION PLAN

I. <u>Description of Behavior</u> to be changed:

- Student fails to turn in homework

II. <u>Operant Level of behavior</u>:

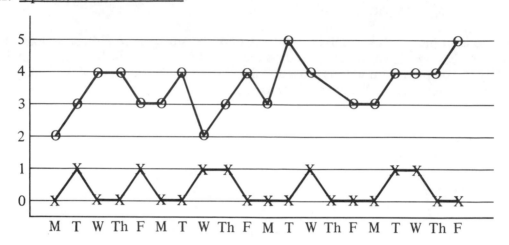

Number of homework assignments = 0
Number of homework assignments completed = X

III. <u>Procedure Used to Change Behavior:</u>

The student is allowed to block out a day on the wall calendar every day that all homework assignments are turned in. He can exchange his blocks on the following ratio:

        1 block   = 30 minutes' basketball time
        2 blocks = Homework pass
        5 blocks = Pocket car
        7 blocks = Michael Jordan poster
     15 blocks = Field trip to Astros game

Follow-Up Activity Sheet 11-6 (Cont.)

IV. <u>Behavior Following the Procedure</u>

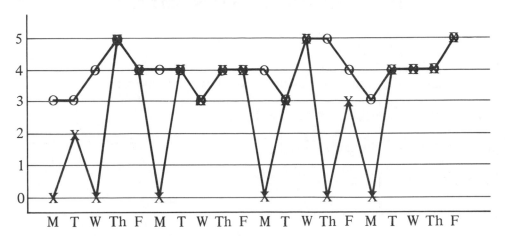

Number of homework assignments = 0
Number of homework assignments completed = X

V. <u>Evaluation of Behavior Modification Program</u>

After the program began, the student's behavior gradually improved over the course of the first week. He turned in all homework assignments on 12 of the 18 days the program has been in operation. Four of the six days he has missed have been Mondays. The teacher now needs to provide some additional intervention, structure, or support to help him improve his record on Mondays.

CHAPTER TWELVE

STANDARDIZED AND TEACHER-MADE MEASUREMENT INSTRUMENTS

CHAPTER OBJECTIVES

Students mastering the content in Chapter Twelve will be able to:

- Identify the characteristics of good tests.

- Evaluate different standardized tests.

- Teach test-taking skills.

- Write test questions.

- Write survey questions measuring affective outcomes.

- Use item analysis to improve test questions.

FOCUS QUESTIONS

1. What are the different uses of evaluation?

   Airasian and Madaus developed a classification system for describing evaluation procedures. They identified four functions of evaluation. These included placement evaluation, formative evaluation, diagnostic evaluation, and summative evaluation. Placement evaluation is concerned with the student's entry behavior before the beginning of instruction. The purpose of placement evaluation is to provide information which places students at the proper position in the instructional sequence and provides the most beneficial method or mode of instruction.

   Formative evaluation is used to provide ongoing feedback to the teacher and student during instruction regarding success and failure. This feedback is helpful in deciding whether changes in subsequent learning experiences are needed and in determining specific learning errors that need correction. Formative evaluation depends on the development of specific tests to measure the particular aspect of instruction that is covered.

   Summative evaluation generally comes at the end of instruction to determine how well students have attained the instructional objectives, to provide information for grading students, and/or to evaluate teacher effectiveness. This type of evaluation usually includes achievement tests, rating scales, and evaluations of student products. Some educators believe that teachers overemphasize this category of evaluation while neglecting the importance of the other three categories. It is important to remember that giving students grades is only a small part of the measurement and evaluation process.

Diagnostic evaluation is used when formative evaluation does not answer all the questions regarding problems students have with certain instructional objectives. It involves special diagnostic instruments as well as observational techniques.

2. What is the difference between norm-referenced and criterion-referenced measurement?

Norm-referenced measurement is the most common method of testing used by teachers and thus receives the most attention in this book. Students' scores on most standardized tests compare their performance to that of their peers. Grading on a curve is another example of norm-referenced measurement.

In recent years, criterion-referenced measurement has gained in popularity. With this method, the performance of a student is measured in terms of the learning outcomes or objectives of the course. In criterion-referenced testing, the teacher concentrates on a limited number of specific objectives. Explicit instructional objectives are necessary because each test item must correspond to a particular objective or criterion which is addressed in the curriculum.

In criterion-referenced measurement, the teacher is primarily concerned with how many items in a set of specific objectives a particular student has mastered. In norm-referenced measurement the test items are written to reflect the objectives and content in a more diffuse manner and result in a larger spread of scores, which is necessary to rank students reliably in order of achievement. Criterion-referenced measurement does not aim for a wide range of scores because the purpose is to have all students master the objectives.

The actual construction of norm-referenced and criterion-referenced tests is similar. Both essay and objective items may be used. The difference lies in the purpose of the tests and the interpretation of the results. Criterion-referenced testing tends to be used more in mastery learning programs when the instructional intent is to raise almost all students to a specified level of achievement. Classroom instruction uses this testing to greatest advantage when the learning outcomes are cumulative and progressively more complex, as in mathematics, reading, and foreign language, and when minimum levels of mastery can be established. When the subject matter is not cumulative, when the student does not need to reach some specified level of competency, and when tests measure success in comparative steps, norm-referenced testing is preferred.

3. Why are both validity and reliability constructs necessary in evaluating tests?

Evaluation specialists have developed specific criteria for judging the quality of various measurement instruments. Two of the most important criteria for evaluating instruments are validity and reliability. Test validity refers to the appropriateness of the interpretation of the test scores with regard to a particular use. Reliability is a qualitative judgment about the consistency of test scores or other evaluation results from one measure to another. For a test to be useful, it must be both valid and reliable. That is to say, the test must measure what it purports to measure, and it must be able to do so consistently. Otherwise, the test results have no meaning.

4. Under what conditions would a test-maker be concerned with each of the following types of validity: content, criterion-related, and construct validity?

Content validity aims for an adequate sampling of a specified universe of content. In constructing a test, the teacher should include test items that sufficiently represent the instructional objectives of the unit and the subject matter. Many students, after analyzing the test questions in their courses, often remark that some material was not even tested on the examination. Such a test may have low content validity.

Criterion-related validity is concerned with two questions: How well does the test judge present ability? How well does the test judge future ability? The typical procedure for reporting criterion-related validity is by the use of a validity coefficient, which reveals the correlation, or relationship, between the test and the criterion. Although the criterion could be another test, it usually is some other type of performance indicator.

The third approach to validity is construct validity. Psychologists develop tests to measure traits and abilities such as intelligence, anxiety, creativity, and social adjustment. These traits are also called constructs. The tests determine the amount of the trait or construct a person possesses.

Although a test may exhibit more than one approach to validity, some tests are constructed with one major source of validity in mind. Content validity is an earmark of teacher-made tests and standardized achievement tests. Criterion-related validity is the main factor in the scholastic aptitude tests used to predict school or college success. Construct validity justifies the use of a test for measuring specific psychological traits or abilities.

5. What is the difference between criterion-related validity and criterion-referenced measurement?

In criterion-referenced measurement, the teacher is primarily concerned with how many items of a set of specific objectives a particular student has mastered. Therefore, the performance of a student is measured in terms of the learning outcomes or objectives of the course. Criterion-related validity is concerned with present ability and prediction of future performance. Criterion-related validity is the main factor in the scholastic aptitude tests used to predict school or college success.

6. Why are different types of reliability used in measurement?

   Reliability is a qualitative judgment about the consistency of test scores or other evaluation results from one measure to another. It is difficult to make good judgments on the basis of unreliable test scores. The methods available for determining reliability are evidence of the recognition that there are different types of consistency. Two important kinds of reliability are consistency over time and consistency over different forms of an evaluation instrument.

   Consistency over time is often referred to as test-retest reliability. In this procedure, individuals take the same test at two different times, and the results of the tests are compared by using a correlation coefficient. If the results are stable, students who score high on the first administration score high again on the second administration. Low achievers score low both times. This consistency is indicated by a high correlation coefficient.

   Consistency over different but equivalent forms of the same test is determined by administering these forms to the same students in close succession and then correlating the resulting scores. The correlation coefficient obtained provides a measure of equivalence indicating the degree to which both forms of the test measure the same aspects of student behavior. A high correlation coefficient would indicate that either test could be used to measure students' knowledge of the material. A low correlation coefficient would indicate that the two forms of the test do not measure the same material or that they differ in the degree of difficulty. This type of reliability is important when using different forms of a test to measure the growth of students over a period.

   A third type of reliability is called split-half. It provides a measure of the internal consistency of the test. It is similar to the equivalent forms method. In the split-half method scores on one half of the test items are correlated to scores on the other half of the test items. The resulting correlation coefficient indicates whether the test is consistent with itself, so to speak.

7. What factors need to be considered in selecting standardized tests?

   It is important for the educational committee responsible for selecting tests in a school district to evaluate the appropriateness of the norm or comparison group provided by the test publishers before selecting a test. In some situations, a test may have as a norm a group with which it would be inappropriate to compare the performance of students in another group. Test norms provide a standard for comparing an individual's relative level of performance on a specific test.

8. What are the strengths and weaknesses of minimum competency testing for students and teachers?

   Many states have passed laws to mandate the establishment of minimum competency testing programs for elementary and secondary school students. The minimum standards are determined by local school districts, or they are established on a statewide basis. The standards are measured by tests given at various grade levels, and the tests must be passed by the time the student expects to graduate. Early testing allows those students who fail one or more parts of the tests to receive remedial instruction designed to help them pass the tests before the completion of the twelfth grade. A student who continues to fail the tests is usually given a "certificate of attendance" rather than a diploma.

Included in the many issues concerning minimum competency testing programs that need to be resolved are the definition of competencies, the specification of minimal competency, and the testing of minimum competence. Not everyone agrees on the identification of "life skills," "essential skills," or "survival skills" that should be required in education. Furthermore, school grades do not correlate highly with economic success; perhaps skills taught in preparation for passing a test will be of little value later on. Nor does everyone agree on appropriate cutoff levels for minimum competency.

While the debate over minimum competency testing for students was occurring, attention moved to the ability of teachers to provide the quality of instruction needed to improve student achievement. Teacher selection and training have come under severe criticism that has focused on the fact that many individuals entering the teaching profession have low or marginal academic ability as measured by such tests as the Graduate Record Examination (GRE). Standards for entering and graduating from accredited teacher education programs are too low, and state certification and school selection processes are inadequate. As a result, many teachers have entered the profession having neither gained nor demonstrated teaching competency and knowledge of basic academic skills.

To combat this problem, every state except Alaska and Iowa have passed laws requiring competency or literacy tests for prospective teachers in such areas as reading, writing, language, and mathematics as a requirement for certification. Some states also assess actual teaching performance as well. The argument often made by proponents of teacher competency tests is that if attorneys, real estate agents, and barbers have to take tests to obtain a license, why should teachers not be required to do the same? Most important, proponents believe that the testing will lead to the improvement of education as a profession.

In addition to the argument that the tests will not necessarily improve the quality of teaching, other criticisms of testing teachers generally fall into two major areas. The tests are not valid, and the standards are not high enough. The validity argument stems from the fact that the tests generally measure not classroom teaching ability but basic academic skills, which don't predict on-the-job success. In the few states that include some measure of actual teaching ability, there are also questions as to whether these assessments can predict teacher effectiveness. If they cannot, the tests will do little to "weed out" inferior teachers. Finally, a good test performance on basic skills does not assure that a teacher is proficient in teaching advanced mathematics or English classes.

The proponents of competency testing for teachers reply to the foregoing arguments by saying that it is not the whole answer to improving the quality of education but that it can be part of the solution. The rest of the solution involves attracting more competent individuals to the profession, screening prospective teachers better, providing more effective teacher education, and instituting effective staff development programs in schools.

9. What are the strengths and weaknesses of standardized testing?

Not all educators are pleased with the extensive use of standardized testing in our nation's schools. Issues of validity and usage are most frequently raised. One of the major criticisms of tests is that they are designed to measure differences among individuals to determine who receives and who is denied certain rewards and privileges. The important question is whether tests are the kind of gatekeepers we want in society. Do educators and employers rely too much on tests, which can be unreliable predictors of future performance? Are there alternatives? Should we rely more on individuals' actual performance rather than on their test performance?

Advocates of the proper use of standardized testing argue that tests also open the gates for some students whose academic records and/or socioeconomic status would not permit them to attend college or enter a special program. In other situations, tests may identify special abilities or talents that encourage students to enter fields they had never before thought about. Some educators believe that the widespread use of the single-answer test item influences students' style of thinking. More specifically, the concern is that many students may believe that all issues or questions can be resolved by finding the one right answer.

On the other hand, well-constructed tests can measure higher-level cognitive skills and can enhance students' thinking. Some educators argue that when teachers learn how and what their students will be tested on, they are less likely to cover important material because they do not believe it will be on the test. In addition, they may be less likely to try new methods of teaching or new resource materials if they believe that students' test results may be affected adversely.

By knowing the general content of a standardized test given at the end of a course, however, a teacher is likely to cover more instructional objectives and help students to attain a higher level of mastery of content than they would if no standardized test were given.

Some critics feel that students make social comparisons to judge their own adequacy and self-worth. Students may come to believe early in their educational careers that they are less capable than their classmates and stop trying to achieve. Many parents have been misinformed by guidance counselors who have told them that their child or adolescent was not "college material," information that may become a self-fulfilling prophecy.

Although some students' self-concepts are negatively influenced by standardized testing, many students are positively influenced by learning that their academic efforts have paid off. With better training, teachers and counselors are less likely to provide inaccurate information about test results to parents and students.

Many schools use test results to assign students to classes based on estimates of learning ability. It has been argued that many students have not learned the necessary test-taking skills, and as a result their ability is underestimated by the tests. The fact that students are assigned to different levels, or tracks, in school often influences the type of education they receive in terms of course content, quality of teachers, and expectations for achievement. Finally, students who score low on standardized tests are likely to be placed with other low-scoring students in homogeneous classes, as compared to heterogeneous classes which include a mix of ability levels.

Perhaps decisions about class or group placement of students should not be made on the basis of any single measurement. Course grades, test scores, work habits, and teacher comments are some of the major sources of information that should be used to make educational decisions. In some situations, standardized tests may indicate that a student has mastered more content than indicated by teacher grades, thus preventing inappropriate placement.

Some test critics believe that although the school has a right to measure achievement, it should not be giving intelligence, personality, and other nonacademic tests. They also say that test results should not be available to individuals other than the students' parents.

At present most school policies specify that nonacademic tests are not usually given to students unless recommended by a counselor or school psychologist after consultation with a parent. Recent privacy laws have attempted to reduce the possibility of anyone receiving test information concerning a student without permission.

10. How do standardized tests differ from teacher-made tests?

Although standardized tests play an important role in measurement and evaluation in education, most tests used in school are developed by classroom teachers. Standardized tests seldom fit the specific content and objectives of a given course. Standardized tests are more appropriate for determining how local achievement compares to national norms, while teacher-made tests are useful for measuring individual classroom instruction.

11. When would you use the following type of tests: multiple-choice, matching, completion, and true-false?

The multiple-choice item has numerous merits. First, it can measure objectives from the knowledge level to the most complex level. Second, the teacher can sample a great deal of information in a relatively short time. Third, scoring is completely objective. The correct answer is not open to interpretation. Last, the inclusion of four or five choices reduces the possibility of obtaining a correct answer through guessing. The matching item is most appropriate for assessing associations. It is not readily adaptable for measuring complex levels of learning. A completion item confronts the students with a statement for which they must supply a missing word or phrase. This type of item emphasizes recall of previously learned material rather than recognition. The advantage of the true-false item is that it tends to be brief. The teacher can ask questions covering a great deal of material and can score the ietms in a short time.

12. What are the advantages and disadvantages of essay and objective tests?

Essay questions are used to their best advantage in measuring higher-order mental processes, such as application, analysis, synthesis, and evaluation. They should not be used to measure knowledge of facts or principles. They provide an opportunity for students to use their own words, style, and organization in dealing with the subject matter of a course.

Teachers should be aware of at least three limitations of essay questions. First is the problem of content validity. An adequate sampling of the content and objectives of a unit or course by essay questions is impossible. These questions take more time to answer than do objective items, limiting the number of questions that can be asked and thus limiting the content coverage of the examination.

Second, subjective scoring makes essay test results lower in reliability than objective tests, which use more precise scoring. A number of extraneous factors can influence a teacher's scoring of an essay question. Handwriting, the use of pen rather than pencil, spelling, and grammatical errors will probably disincline the teacher toward the student. A halo effect (or its opposite), which occurs when a teacher's general impression of the student affects the evaluation of the paper, is an unfortunate possibility. This effect can be either positive or negative.

Last, although essay questions take less time to write than objective questions, this gain is lost in the scoring. For this reason, teachers with large classes often limit essay testing to very specific objectives.

13. How does an item analysis help teachers improve the quality of their tests?

After giving and scoring a test, it is important to determine which items need improvements and which should be omitted from future tests. Item analysis is a method of examining the students' responses to each test item to judge the quality of the test. Both difficulty and discrimination of a given item can be determined. A test item is considered to be good if it is neither too difficult nor too easy, and if it discriminates between the high and low scorers on the test. Item analysis can be applied to any type of test item. The focus here, however, is on multiple-choice tests because of the wide use of item analysis for these types of questions.

CHAPTER OUTLINE

I. ORIENTATION

A. Focus Questions

II. THE USE OF EVALUATION IN CLASSROOM INSTRUCTION

   A. Placement Evaluation
   B. Formative Evaluation
   C. Diagnostic Evaluation
   D. Summative Evaluation

III. JUDGING STUDENT LEARNING: NORM-REFERENCED AND CRITERION-REFERENCED MEASUREMENT

IV. CHARACTERISTICS OF A GOOD TEST

   A. Validity
   B. Reliability

V. STANDARDIZED TESTS

VI. APTITUDE TESTS

VII. ACHIEVEMENT TESTS

   A. Standardized Achievement Tests

      1. Diagnostic tests
      2. Readiness tests
      3. Individual achievement tests

VIII. SPECIAL ACHIEVEMENT TESTING PROGRAMS

   A. National Assessment of Educational Progress
   B. Minimal Competency Testing for Students
   C. Minimal Competency Testing for Teachers

IX. PREPARING STUDENTS FOR TESTS

X. CRITICISMS OF STANDARDIZED TESTING

   A. The Gatekeeper Function

      1. Criticisms
      2. Response

   B. Harmful Effects on Cognitive Style

      1. Criticisms
      2. Response

   C. Effect on Curricula and Change

1. Criticisms
2. Response

   D. Students' Self-Concept and Level of Aspiration

      1. Criticisms
      2. Response

   E. SELECTION OF HOMOGENEOUS EDUCATIONAL GROUPS

      1. Criticisms
      2. Response

   F. Invasion of Privacy

      1. Criticisms
      2. Response

XI. TEACHER-MADE TESTS

XII. PLANNING THE TESTS

XIII. MEASURING AFFECTIVE OUTCOMES

   A. Open-Ended Questions
   B. Questionnaires

XIV. IMPROVING TEST QUALITY THROUGH ITEM ANALYSIS

   A. Index of Item Difficulty
   B. Index of Item Discrimination

XV. THINKING ABOUT THE TEACHING-LEARNING MODEL

KEY TERMS

test (p. 501)

measurement (p. 501)

evaluation (p. 501)

placement evaluation (p. 507)

formative evaluation (p. 507)

diagnostic evaluation (p. 507)

summative evaluation (p. 508)

norm-referenced measurement (p. 509)

criterion-referenced measurement (p. 509)

validity (p. 510)

reliability (p. 510)

content validity (p. 510)

CHAPTER GUIDELINES

The various purposes of evaluation are described in Chapter Twelve. Characteristics of a good test are identified, followed by a critique of several standardized tests currently used in the schools. Instructions for developing a test are presented along with the use of item analysis to improve test questions.

The chapter begins with a description of placement, formative, diagnostic, and summative evaluation, and the types of instructional situations which warrant their administration. Norm-referenced and criterion-referenced measurements are defined. Validity and reliability are two important criteria identified for evaluating the quality of a test. Standardized tests are discussed as being commercially prepared under uniform procedures. The functions of achievement and aptitude tests are described. Specific diagnostic, readiness, and individual achievement tests are listed. Student and teacher minimal competency testing is debated. The chapter focuses on the criticisms of standardized tests and addresses such issues as the gatekeeper function, the harmful effects of testing on cognitive style, the effect of testing on curricular change, students' self-concept, level of aspiration, selection of homogeneous educational groups, and invasion of privacy.

Teacher-made tests are shown to be more advantageous than standardized tests because of their greater relevance to the student's curriculum. A table of specifications for test development is provided. The value of multiple-choice and essay tests are discussed. Item analysis is presented as a technique which examines the effectiveness of a test. Instructions for conducting an item analysis are included. The chapter stresses the importance of standardized and teacher-made tests, as well as other measurement procedures such as observation and teacher expectations.

Supplementary Material

Textbook material on criterion-referenced testing can be supplemented by the work of Berk. His work is especially beneficial in helping teachers make subjective judgments about setting performance standards and determining what constitutes mastery.

Berk, R. A. (1980). <u>Criterion-referenced testing: State of the art</u>. Baltimore: Johns Hopkins University Press.

Berk, R. A. (1986). A consumer's guide to setting performance standards on criterion-referenced tests. <u>Review of Educational Research, 56</u>, 137-172

Instructors can also expand on the information in Chapter Twelve by introducing a discussion of the scholastic aptitude tests which are usually required for admission to college and professional training programs such as medical school and law school. Some tests with which the class might already be familiar are the ACT, the SAT, the GRE, the LSAT and the MCAT. Recently, training courses to improve student performance on some of these tests have proven effective. This evidence could be used to stimulate a debate on whether or not these tests really measure aptitude if, in fact, learning experiences can significantly increase scores.

Marzano and Costa entertain many of these validity issues as they relate to aptitude testing. A recent article of theirs can be used to provide structure to the debate.

Marzano, R. J., & Costa, A. L. (1988). Question: Do standardized tests measure general cognitive skills? Answer: No. <u>Educational Leadership, 45</u>(8), 66-73.

The textbook concepts on minimum competency testing can be expanded by a discussion of the competency testing of teachers. An excellent resource for providing structure to the discussion is an article by Ellwein, Glass and Smith. Their article reports results of a study conducted on competency testing of inservice teachers. The propositions that they present relate to the determination of what constitutes minimum standards, how competency testing can be organized and implemented, and the political and symbolic importance of competency testing. They conclude that significant reforms in this field are not in evidence. They present several themes which seem to support the current status of competency testing.

- Maintaining the image of high standards is crucial.
- Competency testing often repeats screening standards which are already in place.
- Too much importance is placed on initial failure rates.
- There has been a marked contrast between early attempts at testing reform and those efforts which have come later.

Elwein, M. C., Glass, G. F., & Smith, M. L. (1988). Standards of competence: Propositions on the nature of testing reforms. <u>Educational Researcher, 17</u>(8), 4-9.

A discussion of ethics as they relate to the testing process can also be introduced in addition to the other material in Chapter Twelve. In the past, individuals were sometimes given tests without knowing why they were being tested or what the test results would be used for. This practice is no longer acceptable. In addition, schools are subject to open records laws. These laws require that schools share test results with students and their parents when they are requested to do so. Currently, some states such as New York have passed "truth in testing" laws that insure the right of the individual to be provided with not only a copy of the results of the test but also the test questions and their answers. The "truth in testing" laws are somewhat controversial in that they threaten test security, and as such, they raise validity issues.

Discussion Questions

1. Reliability and validity are both terms which are crucial to the development of useful evaluation instruments. What is the difference between reliability and validity? Is it possible to have one without the other?

2. There has been tremendous discussion over the fairness of using standardized tests with minority group children. Numerous attempts have been made to create culture-free or culture-fair tests. None has been overwhelmingly successful. Why do you think it is so difficult to create a test that doesn't discriminate against minority students?

3. Consider that you have a very bright fourth grade student. This boy has completed the Metropolitan Achievement Test. His percentile rank for the complete battery is the 98th. During a parent conference you are going over the test results with his mother and father. The mother notices the grade-level equivalents. She sees that her son's Reading Comprehension grade-level equivalent is 11-6. She asks you what this means. How would you explain it to her?

4. In a discussion of measurement instruments, the emphasis is always on objective measurement. This emphasis holds true for norm-referenced as well as criterion-referenced tests. Even with essay items, the focus is on establishing objective scoring criteria. Do you think there is any place in the evaluation process for subjective judgments as opposed to objective measurements. If so, when and where can subjective data be used to improve the evaluation process?

5. Consider that you are an eighth grade teacher. Five of your students scored at the following percentile ranks on the math section of their achievement test.

John	50%
Jack	60%
Jim	75%
Joe	90%
Jerry	95%

Refer these scores to the normal distribution. Explain the relationship of raw scores, or number of items answered correctly, to the percentile ranks which are assigned to subsequent student performance.

6. Chapter Twelve discusses norm-referenced tests, criterion-referenced tests, achievement tests, and aptitude tests. What are the factors which distinguish these tests from one another. What purpose is each of these tests supposed to serve? Give an example of each kind of test and what function it would serve if it were doing the job it was expected to do.

Audiovisual Aids

Mean, Median and Mode (McGraw-Hill Films, color, 1966, 14 min.). This film uses everyday situations to develop concepts related to the three measures of central tendency.

Statistics at a Glance (Wiley, b&w, 28 min.). This film covers relevant statistical concepts in an informative and interesting way.

FOLLOW-UP ACTIVITIES

1. Identify Your Position on the Importance of Standardized Testing

   Instructors entertaining class debate on the importance of standardized testing might expect some of the following issues to surface as class members defend the two statements presented in this activity.

   a. **Test scores are objective.** They remove personality variables from consideration in the evaluation and placement process. Standardized tests provide the most accurate measure available of how an individual's performance compares to that of same-age peers. Collectively, test scores provide excellent accountability data which can be used to compare teacher effectiveness for teachers, schools, school systems, and states. Parents have a right to know how their children's performance compares to that of others the same age. It is impossible to determine this comparison with criterion referenced measures.

   b. **The public is becoming obsessed with test score mania.** A tremendous amount of student time is wasted in having students prepare for and take standardized tests. These tests have little relevance for instruction, and as such, they are unnecessary in the school setting. Test performance should be irrelevant for pupil placement. Teachers and parents should be able to make valid placement recommendations based on student learning and behavior profiles regardless of what results are obtained on a standardized test.

2. Evaluate Teacher-Made Tests

If a test is not available for use with Follow-up Activity 2, the instructor can ask students to generate a set of test items in a specific content area. These items can then be compiled and analyzed in terms of faulty test construction and to determine whether they measure what they set out to measure.

3. Evaluate Teacher-Made Tests

If an actual test is not available for use with this objective, instructors can require the class to complete Follow-up Activity Sheet 12-3. This assignment specifies a unit of study and requires them to design test items appropriate for evaluating learning at each of the six cognitive levels included in Bloom's Taxonomy of Educational Objectives.

If Follow-up Activity 4 in Chapter Nine was completed, each class member can be asked to design a strategy for evaluating the objectives that were written at that time.

4. Write Exam Questions

Instructors can use the material in Chapter Twelve as the basis for having the class write their own exam. After specifying the chapters covered by the exam, class members can be asked to generate 1 essay item; 10 multiple-choice items, and 5 short-answer, true-false, and matching items. Test items can be critiqued by the class. Collectively these items can become the test bank from which the actual exam is constructed.

5. Use the Mental Measurements Yearbooks

Instructors can alter Follow-up Activity 5 by having the class use one of the mental measurement yearbooks to locate a test which will evaluate students on a particular dimension or characteristic. For example, they might look for a test which:

- measures a student's self-esteem
- diagnoses reading problems
- diagnoses math problems
- assesses interests or vocational suitability
- determines personality characteristics

Additional Follow-up Activities

6. Evaluating Standardized Tests

Have all class members select a standardized test appropriate for use with the student population they intend to teach. Then have them examine the test manual and the test items to determine how well the test addresses each of the eight factors listed on Activity Follow-up Sheet 12-7.

EVALUATING STUDENT LEARNING

DIRECTIONS: Consider that you are a science teacher and have just taught your sixth graders a unit on magnets. List in the spaces provided below how you could evaluate their learning of this concept at each level of Bloom's Taxonomy of Educational Objective: Cognitive Domain.

Cognitive Level	Test Item
Knowledge:	
Comprehension:	
Application:	
Analysis:	
Synthesis:	
Evaluation:	

CRITERIA FOR EVALUATING STANDARDIZED TESTS

DIRECTIONS: Examine the instructor's manual and the test items for a standardized test. Then evaluate the test on each of the variables listed below.

Variable	Effectiveness

1. Description of measured behavior
   - look at the test items, does the test measure what it is supposed to measure?

2. Items per measured behavior
   - does the test have ten items for each behavior it purports to measure?

3. Scope of measurement
   - is the scope broad enough to measure adequately the needed behaviors, but not too broad to evaluate within the time limit and number of behaviors covered?

4. Reliability
   - what are the reliability coefficients for the test scores and subtest scores?

5. Validity
   - what evidence is provided to indicate that the test is valid?
   - what evidence can you find of the test's validity?

6. Comparative data
   - what normative group was used in test standardization?
   - are they representative?
   - when were normative data collected?

7. Ease of administration
   - would the test be easy to administer?
   - how much time does it take?

8. Absence of culture bias
   - do test items include racial or
     sex stereotyping?

Adapted from: Papham, W. J. (1981). <u>Modern educational measurement</u>. Englewood Cliffs, NJ: Prentice-Hall.

CHAPTER THIRTEEN

ANALYZING TEST SCORES AND REPORTING STUDENT PROGRESS

CHAPTER OBJECTIVES

Students mastering the content in Chapter Thirteen will be able to:

- Read and interpret standardized test scores.

- Analyze cumulative records.

- Prepare for and conduct parent conferences.

- Select methods of grading and reporting student progress.

FOCUS QUESTIONS

1. What is the difference between the mean, median, and mode?

   The most familiar measures of central tendency are the mean, the median, and the mode. The mean is the arithmetic average of a set of scores. It is computed by adding the scores and dividing their sum by the number of scores. The median is another measure of central tendency representing the middle score in a distribution. The third measure of central tendency is the mode, the score with the highest frequency of occurrence. All three of these measures provide an indication of the central tendency, but their usefulness often hinges on the character of the score distribution. The mean generally gives the best average of test scores. However, when there are extreme scores at one end of the distribution, the median can better describe the average. The mode is not used as often as the mean and median, but it is appropriate when there are many identical scores.

2. Why is the standard deviation necessary in interpreting test scores?

   The standard deviation is the most important measure of variability because it provides a measure of how dispersed or spread out the scores are around the mean. This statistic is important in understanding scores in a normal curve. If the scores are not distributed over a broad range, the test does not discriminate those students who have learned from those students who haven't.

3. What is the difference between a standard score and a grade-equivalent score?

   The grade equivalent for a raw score indicates the grade placement of students for whom the given score is the average, or norm. Grade-equivalent scores have been popular in the elementary grades because of their apparent ease of interpretation. Another way to interpret raw scores is by the use of a standard score expressed in terms of standard deviation units. These scores indicate how far from the mean of the distribution a given score appears. They are based on equal units of measurement; therefore, you can average standard scores.

4. How is the standard error of measurement used in analyzing test scores?

   This statistic is an estimate of the amount of error in a test score. The standard error of measurement keeps us aware of the inaccuracy of test scores and helps us to compare students. The standard error of measurement creates a range within which the student's true score probably lies.

5. What is the difference between norm-referenced and criterion-referenced measurement?

   Norm-referenced tests compare a given student's performance on a series of tasks with the performance of a random sample of students the same age. A criterion referenced test compares a given student's performance to a mastery level of a specified curriculum such as a sequence of instructional objectives.

6. What are the advantages and disadvantages of the following type of grading systems: contracts behavioral mastery reports, and pass-fail, and parent-teacher conferences?

   A behavioral report permits a degree of communication to the parent not possible with other systems. By specifically identifying those skills and abilities the student has attained, the report puts the parents in a better position to judge the quality of their child's education. The use of this approach drives home its limitations. In highly structured subjects like mathematics, it is possible to identify and report student progress in a specific domain of learning outcomes. In loosely defined subjects like social studies, the domain of learning outcomes is difficult to assess and there is no clear hierarchical structure. A second deficiency in behavioral mastery reports is the problem of identifying all instructional objectives in terms of student outcomes. Third, it is difficult to specify meaningful standards of performance for many objectives.

   A system of grading that is most appropriate at the junior high and high school levels is individualized contracts. These allow students to determine how much effort they wish to expend on school tasks. The advantage of this system is that students know exactly what is expected of them in order to achieve different grades. In addition, it can reduce anxiety because students know their performance level and what can be done to increase their grades. Pass-fail grading removes the competitive pressures of better grading and permits students to explore new subject areas without fear of receiving low grades. This system is limited in that it provides little information about student learning. In addition, students may not complete assigned readings or they may do just enough to get by in lieu of attempting to attain a high level of competency in the course.

7. What are the factors that should be considered in promotion and retention decisions?

   In general, researchers reviewing studies on the effects of retention have concluded that it does not lead to improved achievement and better personal adjustment. When students with similar problems and backgrounds are compared, the students who are retained appear to do as well as those who are promoted.

Lieberman developed the Decision-Making Model for Ingrade Retention. This model identifies variables that a committee should consider in three important categories. These categories are child, family, and school. Child factors include basic skills competency, physical disability, academic potential, chronological age, and the nature of the problem. Family factors include geographical moves, attitude toward retention, age of siblings, and sibling pressure. School factors include a system attitude for retention, teacher attitude on retention, and availability of remedial services.

CHAPTER OUTLINE

I. ORIENTATION

    A. Focus Questions

II. FREQUENCY DISTRIBUTION

III. MEASURES OF CENTRAL TENDENCY

    A. Mean
    B. Median
    C. Mode
    D. Standard Deviation

IV. INTERPRETING TEST SCORES

    A. Percentile Rank
    B. Grade Equivalent
    C. Standard Score

V. NORMAL DISTRIBUTION

VI. STANDARD ERROR OF MEASUREMENT

VII. THE CUMMULATIVE RECORD

VIII. GRADING AND RECORDING STUDENT PROGRESS

    A. Basing Grades on the Normal Distribution
    B. The Inspection Method

        1. Combining data in assigning grades

    C. Basing Grades on Predetermined Levels of Achievement
    D. The Contract System
    E. Behavioral Mastery Reports
    F. Pass-Fail Grading
    G. Parent-Teacher Conferences

IX. GRADES: HELP OR HINDRANCE

X. PROMOTION AND RETENTION OF STUDENTS

XI. THINKING ABOUT THE TEACHING-LEARNING MODEL

KEY TERMS

frequency distribution (p. 548)	grade-equivalent score (p. 551)
measures of central tendency (p. 548)	standard score (p. 551)
mean (p. 548)	z score (p. 553)
medium (p. 548)	t score (p. 553)
mode (p. 548)	deviation IQ (p. 554)
variability (p. 550)	normal distribution (curve) (p. 554)
range of scores (p. 550)	stanines (p. 555)
standard deviation (p. 550)	standard error of measurement (p.555)
raw score (p. 551)	cumulative record (p. 557)
derived scores (p. 551)	norm-referenced evaluation (p. 563)
percentile rank (p. 551)	behavioral mastery reports (p. 566)

Chapter Guidelines

Chapter Thirteen provides instruction on how to interpret and report test results to students and parents, and how to make instructional decisions based on the information collected.

Several definitions are presented with illustrations to help teachers read and interpret standardized test scores. Frequency distributions, mean, median, mode, and standard deviation are explained. Raw scores are differentiated from standard scores. discussion of standard scores is elaborated with procedures for calculating z and t scores. Directions for interpreting percentile ranks and grade-equivalent scores are provided. The bell-shaped curve and stanine scores are described to represent the normal distribution of human characteristics. To assess the amount of error in a test score, the standard error of measurement is defined.

Various grading approaches are presented. Basing grades on the normal distribution curve or on predetermined levels of achievement are compared. The inspection method, contract system, and pass-fail grading are other alternatives which are discussed.

Reporting test results and grades during parent conferences is suggested. Guidelines for preparing and conducting a conference are also included in this chapter.

The value of assigning grades for student achievement is considered along with promotion and retention issues. Historical viewpoints and litigation relating to these topics are designed to stimulate teachers in developing and/or evaluating their own perceptions. Chapter Thirteen concludes with a discussion of the parent-teacher relationship, how to establish and maintain a working rapport with parents, and the effects of the evaluation system on student motivation.

Supplementary Material

Instructors wishing to expand on the content included in Chapter Thirteen could do so by utilizing the research results of a study conducted recently by Foribi-Parizi and Campbell. According to their findings some commonly held notions about constructing objective test items are unfounded. For example, multiple-choice items which offer four response choices are not superior to those items which include three response choices. Also, the placement of the blank space for fill-in-the-blank items is largely irrelevant. The blank does not necessarily need to be at the end of the sentence.

Foribi-Parizi, R., & Campbell, N. (1983). Classroom test writing: Effects of item formation test quality. Elementary School Journal, 83(2), 155-160.

Instructors wanting to provide the class with additional skill in evaluating instructional objectives at the higher levels of Bloom's Taxonomy can consult the Handbook for Normative and Summative Evaluation. The book offers a detailed description of the different purposes of evaluation as well as many practical suggestions for evaluating higher level cognitive skills in an objective format.

Bloom, B. J., Hastings, J. T., & Madaus, G. F. (1971). Handbook for formative and summative evaluation. New York: McGraw-Hill.

The work of Gronlund also provides an excellent source of additional information in the area of evaluation. He addresses many of the issues necessary for selecting as well as designing evaluation instruments. Below are listed six principles which must be considered in the use of achievement testing.

Principles of Achievement Testing

1. The test must measure learning objectives which eminate from instructional objectives.

2. The sample of items must be representative of the learning tasks which served as the basis for instruction.

3. The test items must be appropriate for measuring the learning objectives.

4. The achievement test chosen must fit the basic purpose for which the results will be used.

5. The test reliability and validity must be considered, and the results for a given student must be cautiously interpreted.

6. The test must have the potential to be used to improve learning.

Gronlund, N. E. (1985). <u>Measurement and evaluation in teaching</u> (5th ed.). New York: Macmillan.

Gronlund, N. E. (1988). <u>How to construct achievement tests</u> (4th ed.). Englewood Cliffs, NJ: Prentice-Hall.

Instructors can introduce students to the Contract System of grading. This system allows students to agree beforehand to work for a specific grade. According to the Contract System the type, quantity, and quality of work to be completed in order to earn a particular grade is clearly specified before any of the work is begun. Contracts can set grading standards for an entire class or the contracts can be negotiated individually. Some contracts include a revision option which allows the student to modify and improve work that is turned in if quality standards are not met. A discussion of contracting for student grades could be related to the principles of behavioral contrasting which were presented in Chapter Eleven.

Discussion Questions

1. The 11th grade math teacher at N. Line High School is sick and tired of students forgetting their homework, turning in projects late, not writing their names on the paper, and so on. The teacher has implemented a new grading policy designed to make the students more responsible. It includes the following points:

   * missed homework - zero averaged in with six weeks grades
   * turning in paper without name - minus 10 points
   * late projects - grade drops one letter per day

   How do you feel about the math teacher's policy. Do you think the students' math grades should reflect their memory, responsibility, and punctuality traits? How does this policy interface with the purposes of evaluation?

2. Consider that you are a superintendent in a local school district. You are committed to the prospect of ungraded education. You have formulated the goal of creating an ungraded school district, but you are not in any hurry to make the change. In fact you are allowing ten years to accomplish this feat. How would you proceed? Provide a step-by-step plan of how you might convert your district to an ungraded system.

3. When ungraded systems have been considered, frequently it is the parents who are most opposed. What are some of the reasons that you can think of that parents would be against ungraded schools?

4. Grades have been the subject of frequent criticism. Some professionals in the field of education even feel that they should be eliminated. What are some strategies for conducting educational evaluation which do not result in assigning grades?

5. Students in elementary and secondary schools are generally required to be there by law, while students in post secondary training programs are often selected on the basis of aptitude and are attending from choice. Does this fact have any implication

for evaluation. In other words, should instruction be structured differently for students who must attend instruction regardless of whether they have the ability to compete?

6. Consider the strengths and weaknesses of essay and objective test items. What criteria might you apply when deciding to utilize one or the other or a combination of these test items to evaluate student learning?

Audiovisual Aids

Four Keys to Classroom Testing (Research Press, 1984). This instructional package contains both film strips and audiocassettes. It addresses issues in planning, constructing, assembling, and scoring teacher-made tests to assess classroom learning.

Report Card (Harcourt Brace Jovanovich, color, 1970, 12 min.). This film explores problems which are likely to arise when teachers utilize different grading philosophies and procedures.

Test Interpretation (CAR, filmstrip, cassette)
Introduction to the language of testing. Designed for the person who has had little training in tests and measurement and who needs some knowledge.

Using Test Results (Educational Testing Service, b&w, 1965, 15 min.)
Shows what can be done with data obtained from standardized tests in guiding students.

FOLLOW-UP ACTIVITIES

1. Interpret Achievement Test Scores

   Class members engaged in this activity should make the following observations with respect to the achievement test scores presented.

   * Mary Simmons scored closest to the average third grader in the October testing.
   * Fred Sims was more than a year above third grade level in word knowledge.
   * Fred Sims scored very well in reading.
   * About 40 percent of the students in the country are estimated to score higher in word knowledge than Mary Simmons.
   * Fred Sims' stanine score was second from the top in word knowledge

2. Interpret Information from a Cumulative Record

   Class members could be expected to make the following observations and recommendations based on the information in Fred North's cumulative record.

   * Fred's potential for performance-type activities should be considerably greater (over one standard deviation) than his potential for verbal-type activites.
   * Fred's WISC-R score and his CTMM score yielded similar results.
   * Fred's achievement scores are relatively consistent with his aptitude scores.
   * Fred's academic record is roughly what would be predicted from his standardized test scores.
   * Improved work habits might result in somewhat better grades for Fred.

3. Interpret a Grade Summary Sheet

As the class interprets the grade summary sheet included in Follow-up Activity 3, they might be expected to make the following observations.

- The grades of Sally Ames, Sid Brooks, Sam Debs, Tom Williams, and John Young seem fairly consistent. The other students did not appear to get the grade they deserved. It is difficult to tell without knowing the exact contribution each activity was supposed to make toward the final grade.
- Billy Colton and Alice Zimmer seemed to receive a higher grade than they earned, while Sally Courtis received a slightly lower grade than she earned.
- Tom Williams and John Young had the same performance and received the same grade, but their grades seemed lower than would be expected.
- This grading system needs to be structured so that the relative contribution of each item is clearly shown.

4. Evaluating Grading Methods and Procedures

This activity could be altered to demonstrate the motivational properties of grading. For example, the instructor could make a library assignment. The class could be told that the assignment would serve as the basis of the next class discussion but that it would not be graded. During the next class period, the instructor could administer a cursory screening quiz, such as having students identify the main ideas in the reading assignment. The quiz should be simple enough to discriminate those who read the assignment from those who did not. The low number of people completing a non-graded library assignment should demonstrate to the class the motivational properties of grades to persons who are the product of America's educational system.

Additional Follow-up Activities

5. Comparing Different Grading Systems

Reproduce and distribute copies of Follow-up Activity Sheet 13-5 to each number of the class. Then ask them to assign number and letter grades to each student using both a criterion-referenced evaluation system and a norm-referenced evaluation system. After the activity is completed have the class compare the impact of these different grading policies on individual student's grades.

6. Finding Measures of Central Tendency

Refer the class to the distribution of raw scores which are displayed in Follow-up Activity Sheet 13-5. Have them create a frequency distribution for these scores. Then have them locate the mean, the median, and the mode. Ask the class what conclusions they can draw about the test based on its measure of central tendency.

COMPARING DIFFERENT GRADING SYSTEMS

DIRECTIONS: Below is a list of raw scores that students made on a 50-item multiple-choice test. Assign grades to each raw score based on a criterion-referenced system and a norm-referenced system.

Raw Scores	Criterion-Referenced Grades	Norm-Referenced Grades
Student 1, 41		
Student 2, 37		
Student 3, 44		
Student 4, 41		
Student 5, 41		
Student 6, 42		
Student 7, 33		
Student 8, 39		
Student 9, 39		
Student 10, 45		
Student 11, 40		
Student 12, 43		
Student 13, 38		
Student 14, 40		
Student 15, 40		
Student 16, 39		
Student 17, 37		
Student 18, 32		

TEST ITEMS

Table of Contents

189

Introduction

A summary of the items written to assess the material covered in <u>Applying Educational Psychology in the Classroom</u> (4th ed.) is presented in Table 1. There are a total of 581 items. The items are grouped by chapter and learning process required to solve an item. The learning process level of an item was determined by a panel of educational psychologists with expertise in the areas of measurement, learning theory, development and personality. The learning processes used were:

a) recall of facts, terms, or principles (R),
b) understanding of facts and principles (U), and
c) application of facts and principles (A).

Items were written in either multiple-choice or essay format. For multiple-choice items, the student should be directed to select the <u>best</u> answer. For essay items, suggested answers are provided. It should be noted that these answers represent only a minimal response to the essay questions; instructors may desire greater elaboration of response from their own students.

After each item is a set of numbers, e.g., U,A,(13). The first capital letter represents the learning process level measured, the second capital letter signifies the correct response to the item. The number(s) in parentheses is(are) the page(s) of the text where the correct answer may be located.

Relating items to both specific objectives and specific pages in the tests allows the teacher the flexibility of providing students with a table of specifications that may aid in their studying. It also provides the instructor with a guide to providing feedback to students who incorrectly answer certain items. The instructor can point out the page(s) from which the item was developed and have the students re-read those pages.

Table 1

Table of Specifications for Test Items for

Applying Educational Psychology in the Classroom

Number of Items = 581

Chapter		Recall	Learning Processes Understanding	Application	Total
1.	The Teacher as Decision Maker	6	9	10	25
2.	Intelligence and Cognitive Development	14	20	16	50
3.	Cognition, Culture, and Language	17	12	13	42
4.	Social and Personal Development	23	16	11	50
5.	Exceptional Children	31	9	6	46
6.	Behavioral Approaches to Learning	23	23	6	52
7.	Cognitive Approaches to Learning	24	19	19	62
8.	The Humanistic Perspective	25	17	5	47

Learning Processes

Chapter		Recall	Understanding	Application	Total
9.	Planning for Instruction	18	22	13	53
10.	Motivation	12	21	5	38
11.	Classroom Management and Discipline	18	14	7	39
12.	Standardized and Teacher-Made Measurement Instruments	13	17	12	42
13.	Analyzing Test Scores and Reporting Student Progress	12	9	14	35
Total Items		236	208	137	581

CHAPTER 1

THE TEACHER AS DECISION MAKER

1. A teacher's classroom behavior can best be predicted from an analysis of his or her

   A. knowledge of psychological theories and principles.
   B. personal beliefs about the teaching-learning process.
   C. knowledge of student characteristics and classroom management skills.
   D. personality characteristics.

   R,B,(2)

2. Teachers who produce more student learning also demonstrate

   A. good classroom management skills.
   B. more knowledge of psychological principles.
   C. fewer personal beliefs about the teaching-learning process.
   D. authoritarian personalities.

   R,A,(3)

3. Mr. Good has decided to teach his class a unit on North American Indian tribes. In preparation for this lesson, he should first determine

   A. what instructional strategy he will use.
   B. what instructional materials he will use.
   C. how he will evaluate student performance.
   D. what the students already know about the topic.

   A,D,(4)

4. In assessing a student's entry level in arithmetic, a teacher should first determine the

   A. student's attitude toward arithmetic.
   B. goals and objectives related to arithmetic instruction.
   C. student's previously demonstrated rate of learning.
   D. student's present level of understanding in arithmetic.

   R,D,(5)

5. The formulation of instructional objectives should be most influenced by

   A. available evaluation instruments.
   B. academic content of the subject matter to be taught.
   C. competencies of the teacher.
   D. the expectations the teacher has for different learners.

   A,B,(5)

6. To help her students learn the multiplication tables, Mrs. Evans teaches her students how to use strategies to increase memory. This is an example of

   A. adapting instruction to the characteristics of the learner.
   B. matching teaching strategies to the type of learning task.
   C. using effective classroom management.
   D. matching student characteristics to the learning objective.

   A,B,(5)

7. The teacher grouped his class on the basis of general ability and gave independent activities to the more able students, while spending most of his time with the less able groups. This is an example of

   A. adapting instruction to the characteristics of the learner.
   B. matching teaching strategies to the type of learning task.
   C. using effective classroom management.
   D. matching student characteristics to the learning objective.

   A,A,(7)

8. Because most of her students are poor readers, Mrs. Evans teaches a lesson on nutrition with the help of a picture chart. This strategy best illustrates

   A. adapting instruction to the individual differences of learners.
   B. selecting an instructional method that best fits the objective of the lesson.
   C. assessing the prior knowledge of learners.
   D. effective classroom management.

   A,A,(7)

9. After teaching a unit on North American Indian tribes, Mr. Good will be able to best evaluate student learning by

   A. comparing test scores to scores on a previous unit.
   B. evaluating student attitude during the unit.
   C. comparing student outcomes to instructional objectives.
   D. evaluating student rate of learning.

   A,C,(9)

10. Specific instructional methodologies may vary for the same instructional content because of

    A. individual differences of students.
    B. teachers' personal beliefs about the teacher-learning process.
    C. teachers' knowledge of principles of learning.
    D. all of the above.

    U,D,(7-9)

11. Evaluation of student performance is most important and should occur

    A. at the beginning of instruction.
    B. at the end of instruction.
    C. throughout the instructional process.
    D. only at the end of major units of instruction.

    R,C,(9)

12. Mrs. Jones has a well-organized classroom that runs smoothly. Mr. Smith's classroom is not as well organized, but his concern for his students is readily apparent. Research indicates that most likely

    A. Mr. Smith will produce higher student gains than Mrs. Jones.
    B. Mrs. Jones will produce higher student gains than Mr. Smith.
    C. both teachers will produce approximately equal gains.
    D. it is not possible to predict which teacher will produce the greatest gains.

    A,B,(8-9)

13. Mr. Woble is disappointed in his students' performance at the end of a unit on metric measurement. In evaluating the students' outcome, he would be wise to consider the need to

    A. revise the objectives for his students.
    B. acquire more knowledge of psychological principles.
    C. assess student attitudes toward himself as a teacher.
    D. assess his personal beliefs about the teaching-learning process.

    A,A,(9)

14. Instructional decisions should be related to

    A. content area, behavior of the learner, and experience of the teacher.
    B. learning task, content area, and behavior of the teacher.
    C. behavior of the learner, behavior of the teacher, and experience of the teacher.
    D. learning task, behavior of the learner, and behavior of the teacher.

    R,D,(4-9)

15. Ms. Riley, a student-teacher and a staunch advocate of student-centered learning, is sent by her college instructor to observe the classroom of a teacher who is known to be highly directive in her teaching approach. In this situation, you would expect Ms. Riley's observations to be mostly affected by her

    A. knowledge of instructional methodology.
    B. personality characteristics.
    C. knowledge of student characteristics and classroom management skills.
    D. personal beliefs about the teaching-learning process.

    U,D,(16)

16. A concern with the needs and learning of individual students is most frequently exhibited by

    A. beginning teachers.
    B. teachers with no personal biases.
    C. teachers with years of experience.
    D. teachers who have a clear model of the variables that influence the effectiveness of their instruction.

    U,C,(18)

17. Beginning teachers are most likely to be concerned with

    A. students' achievement gains.
    B. mastery of curriculum content.
    C. professional growth and stimulation.
    D. peer and student views of them as a teacher.

    U,D,(18)

18. As beginning teachers gain more experience, their classroom management style is likely to

    A. become more authoritarian.
    B. become less controlling.
    C. change very little.
    D. change in relation to their personality characteristics.

    R,A,(18)

19. Your car depreciates systematically in resale value with each year of use. If you were to determine the correlation of the variable resale value and year of use to establish a relationship between them, you would expect the r of the two variables to indicate

    A. a high negative relationship.
    B. a high positive relationship.
    C. a low positive relationship.
    D. no relationship.

    A,A,(29)

20. Of the following correlation coefficients, which would lead to the most accurate prediction?

    A. .90
    B. +.25
    C. -.20
    D. -.95

    U,D,(29)

21. The research personnel at a school district observe a strong relationship between speech problems and spelling difficulties. It is decided that the best approach to improving spelling scores will be to increase speech training. The assumption most likely to be in error would be

    A. environmental change remedies heredity.
    B. measures of speed and spelling were valid.
    C. speech can be improved through instruction.
    D. correlation implies causality.

    U,D,(29)

Essay Questions:

1. Why is it important for teachers to examine their personal beliefs about the teaching-learning process?

Suggested Answer:

Teachers should examine their personal beliefs about the teaching-learning process because it is these beliefs that lead them to make decisions that affect how students learn in school. Examining personal beliefs also helps teachers evaluate and modify their own teaching practices.

U,(1-4)

2.   Mr. Ready, a beginning high school math teacher, is preparing for his new classes in September. What advice would you offer Mr. Ready to help him decide what instructional objectives to teach his new students?

Suggested Answer:

In deciding what instructional objectives to teach, Mr. Ready should first determine the entry-level behavior of his students so he will know what it is they need to learn. He should then decide what behaviors his students will engage in to learn the new material. From this information, Mr. Ready will be well prepared to develop objectives that are relevant to both the material he is teaching, and to the students he is instructing.

A,(4-7)

3.   How do description, feelings, and inferences interact to influence a teacher's observation of student behavior?

Suggested Answer:

A teacher's description of a student's behavior is often influenced by the teacher's past experiences, biases, and prejudices. This can lead the teacher to make mistaken inferences about the student's behavior that have little to do with the actual way in which a student is acting. Thus, in observing student behavior, a teacher should learn to separate description of behavior from his/her own feelings and inferences.

U,(16-17)

4.   Many beginning teachers change from a humanistic to a custodial orientation in their classroom management style during their first years of teaching. What accounts for this change?

Suggested Answer:

Because of the socialization processes in school, teachers are expected to keep their students under control and to run well-managed classrooms. Faced with this expectation, beginning teachers often become less humanistic and more authoritarian. Beginning teachers are also concerned with personal adequacy and thus are anxious to demonstrate their ability as good classroom managers.

U,(18)

CHAPTER 2

INTELLIGENCE AND COGNITIVE DEVELOPMENT

1.   The psychometric approach to intelligence differs from the Piagetian and information processing approaches by focusing on the

    A. specific processes that emphasize how we think.
    B. developmental processes that occur over time.
    C. mental structures that determine intelligence.
    D. maturation factors that contribute to learning.

                                                    U,C,(34)

2.   Spearman theorized that an individual

    A. possesses only a general factor of intelligence.
    B. will be weak in general intelligence if a specific factor is extremely high.
    C. must have a high general factor of intelligence in order to have a high specific factor.
    D. can have a high specific factor while not high in general intelligence.

                                                    R,D,(35)

3.   In contrast to Spearman, Thorndike believed that intelligence was

    A. a single-factor.
    B. measurable through any test.
    C. a composite of specific abilities.
    D. mainly abstract ability.

                                                    R,C,(36)

4.   Thorndike and Thurstone disagreed on the

    A. number of specific factors.
    B. the existence of a general factor.
    C. both A and B.
    D. measurability of intelligence.

                                                    U,A,(36)

5. Robin's ability to handle "story problems" in arithmetic and her ability to comprehend paragraph meaning would suggest to Spearman that _____ was present.

   A. a general factor
   B. figural content
   C. associative memory
   D. word fluency

   A,A,(35)

6. Gail's classroom has been designed on the <u>Structure of Intellect</u> model, thus her teacher will assess the

   A. content of the task.
   B. discovery and recognition of information.
   C. forms of the processed information.
   D. all of the above.

   A,D,(36)

7. An example of divergent thinking, according to the Guilford model, is

   A. correctly responding to a multiple-choice item.
   B. repeating accurately what your parents have taught you.
   C. deriving a new alternative solution to a puzzling problem.
   D. none of the above.

   U,C,(37)

8. Binet's intelligence test is based on comparisons of:

   A. children within a particular age group.
   B. average children with slow children.
   C. children of different age groups.
   D. children with adolescents.

   R,A,(38)

9. Guilford's revised model of the <u>Structure of the Intellect</u> contained _____ different factors.

   A. 2
   B. 7
   C. 60
   D. 180

   R,D,(36)

10. Binet's intelligence test focused on

    A. the seven primary abilities.
    B. no particular theory.
    C. structuralism.
    D. the three specific factors.

    R,B,(38)

11. The WISC-R test differs from the revised Stanford-Binet test in that it:

    A. tests large groups of students at one time.
    B. includes subtests that range from easy to difficult.
    C. uses different tests for children of different ages.
    D. requires a trained examiner to administer the test.

    U,B,(39)

12. In his parent conferences, Mr. Cares wishes to be as "research" honest with parents as possible. Mr. Cares will probably tell parents that _____ best predicts school achievement.

    A. personality factors
    B. motivation
    C. physical health
    D. intelligence

    A,D,(40)

13. Intelligence tests are primarily used to:

    A. measure innate abilities.
    B. assist educational development.
    C. predict academic success.
    D. motivate student efforts.

    R,C,(40)

14. A group of concerned college professors have won a grant to develop a test that will involve no biases in measuring the intelligence of children from several different cultural backgrounds. What do you predict the outcome of the standardization results will be?

    A. All groups may score about the same.
    B. The test could be helpful to teachers in program planning.
    C. The results may not be significantly related to school activities.
    D. Reverse discrimination could occur.

    A,C,(44)

15. Arthur Jensen believed that

    A. lower-class children will never be equal to middle-class children.
    B. educational programs must be related to the thinking processes of children.
    C. environmental changes can greatly enhance intellectual development.
    D. all abilities are equally distributed among all social class groups.

    R,B,(46)

16. Intelligence is the concern of psychologists, geneticists, and educators. Which of the following would allow the most flexible classroom approach?

    A. Genetic limits prevent any significant increase in IQ through environmental stimulation.
    B. The limits of intelligence are set only by the limits of the environment.
    C. The limits of intelligence can be predicted through neither genetic inheritance nor degree of environmental stimulation.
    D. Intelligence can be increased through environment up to the natural limits.

    A,B,(46)

17. A main criticism of compensatory education programs is that

    A. too much money is being spent on one group.
    B. achievement gains are too short lived.
    C. parental involvement is missing.
    D. there are too many untrained educators.

    U,B,(45)

18. Twin studies suggest that

    A. the relationship between people's IQ level increases as their genetic similarity increases.
    B. environment plays an unimportant role in determining intelligence.
    C. genetic factors are the strongest determinant of human intelligence.
    D. both genetic and environmental factors contribute equally to intelligence.

    R,A,(46)

19. Ron's instructor in teacher education wants Ron to remember at least the fundamentals of Piagetian theory. She will emphasize the

    A. limits set by developmental stages.
    B. qualitative differences between different age groups.
    C. shift from concrete to abstract thinking.
    D. all of the above.

    A,D,(47)

20. Scott has figured out that if he considers possible answers one by one, using what adults call "the process of elimination," he will arrive at the best answer. Piaget would call this repeatable behavior pattern

    A. content analysis.
    B. function.
    C. scheme.
    D. equilibrium.

    A,C,(47)

21. The use of an existing mental structure to deal with some problem is called

    A. assimilation.
    B. accommodation.
    C. equilibrium.
    D. disequilibrium.

    R,A,(48)

22. Which of these does not fit into Piaget's definition of a scheme?

    A. An arithmetic process
    B. Grasping a pencil
    C. A good tennis serve
    D. A chance event

    U,D,(47)

23. In working with a child in mathematics, you find that he tends to relate his learning to what he already knows. In Piagetian terms, the process he is using is

    A. reversibility.
    B. seriation.
    C. accommodation.
    D. assimilation.

    A,D,(48)

24. When teaching children at the preoperational stage, instruction should

    A. emphasize the manipulation of concrete objects.
    B. emphasize rote learning.
    C. teach theory first.
    D. teach combinational thinking.

    U,A,(50)

25. According to Piaget, one factor that influences cognitive development is

    A. external stimulus.
    B. environmental feedback.
    C. physical actions.
    D. personal expectation.

    R,C,(50)

26. According to Piaget, which of the following represents the order of cognitive development?

    A. Sensorimotor, preoperational, concrete operations, formal operations
    B. Primitive, egocentric, socialized, formal thought
    C. Egocentric, socialized, concrete operations, formal operations
    D. Sensorimotor, concrete operations, preoperational, formal operations

    R,A,(50)

27. Brian is now able to sort blocks on the basis of two characteristics, color and length. He is demonstrating

    A. accommodation.
    B. adaptation.
    C. decentering.
    D. organization.

    A,C,(53)

28. Q: "Do you have a brother?"
    David: "Yes. His name is Robert."
    Q: "Does Robert have a brother?"
    David: "No."

    The above dialogue indicates David is in the

    A. preoperational stage.
    B. concrete operational stage.
    C. formal operational stage.
    D. immature stage.

    A,A,(51)

29. When a group of pennies is rearranged and a child fails to understand this task, he has failed to develop

    A. associativity.
    B. conservation of number.
    C. law of pragnanz.
    D. insight.

    A,B,(53)

30. In Piagetian terms, the parallel play of young children is often

    A. centering.
    B. social.
    C. egocentric.
    D. transitive.

    U,C,(53)

31. Dogs eat.
    People eat.
    Therefore people are dogs.

    The above thinking is an example of

    A. inductive reasoning.
    B. transductive reasoning.
    C. deductive reasoning.
    D. stupidity.

    A,B,(53)

32. What is an important characteristic of the concrete operational child as opposed to the preoperational child's thought?

    A. Myths are accepted uncritically.
    B. The child is tied to personal experience.
    C. The child has no interest in social causes.
    D. Thought processes take precedence over perceptions.

    U,D,(54)

33. If my dog is bigger than your dog, your dog is smaller than Robyn's dog, and Robyn's dog is the largest of the group, whose dog is smallest? This question poses a problem in

    A. associativity.
    B. reversibility.
    C. centering.
    D. seriation.

    A,D,(56)

34. Senior high school youngsters will probably profit more from classes in higher mathematics than younger students because they have the ability to

    A. decenter.
    B. think abstractly.
    C. associate.
    D. perform transitivity.

    U,B,(56)

35. One of the major criticisms of Piaget's theory is that he may have

    A. underestimated the intellectual abilities of the preschool child.
    B. underestimated the formal operations thinking of adolescents.
    C. reversed the order of the stages of development.
    D. relied too much on factor analysis.

    R,A,(59)

36. According to Piagetians, for maximal learning, educational materials should

    A. be slightly above the child's cognitive level.
    B. be one level below the child's cognitive level.
    C. include formal operations thinking.
    D. match the child's cognitive ability.

    R,D,(61)

37. A teacher who takes a position opposite to the majority of students in class may be applying Piaget's notion of

    A. assimilation.
    B. discentration.
    C. disequilibrium.
    D. identity.

    U,C,(61)

38. In a Piagetian classroom, the role of the child includes

   A. listening, recording, and repeating.
   B. cooperative learning with group interaction.
   C. self direction and inquiry.
   D. memorization, recognition, and recall.

   A,C,(60)

39. Fischer differs from Piaget in that he

   A. emphasizes the role of learning in cognitive development.
   B. focuses on the role of memory capacity in cognitive processes.
   C. finds that cognitive development is based on domain-specific subjects.
   D. hypothesizes that children actively process information by the use of relations.

   U,A,(64)

40. Sternberg can be distinguished from such other theorists of intelligence such as Spearman and Guilford by his interest in

   A. specific factors in intelligence.
   B. general factors in intelligence.
   C. the way in which general intelligence is manifested.
   D. how information is mentally represented and processed.

   R,D,(65)

41. Neo-Piagetians differ from Piaget in that they

   A. emphasize the role of learning in cognitive development.
   B. focus on the role of memory capacity in cognitive processes.
   C. find that cognitive development was based on domain-specific subjects.
   D. hypothesize that children actively processed information by the use of relations.

   U,A,(64)

42. The information processing approach holds that

   A. what is learned indicates the abilities and processes of the learner.
   B. how a person learns is more important than what a person learns.
   C. standardized intelligence tests reflect underlying processes used during learning.
   D. the processes involved in problem solving are consistent across all learners.

   U,B,(65)

43. According to Sternberg, componential intelligence

   A. refers to how individuals face new situations where insight and creativity are brought to bear.
   B. refers to social intelligence or "street smarts" or the environment where learning occurs.
   C. refers to the mental components involved in analytical thinking.
   D. refers to the mental components involved in self-management in the classroom.

   U,C,(67)

44. Gabriel has recently transferred to a new school and has had very little trouble adjusting to his new class. According to Sternberg, Gabriel's behavior would be indicative of

   A. componential intelligence.
   B. experiential intelligence.
   C. contextual intelligence.
   D. general intelligence.

   U,C,(68)

45. Tracking within the classroom involves

   A. the placement of students with different educational needs into common classes.
   B. the provision of special programs for students at different ability levels.
   C. the placement of low ability students with high ability students for social development.
   D. the development and assessment of individualized educational programs for each student.

   A,B,(69)

46. According to research findings, students benefit the most from which of the following types of school or classroom instruction?

   A. School-wide tracking
   B. Within-classroom grouping
   C. Individual learning centers
   D. All of the above

   U,B,(69)

Essay Questions:

1. How do information-processing and psychometric theorists differ in their approach to understanding intelligence?

Suggested Answer:

Psychometric theorists attempt to understand intelligence by identifying the factors or mental structures that are responsible for individual differences on intelligence tests. Information-processing theorists focus on the underlying mental processes that contribute to individual differences in intelligence. Another way of describing this difference is that the psychometric perspective assesses what we know (the product), whereas the information-processing perspective emphasizes how we think (the process).

2. How do you explain the fact that intelligence is a better predictor of academic achievement in school than it is of job performance or financial success?

U,(34)

Suggested Answer:

Intelligence better predicts academic achievement because it is primarily measured by tests that are designed to determine a student's academic potential. Since many intelligence tests incorporate tasks that are similar to those found in the school curriculum, they will correlate more highly with school performance than other types of achievement outside of school, such as job performance or financial success.

U,(40-41)

3. How would the low intelligence scores of lower-class children be explained by critics of intelligence tests who claim that such tests are culturally biased?

Suggested Answer:

Such critics argue that since intelligence tests emphasize verbal rather than other kinds of mental abilities, the tests favor middle-class over lower-class children. The development of verbal ability is not as stressed by the lower-class as it is by the middle-class, so lower-class children will inevitably score poorly on these tests, regardless of their true verbal potential.

U,(42)

4. During a classification task, Scott is shown an apple, a red ball, and an orange. Asked which of the objects go together, he selects the apple and ball. What Piagetian stage of cognitive development is Scott demonstrating and why?

Suggested Answer:

Scott is demonstrating the preoperational stage of cognitive development. At this stage, children's classification skills are not well developed. Also, they tend to think concretely and usually focus on irrelevant aspects or attributes of an event or object. Thus, Scott chose the apple and ball because they are alike in color, but failed to notice that the apple and orange are more closely related as fruits.

A,(51)

CHAPTER 3

COGNITION, CULTURE, AND LANGUAGE

1. Research on conceptual tempo has indicated that students may vary in

    A. their response times.
    B. their attention spans.
    C. the amount of help they need
    D. their reactions to new tasks.

    R,A,(81)

2. Impulsive students can often be identified by their

    A. desire to attract attention.
    B. inability to do the work.
    C. increased number of reading errors.
    D. dislike of the teacher.

    U,C,(81)

3. A teacher has suggested that you may be a reflective learner because you have difficulty

    A. finishing your math in the allotted time period.
    B. with physical education activities.
    C. remembering the states and their capitals.
    D. generating hypotheses, given particular premises.

    A,A,(81-82)

4. Laurie's tendency to have many errors but to be the first finished on a math test would suggest that she

    A. is probably a reflective responder.
    B. performs better on reading and memory tasks.
    C. has an ability deficiency causing poor achievement.
    D. is probably an impulsive responder.

    A,D,(81-82)

5. Cognitive styles may be responsible for

    A. poor teacher-student communication in the classroom.
    B. poor scores on reading, intelligence and achievement tasks.
    C. poor adjustment of a student to classroom instruction.
    D. all of the above.

    U,D,(80-85)

6. Sarah's ability to find hidden patterns suggests that she is

    A. left brained.
    B. field independent.
    C. reflective.
    D. bicognitive.

    A,B,(84)

7. The more independent the person is of distracting elements, the more

    A. global the person is.
    B. analytical the person is.
    C. the person is sensitive to other needs.
    D. the person is involved with other students.

    A,B,(83)

8. The research on field dependence/field independence indicates that field-dependent persons

    A. score higher on IQ tests.
    B. are more aloof than field-dependent persons.
    C. are better at learning abstract material.
    D. are better at learning social material.

    R,D,(83)

9. When a child has difficulty interpreting maps, it is possible that the student is

    A. analytical.
    B. field dependent.
    C. impulsive.
    D. field independent.

    A,B,(83-85)

10. The best description of the contrasting functions of the right and left hemispheres of the brain is

   A. creative versus intuitive.
   B. logical versus verbal.
   C. intuitive versus logical.
   D. emotional versus intuitive.

   R,C,(86)

11. Levy disagrees with certain claims made by proponents of right brain stimulation. Levy believes that

   A. both hemispheres of the brain work together.
   B. students learn with only one side of the brain.
   C. the right brain focuses on speech and logic.
   D. the two parts of the brain house distinct functions.

   A,A,(86)

12. Understanding the functions of both sides of the brain has which of the following implication for education?

   A. Whole brain learning may be attained by different individuals using different methods.
   B. Whole brain learning is still best when educators teach with the left side of the brain in mind.
   C. Whole brain learning is best when math concepts are taught with equations first.
   D. Whole brain learning is attained by individuals using similar methods.

   U,A,(87)

13. Fluency, flexibility, originality and elaboration are all characteristics of

   A. field-independent thinkers.
   B. analytical thinkers.
   C. divergent thinkers.
   D. convergent thinkers.

   R,C,(88)

14. Creative children approach learning tasks with

    A. humor and playfulness.
    B. rigidity and structure.
    C. short attention spans.
    D. preoccupation with others' opinions.

    R,A,(88)

15. According to Aptitude-Treatment-Interaction research, you would expect low ability students to do best when

    A. choosing their own method of learning.
    B. they impose their own structure on learning tasks.
    C. learning tasks are structured by the teacher.
    D. they are free to work alone.

    R,C,(89)

16. Matching instruction to the student's cognitive style is difficult because

    A. instructors usually don't have a particular style of their own.
    B. students don't enjoy instructional styles from which they learn the least.
    C. matching styles may increase achievement but only short term.
    D. there are hundreds of possible combinations of learning styles and instruction.

    A,D,(89)

17. Proponents of the "cultural differences approach" differ from the "secondary cultural discontinuity approach" in that they believe that some academic difficulties experienced by minorities

    A. occur as a result of differences between school culture and home culture.
    B. occur as a result of involuntary migration of some minorities to the United States.
    C. occur as a result of the limited occupational opportunities available to the minorities.
    D. occur as a result of the lack of parental involvement in education.

    U,A,(89-90)

18. Because of the current migration of varied cultures to the United States, public schools are faced with which of the following new problems?

A. Students' language often is different from that of the classroom.
B. Students' value systems differ from that of main-stream America.
C. Students may not be acquainted with the basic rules of the school and classroom.
D. All of the above.

R,D,(92-95)

19. A common problem for teachers with culturally diverse classrooms is that they might

A. make mistakes estimating students' academic and future success potentials.
B. need to modify the students' behavior to be like others in the classroom.
C. need to stop using class recitation as a teaching method.
D. need to completely accommodate to the children's learning preferences.

A,A,(93)

20. Non-Standard English

A. is a dialect that deviates from standard English in pronunciation, vocabulary, and grammar.
B. is a defective form of standard English and detrimental to learning.
C. should not be recognized as a proper dialect in the classroom.
D. is an uncomplicated way to express abstract concepts.

R,A,(94)

21. According to Labov

A. children using non-standard english do not need additional verbal skills training.
B. differences in linguistic forms may lead to problems in the classroom.
C. schools should not accommodate instructional programs to differences in language.
D. speaking and understanding are identical aspects of language development.

U,B,(94)

22. In order to improve academic performance among lower SES children, Labov would likely support

   A. matching school programs to students' strengths.
   B. implementation of Head Start expansion plans.
   C. formal instruction in middle-class verbal style.
   D. none of the above.

   U,A,(95)

23. According to research findings, teachers in culturally diverse classrooms should be concerned about the possible negative effects of

   A. cooperative learning.
   B. public recitation.
   C. individual projects.
   D. student workbooks.

   R,B,(95)

24. In teaching reading to students who speak non-standard English, research supports that teachers should emphasize

   A. phonetics over comprehension.
   B. comprehension over phonetics.
   C. spelling over reading.
   D. English-only instruction.

   R,B,(95)

25. Lesser believes that a student's cultural background

   A. influences intellectual ability, thinking style and interests.
   B. determines the performance ability of middle-class children but not lower-class children.
   C. results in differences in patterns of ability between children.
   D. does not influence the academic success or ability of children.

   A,A,(97)

26. All of the following were important factors in modifying classroom instruction in the Kamehameha Early Education Program (KEEP) except

   A. social organization.
   B. cognition.
   C. testing.
   D. motivation.

   R,C,(101)

27. The Kamehameha Early Education Program (KEEP) modified

A. the social organization of the classroom.
B. the object orientation of the classroom.
C. the holistic orientation of the classroom.
D. none of the above.

R,A,(100)

28. When a teacher decides to present small segments of a story and discuss its meaning in terms of the lives of the students rather than emphasize word identification skills, the teacher is concerned primarily with the students'

A. intelligence.
B. social development.
C. cognitive style.
D. ability level.

R,C,(99)

29. Vygotsky's believes that

A. development usually precedes the child's learning.
B. learning usually precedes the child's development.
C. developmental stages determine quality of thinking.
D. with assistance, abilities may be internalized.

R,B,(103)

30. According to Vygotsky, what role does social interaction play?

A. It provides a tutoring process for students.
B. It guides the thinking of less capable students.
C. It allows expertise to interact during learning.
D. all the above.

A,D,(104)

31. A teacher who is interested in applying Vygotsky's notion of the zone of proximal development in the classroom would use which of the following teaching methods?

A. Spelling quizzes
B. Competitive games
C. Individual learning projects
D. Peer tutoring

A,D,(104)

32. The zone of proximal development is the area where a child may solve a problem

    A. in a particular part of the room.
    B. with the support of another person.
    C. alone.
    D. with the use of reference materials.

    U,B,(103)

33. A teacher who is interested in applying Krashen's natural approach to second language acquisition would emphasize

    A. the importance of learning the formal rules of a language.
    B. the correction of the student's grammatical errors.
    C. activities that focus on the comprehension of language.
    D. activities that focus on the production of language.

    A,C,(105)

34. Krashen's natural approach to language instruction

    A. separates relevant subject matter from creative subject matter.
    B. distinguishes between two different linguistic systems.
    C. holds that the key to language acquisition is to maximize the output.
    D. proposes that one acquires the rules of language through study.

    U,B,(105)

35. Which of the following exercises would Krashen recommend to help students learn to speak another language?

    A. Reports on home activities
    B. Workbooks focusing on correct grammatical usage
    C. Copying widely used words from the blackboard
    D. all the above

    A,A,(105)

36. Motherese is

    A. a complex form of communication.
    B. composed of correct form and grammar.
    C. expresses complex and abstract thoughts.
    D. none of the above.

    R,D,(105)

37. Bilingual programs have been found to be more effective than English-only instruction when

   A. students learning English are of high ability.
   B. bilingual instruction is implemented in the early grades.
   C. English speaking students are segregated from non-English speaking students.
   D. bilingual instruction is well organized and taught by teachers who are proficient.

   R,D,(106)

38. The "sink or swim" approach to language instruction

   A. does not undermine the cultural identity of minority students.
   B. stops cultural groups from retaining their primary language.
   C. was partially responsible for the high rate of high school dropouts among minority students.
   D. enhanced the value of minority students' primary language.

   U,C,(107)

39. The development of students' language skills may be facilitated when they have

   A. opportunities to play and talk with one another.
   B. encouragement to formulate their own messages.
   C. exposure to the meaning of words in a variety of contexts.
   D. all the above.

   R,D,(109)

Essay Questions:

1. Describe the relationship between student achievement and preference or enjoyment of instructional methods.

Suggested Answer:

   ATI research indicates that students often report enjoying instructional methods from which they learn the least. High ability students, for example, like more structured methods even though they learn better with more permissive methods. On the other hand, low ability students often prefer to learn with more permissive methods, but seem to learn best with methods that are more controlling.

   U,(88-89)

2. How can teachers make modifications in the social organization of their classrooms to make their instruction more culturally compatible with the home experiences of some of their students?

221

Suggested Answer:

Some students find it difficult to learn in a classroom where they are expected to recite in front of the whole class even when they are unprepared or where they must wait until the teacher is finished speaking until they can respond. Teachers can use cooperative small groups to encourage students to work together rather than encourage competition in the classroom. Teachers can also use the groups to enhance students' language development and allow them the opportunity to discuss academic content in a more relaxed environment. The result of this intervention is that, in time, students may feel more comfortable speaking in front of the class.

U,(95-96)

3. Mrs. Waters is assigned a class with a large number of students whose primary language is not English. What advice would Krashen give her about her approach to English instruction?

Suggested Answer:

Spend time providing students with opportunities to listen to and use English in their daily experiences. Make sure their language experiences are comprehensible, interesting and/or relevant. Keep the vocabulary simple and use repetition frequently. Don't worry about the students' correct use of grammar or their pronunciation. Students learn more about a language than they can verbalize. For this reason, teachers can't always judge a student's progress in a language by what he or she says in class.

U,(105-106)

CHAPTER 4

PERSONAL AND SOCIAL DEVELOPMENT

1. A central theme in Erikson's theory is that

   A. each crisis cannot be completely resolved.
   B. although crises are represented on a continuum, the resolutions must be positive.
   C. the way developmental issues are resolved in one stage will influence the resolution of issues in other stages.
   D. the resolution of each crisis does not affect one's basic identity.

   R,C,(119)

2. The degree to which parents allow their children freedom to attempt new tasks and challenges impacts most directly on which one of the following psychosocial crises?

   A. Autonomy vs. shame
   B. Initiative vs. guilt
   C. Industry vs. isolation
   D. Identity vs. identity confusion

   U,B,(121)

3. When a student drops out of school to assume adult responsibilities, he or she is relinquishing a

   A. psychosocial crisis.
   B. psychosocial moratorium.
   C. developmental stage.
   D. positive identity.

   U,B,(122)

4. A teacher is concerned about a student who will not turn in work unless he does it perfectly and works constantly for high achievement and recognition. He no longer participates in extracurricular and social activities but spends most of his time on school work. This student is probably dealing with the psychosocial crisis of

   A. industry vs. inferiority.
   B. initiative vs. guilt.
   C. identity vs. identity confusion.
   D. intimacy vs. isolation.

   U,A,(122)

5. According to Marcia, the criteria for attainment of a mature identity are based on

    A. occupational opportunities after school.
    B. experiences of crisis and commitment.
    C. parental styles of child-rearing.
    D. an atmosphere of freedom and protection.

    R,B,(123)

6. Heather has not made any decisions regarding what she wants to be when she grows up and has not yet experienced any identity crisis. The stage of her identity most closely resembles that of

    A. identity foreclosure.
    B. identity achievement.
    C. identity moratorium.
    D. identity diffusion.

    U,D,(124)

7. Bill plans to be a teacher. He has always been told by friends and family that he interacts well with children. Bill's father is a teacher and he has never questioned his expectation that he become a teacher. Bill's identity state is one of

    A. achievement.
    B. moratorium.
    C. diffusion.
    D. foreclosure.

    A,D,(124)

8. Susan is a high school senior and is applying to a college. Her mother thinks she should study nursing, and her father thinks she should major in biology. Susan thinks she is interested in exercise science. However, her best friend is an exercise instructor at a local health club and Susan also is considering getting a job at the club. Susan is probably in which identity state?

    A. moratorium
    B. achievement
    C. foreclosure
    D. crisis

    A,A,(124)

9. Jennie feels that by teaching her children to be sensitive to the needs of others, they will, in time, raise thoughtful children, too. This belief is an example of

    A. stagnation.
    B. generativity.
    C. intimacy.
    D. integrity.

    U,B,(125)

10. According to Erikson, the development of women's identity

    A. does not differ from the developmental trend of males.
    B. comes from marriage and the men they marry.
    C. is determined by their knowledge, competencies, and values.
    D. lags behind men after high school.

    U,B,(125)

11. A criticism of Erikson's theory is that he fails to realize that women tend to focus on which one of the following aspects of identity development?

    A. Historical
    B. Verbal
    C. Occupational
    D. Interpersonal

    R,D,(125)

12. Students in the early grades are resolving the crises of initiative versus guilt and industry versus inferiority. Therefore, these students need

    A. to see failure as a natural part of the learning process.
    B. more help when choosing learning activities.
    C. to succeed more at their tasks.
    D. to depend on adult direction.

    U,A,(126)

13. Research has shown that gender differences exist in the classroom because

    A. there are real differences in ability between boys and girls.
    B. boys try to avoid failure in academic tasks whereas girls don't.
    C. role training and social expectations differ for boys and girls.
    D. girls set their achievement sights too high but boys are more realistic.

    U,C,(127)

14. The book, The Cinderella Complex, concerns the socialization of women. The author believes that the women of today are

   A. freeing themselves from traditional aspects of sex-role stereotyping.
   B. earnestly being encouraged to achieve their own full potential.
   C. finally being trained out of their dependency role.
   D. still being made to feel successful only if they are married.

                                                           R,D,(127-128)

15. Research in gender differences shows that females are more likely than males to

   A. attribute failures to factors such as luck or difficulty of the task.
   B. use ability as an explanation for their successes.
   C. select difficult tasks rather than easy tasks.
   D. avoid the possibility of failure.

                                                           U,D,(128)

16. The term androgynous describes individuals who

   A. choose the most appropriate response to a given situation.
   B. can't act assertively no matter what situation they find themselves in.
   C. are low in both independent and nurturing types of traits.
   D. impose stereotypic meaning into their daily perceptions.

                                                           R,A,(128-129)

17. If Johnny is not learning to read, what effect may introducing him to a male reading teacher have on his reading difficulty?

   A. It may alleviate the problem because a male teacher is more likely to enforce strict discipline.
   B. It may help Johnny by providing him with a model.
   C. It wouldn't help because some girls still cannot read although the teacher is female.
   D. It wouldn't help because reading has nothing to do with sex roles.

                                                           A,B,(132)

18. Which of the following explanations is not consistent with a socialization explanation of gender differences?

   A. Boys have superior ability and superior math reasoning.
   B. Boys have more confidence in their ability to learn math.
   C. Boys take more higher level math courses.
   D. Boys perceive math as a more useful subject than do girls.

                                                           R,A,(130)

19. Major differences in the classroom behavior of males and females appear to be caused by

    A. developmental differences.
    B. societal expectations.
    C. educational levels.
    D. sexual dominance.

    R,B,(133)

20. According to recent research, which of the following factors contribute to an amplification of gender differences within the school environment?

    A. The age of the students
    B. Differentiation in the division of tasks within the classroom
    C. The students' academic ability
    D. The socioeconomic status of the students

    R,B,(133)

21. The "feminization" of the elementary school appeared to be caused by

    A. female teachers' innate preference for female students.
    B. preponderance of female teachers.
    C. institutional expectations of the school.
    D. boys' preference for "hands-on" activities.

    R,C,(134)

22. Which of the following is not true about teacher-student interaction with male and female students?

    A. Teachers see females as calmer, more attractive, and more cooperative.
    B. Teachers see males as aggressive, active, and inattentive.
    C. Teachers criticize boys more frequently and give them low grades.
    D. Teachers estimate the potential of girls as equal to that of boys.

    A,D,(134)

23. Miss Rice is a principal of an elementary school. Because she is aware of some research that indicates that female teachers favor girls over boys, she has made a commitment to hire male teachers for her two new positions in an attempt to balance her staff. Which of the following may Miss Rice have overlooked?

    A. Male teachers are hard to find for elementary jobs.
    B. Male teachers have been shown to treat males more fairly than female teachers.
    C. Male teachers hold higher expectations for boys than for girls of equal ability.
    D. Male teachers have not been shown to treat males more fairly than female teachers.

    U,D,(135)

24. Brophy and Good have argued that gender differences are a result of

    A. student effects on teachers more than teacher effects on students.
    B. female teachers' bias against their male students.
    C. girls gaining their teachers' attention more effectively than boys.
    D. boys receiving less attention in the classroom than girls.

    R,A,(135)

25. Which of the following statements is not true regarding the most recent findings of gender differences within the classroom?

    A. Males receive less attention and interact less with teachers than females.
    B. Females may receive better instruction in reading.
    C. Males may receive better instruction in math.
    D. Males are socialized by teachers to be independent and self-reliant; females are socialized to be conforming.

    R,A,(134-135)

26. In attempting to reduce sex-role stereotyping, teachers should

    A. help children become more aware of sex-role stereotyping.
    B. allow students to self-select materials and people with whom to work and play with.
    C. encourage children to learn to work together.
    D. all the above.

    R,D,(136-138)

27. Self-concept is defined as

   A. the value or judgments individuals place on self.
   B. the total organization of the perceptions individuals have of the self.
   C. a multifaceted entity that is unstable.
   D. none of the above.

   R,B,(138)

28. Mary and Jane are both students from disadvantaged homes. On a test of self-concept, Mary was shown to have a high self-concept, and Jane, a low self-concept. Although the test they were given may be accurate, one nevertheless should consider that

   A. self-concept tests are not subject to validation study.
   B. females usually have a low self-concept.
   C. most disadvantaged children enter school with a low self-concept.
   D. more than one type of self-concept may be involved.

   A,D,(139)

29. You have been reviewing an educational proposal that claims that the project will "raise student self-concept." In consideration of what you have learned of self-concept characteristics, the proposal writer should have

   A. known that self-concept is stable and fixed.
   B. written "general self-concept."
   C. been more explicit about "self-concept."
   D. written "achievement self-concept."

   A,C,(139)

30. One characteristic of persons with low self-esteem is the tendency to

   A. forge ahead unprepared into new territory.
   B. limit activities in new learning situations.
   C. impose ideas upon other people.
   D. present and defend personal views.

   R,B,(142)

31. Mark believes he cannot achieve in school. He avoids assignments. Thus, he fails to practice and does poorly on tests. This reinforces his low self-concept. This process is an example of

    A. the low self-concept paradox.
    B. having a middle-class teacher.
    C. the self-fulfilling prophecy.
    D. heredity vs. environment.

    U,C,(142)

32. A students' self-concept may be molded by

    A. the image that the student has of his or her own body.
    B. others' reactions to his or her physical appearance.
    C. mass media presentations of beautiful bodies.
    D. all of the above.

    R,D,(142-143)

33. According to the research on rate of development affecting self-concept, which group of girls expresses a more positive self-concept about themselves?

    A. Early-maturing girls
    B. Mid-maturing girls
    C. Late-maturing girls
    D. No differences were found regarding self-concept between levels development.

    R,B,(144)

34. In planning a school setting that affects students' self-esteem, which of the following situations should probably be avoided?

    A. Having twelve-year-old boys and girls remain in the sixth grade elementary classes.
    B. Placing twelve-year-old boys and girls in seventh grade junior high school classes.
    C. Encouraging body building and fitness classes in the junior high curriculum.
    D. Encouraging dating and modeling of high school activities for junior high school students.

    U,D,(145)

35. Pubertal girls experience more stress when they move from sixth grade to seventh grade in a new school compared to boys of the same age. Simmons and her colleagues believe that this finding is due to the fact that

    A. girls rely more on opinions of others to determine their self-esteem.
    B. girls rely less on "looks" as a factor in sixth grade but not seventh grade.
    C. girls view their body changes as an improvement in their appearance.
    D. junior high is more supportive and less competitive compared to elementary school.

    R,A,(145)

36. Which of the following factors have been identified as causes for the difficulty many students face when they change schools?

    A. Timing and nature of transition
    B. Timing and socioeconomic status of students
    C. Nature of transition and socioeconomic status of students
    D. Ability level and racial mix of students

    R,A,(145)

37. Which of the following behavior patterns do authoritative parents have for raising their children?

    A. These parents attempt to control their children's behavior. They value obedience and favor punitive measures.
    B. These parents allow their children to regulate their own behavior. They rarely punish their children and avoid the exercise of control.
    C. These parents attempt to direct their children's activities by establishing rules and standards. They are loving and respectful.
    D. These parents use harsh and inconsistent discipline. They do not monitor or supervise their children's activities.

    R,C,(147)

38. Research has found that the families of antisocial children

    A. use strong but consistent discipline.
    B. don't adequately monitor or supervise children's activities.
    C. consistently use punishment for deviant behavior.
    D. do not permit their children to be aggressive with family members.

    A,B,(147)

39. All of the following are factors that have been found by researchers to be important determinants of child abuse except

   A. the fact that a child is handicapped.
   B. marital problems.
   C. interracial marriages.
   D. parental knowledge of child development.

   R,C,(148-149)

40. All of the following may be symptoms of child abuse except

   A. evidence of new injuries before previous injuries heal.
   B. burns from cigarettes or burns with well-defined parameters.
   C. inappropriate clothing for the weather.
   D. poor mathematical reasoning.

   R,D,(149)

41. Which of the following statements is not true regarding children and stress?

   A. Pediatricians report a greater incidence of chronic psychosomatic complaints in stressed children.
   B. Children feel stressed when they are expected to deal with divorce and single parenthood without difficulty.
   C. Children deal with stress better than adults and display anger more easily.
   D. Some children show symptoms of stress even with low stress loads.

   A,C,(150-151)

42. The rate of suicide among adolescents has increased 300 percent during the past 30 years. A stressor that is the highest predictor of teen suicide is a

   A. history of physical and sexual abuse.
   B. separation from one or both parents.
   C. problem with failing in school.
   D. feeling of alienation from peers.

   A,A,(153)

43. Which of the following is true when analyzing the effects of maternal employment on children?

    A. Employed mothers are too tired and therefore spend less time with their children compared to nonemployed mothers.
    B. Employed mothers have children that are more independent compared to nonemployed mothers.
    C. Children of employed mothers experience more detrimental effects compared to children of nonemployed mothers.
    D. Both A and C.

    U,B,(154-155)

44. Megan is a fourteen-year-old whose parents are just divorcing. According to Wallerstein and Kelly, which of the following statements would best describe her behavior?

    A. Megan acts afraid even when her mother goes to work and she often has trouble sleeping.
    B. Megan cries every day and although she was a good student, her grades are slipping.
    C. Megan spends more time with her friends at their home than she does with her own family.
    D. Megan feels sorry for her mother and acts angry at her father when he comes to visit.

    U,C,(155-156)

45. Which of the following statements about latchkey children is true?

    A. Latchkey kids are maladjusted and do poorly in school.
    B. Latchkey kids are less afraid and anxious but more independent than children who are supervised after school.
    C. Latchkey kids are less susceptible to peer pressure because they are alone.
    D. Latchkey kids are less fearful when they have structured activities to complete while alone.

    A,D,(157)

46. A parent notices that her son appears to be more helpful at home after watching a television program that focused on cooperative behavior. The child's behavior is an example of how television can develop which of the following type of behavior?

A. Presocial
B. Prosocial
C. Preoperational
D. Proactive

U,B,(158)

Essay Questions:

1. Why is it important for educators to study Erickson's stages of psychosocial development?

Suggested Answer:

Erickson's stage theory can help teachers be aware of and understand the different type of psychosocial conflicts students encounter at various developmental periods. This awareness may aid teachers in their instructional as well as interpersonal interactions with students. For example, at the elementary level, students are resolving the crisis of initiative versus guilt and industry versus inferiority. Teachers can help students overcome these crises by helping students learn to explore their environment, and meet and master new tasks and new challenges successfully.

U,(126-127)

2. How can teachers negatively influence the educational development of females?

Suggested Answer:

Research on teacher-student interaction has shown that males receive more attention from teachers than females. Males are both praised more and punished more by teachers; asked more questions; initiate more contact; and called on more often by teachers. Since inquiry and questioning are important conditions of learning, lower rates of initiation and general interaction during instruction can place females at a disadvantage.

R,(144-146)

3. Susan is an overweight student who is in her first year of junior high school. Her parents are concerned that she spends much of her time alone, is critical of her appearance, and has difficulty making friends. They visit the school counselor at the junior high to discuss their concerns. Based on research findings in Chapter 4 (Personal and Social Development), how can the counselor explain what development factors are influencing Susan's behavior?

Suggested Answer:

Susan's self-concept is strongly influenced by her body image. Her weight problem is probably one factor contributing to her low self-image. Entrance into junior high school may have negatively affected her self-image. Girls value sociability and appearance, and when they move to a new school, they are faced with an entirely new reference group in which the peers who are evaluating them are less well known. As a result, girls tend to have lower self-images when compared to a comparable group who attend a school with students in grades 6, 7, and 8.

A,(142-143)

4. How do parents' child-rearing practices influence their children's behavior?

Suggested Answer:

Baumrind has identified three categories of parenting styles--the authoritarian, the permissive, and the authoritative. She has found that how parents attempt to control their children's behavior and attitudes is an important factor influencing their children's behavior. Authoritarian parents who attempt to control their children's behavior and attitudes to conform to strict rules of conduct by using punitive measures produce children who are more discontented, withdrawn, and distrustful. Permissive parents make few demands on their children, allowing them to regulate their own behavior. Their children tend to be the least self-reliant, explorative, and self-controlled of the three categories of parenting styles. Finally, authoritative parents who try to direct their children's activities by establishing firm rules and standards but are willing to discuss the reasons behind their regulations produce children who are the most self-reliant, self-controlled and contented of the three categories of parenting styles.

R,(146-147)

CHAPTER 5

EXCEPTIONAL CHILDREN

1. The term "exceptional" refers to a student whose performance is significantly

   A. above the average student.
   B. below the average student.
   C. similar to the average student.
   D. above or below the average student.

   R,D,(166)

2. The term "disability" refers to

   A. the difficulties faced by an individual because of a physical problem.
   B. a behavioral characteristic that distinguishes an individual from other individuals.
   C. a physical problem that leads to a reduction in the ability to perform certain tasks that others can perform.
   D. any student whose performance significantly departs from the average or typical student.

   R,A,(166)

3. All but <u>one</u> of the following apply to a group of students with a common specific handicap (e.g., cerebral palsy).

   A. They are a homogeneous group.
   B. They are a heterogeneous group.
   C. They will benefit from positive interaction with peers.
   D. They are protected by due process guarantees.

   R,A,(167)

4. According to the U.S. Office of Education, almost half of the children in special education are categorized as

   A. mentally retarded.
   B. behavior disordered.
   C. learning disabled.
   D. speech disordered.

   R,C,(168)

5. All of the following are potential disadvantages of labeling except

   A. categories can relate diagnosis to specific treatment.
   B. labels may make others react to or hold expectations for a handicapped child.
   C. labels might lead to peer rejection of a handicapped child.
   D. a labeled child may develop a poor self-concept.

   R,A,(170)

6. Steven and Laurie were both referred for a special education evaluation. Steven, a third grader, has difficulty finding his way around school and dressing himself properly. His IQ score is 68. Laurie, a first grader, is far behind her peers academically, but gets along well with them socially and is one of the most responsible students in her class. Her IQ score is 65. Which of the following statements is not true?

   A. Laurie appears to have better adaptive behavior than Steven.
   B. Both adaptive behavior and intellectual functioning need to be considered in a diagnosis of mental retardation.
   C. They both qualify for the Educable Mentally Retarded program because of their test scores.
   D. Not being able to dress himself is an indication that Steven has deficits in adaptive behavior.

   A,C,(171)

7. Which of these instruments does not evaluate adaptive behavior?

   A. Stanford Binet
   B. AAMD
   C. SOMPA
   D. Vineland Social Maturity Scale

   R,A,(172)

8. Which of the following categories of mental retardation would be most likely to learn to read and write?

   A. Moderately retarded
   B. Severely retarded
   C. Mildly retarded
   D. Profoundly retarded

   R,C,(171-172)

9. Characteristics of EMR students include

   A. need for drill and repetition, but once material is learned it is usually not forgotten.
   B. poorer functioning in a structured environment than in an unstructured environment.
   C. ability to maintain attention and work at a dull task.
   D. poor motivation due to past failures encountered.

   R,D,(172)

10. A teacher who has two EMR students in her regular class for math should

    A. not worry too much about the sequence of the tasks she presents to them.
    B. provide many opportunities to practice with flash cards.
    C. not allow these children to talk aloud as they work because they might disrupt others in the class.
    D. provide feedback and reinforcement only at the end of the day.

    U,B,(173)

11. The term "discrepancy" as applied to the identification of students with specific learning disabilities refers to a discrepancy between a child's

    A. academic achievement level and the average academic achievement level for his age.
    B. intellectual ability level and the average intellectual ability level for his age.
    C. intellectual ability level and adaptive behavior level.
    D. academic achievement level and intellectual ability level.

    R,D,(174)

12. A second grade teacher notices that one of her students seems to be easily distracted and moves constantly in his seat during class. He does not read fluently and often reverses letters and words. He also has difficulty copying words from another paper or from the board. This student may be showing signs of a

    A. behavioral disorder.
    B. learning disability.
    C. hearing impairment.
    D. language disorder.

    A,B,(Table 5.2,175)

13. According to current research, which of the following approaches to dealing with learning disabilities is most successful?

    A. Direct instruction in learning strategies
    B. Indirect instruction to try to remediate the learning disability itself
    C. Indirect instruction in subject matter
    D. None of the above

    R,A,(177)

14. Which of the following could be exhibited by a child having a behavior disorder?

    A. Frequent fights on the playground
    B. Inappropriate behavior, but adequate academic achievement
    C. Withdrawal and passive behavior
    D. Both A and C

    R,D,(178-179)

15. Which of the following statements is <u>false</u> concerning behavior disordered children in the regular classroom?

    A. The teacher should provide frequent rewards for appropriate behavior.
    B. Firm expectations for appropriate behavior and consistent consequences should be communicated to the child.
    C. Behavioral expectations should be relaxed since it has already been determined that they have difficulty controlling their behavior.
    D. The environment should be modified whenever possible to eliminate negative influences.

    U,C,(180)

16. The type of specialist most likely to provide needed services to a hearing impaired child is one who specializes in

    A. speech and language disabilities.
    B. physical disabilities.
    C. learning disabilities.
    D. mental retardation.

    R,A,(181)

17. Which of the following is not true of hearing impaired children?

   A. They have problems with social interaction.
   B. Their thinking processes are different than those of children with normal hearing.
   C. They can function effectively with the correct communication method.
   D. If is often difficult to diagnose children with hearing impairments.

   R,B,(181)

18. When providing instruction to a hearing impaired child in the regular classroom, the teacher should

   A. not make any adjustments or modifications in teaching.
   B. utilize the child's visual modality whenever possible.
   C. exaggerate movements of the mouth when speaking to facilitate lipreading.
   D. not insist on special seating arrangements since that might make the student self-conscious.

   R,B,(182)

19. Which of the following should be avoided when dealing with a visually impaired student in the classroom?

   A. Encourage interpersonal interaction between the visually impaired student and his or her sighted peers.
   B. Help the visually impaired student take care of his or her materials.
   C. Treat the visually impaired student the same as sighted students.
   D. Give the visually impaired student the same kinds of tasks or responsibilities as sighted students.

   R,B,(185)

20. A first grade student appears to have a very limited vocabulary. She uses poor sentence structure with multiple grammatical errors. When asked a question, she frequently gives inappropriate responses or has difficulty explaining what she wants to say. This child may have which of the following problems?

   A. Hearing impairment
   B. Speech disorder
   C. Language disorder
   D. Learning disability

   A,C,(Table 5.3,187)

21. Which of the following would students with severe physical health disorders be most likely to exhibit in addition to health problems?

   A. Mild retardation
   B. Learning disabilities
   C. Speech and language disabilities
   D. Social/emotional problems

   R,D,(188)

22. Mr. Williams, a high school English teacher, is disturbed that one of his brightest students (IQ = 130) has a C average in his creative writing class. Mr. Williams believes that the student has a poor attitude. Which of the following is the most likely alternative explanation?

   A. The student does not value creative endeavors.
   B. The student's IQ does not guarantee creativity.
   C. The student has an emotional block toward creative writing.
   D. The student is creative only in numerical tasks.

   U,B,(191)

23. In attempting to identify creative students, teachers should look among

   A. their high achieving students.
   B. those students with somewhat "neurotic" tendencies.
   C. those students who come up with unexpected, unusual comments.
   D. those students who are serious-minded and highly structured.

   R,C,(193)

24. According to Renzulli, which three characteristics appear to be necessary for truly gifted performance in any field?

   A. High ability, high creativity, and high task commitment
   B. Average ability, average creativity, and average task performance
   C. High ability, high creativity, and average motivation
   D. High ability, average creativity, and high task performance

   R,A,(193)

25. Which of the following programs would qualify as an "enrichment program" for gifted students?

    A. Placing all students with IQ scores above 130 in the same class.
    B. Giving gifted students special projects to work on independently.
    C. Using gifted students as peer tutors for less able students.
    D. Allowing students more time to complete their homework.

            U,B,(193)

26. Which of the following programs would qualify as an "accelerated program" for gifted students?

    A. Teaching gifted students research skills.
    B. Giving gifted students freedom to choose their own homework assignments.
    C. Allowing a child to skip a grade.
    D. Giving gifted students special projects to work on independently.

            U,C,(194)

27. PL 94-142 requires all but <u>one</u> of the following for all handicapped children.

    A. Free appropriate education
    B. Due process guarantees
    C. Education in nonhandicapped programs
    D. An Individualized Educational Program (IEP)

            R,C,(196)

28. Recent legislation has

    A. given schools guidelines for excluding handicapped students.
    B. increased due process protection for handicapped students.
    C. decreased parental involvement.
    D. encouraged special separate schools for handicapped students.

            R,B,(197)

29. PL 94-142 prohibits the results from group intelligence tests being used as the sole criteria for

    A. placement in special education programs.
    B. grouping students into homogeneous groups.
    C. developing curricula.
    D. advising students.

            R,A,(197)

30. If parents of handicapped children are not satisfied with their child's educational program, they may

    A. file a complaint.
    B. initiate a fair hearing.
    C. obtain an independent outside evaluation.
    D. all of the above.

    R,D,(197)

31. The primary function of an IEP is to

    A. hold parents accountable for special education program results.
    B. serve as a contract between parents and school.
    C. limit the range of services parents can demand for their child.
    D. provide an appropriate individualized program for each handicapped child.

    U,D,(197)

32. Which of the following is not a step taken before an IEP is written?

    A. The classroom teacher initiates a referral.
    B. A committee reviews the request for referral and conducts a preliminary screening.
    C. A comprehensive assessment of the student is completed.
    D. The student is placed in a special education class to assess his or her disability.

    R,D,(197-198)

33. Handicapped children should be in regular classes

    A. even if the IEP stipulates a special class.
    B. to the extent that it is appropriate.
    C. at all times.
    D. only for certain class periods of the day.

    R,B,(198-199)

34. The continuum of educational environment options allows educators to

    A. fund a broad range of programs.
    B. transfer students so they have a different teacher every year similar to regular students.
    C. match individual needs of the child to an appropriate environment.
    D. minimize disruption for nonhandicapped peers.

    R,C,(199)

35. Which of these placements is the most restrictive educational environment?

A. Regular class with support services
B. Residential facility
C. Special school
D. Special class

R,B,(Fig. 5.1,200)

36. According to recent research, which of the following statements regarding mainstreaming is not true?

A. Mainstreaming is an attempt at providing different alternatives for handicapped students.
B. Even when individualized instruction is used, mainstreamed students perform worse than students in special education classes.
C. Placing handicapped and nonhandicapped students together can actually result in lower acceptance for the handicapped.
D. Acceptance of the handicapped students can be improved when teachers structure their classroom to help these students exhibit more appropriate behavior.

U,B,(201)

37. The proponents for the regular education initiative argue that

A. special education instruction is no longer needed.
B. special education students should be educated separately from their normal-achieving peers.
C. "pull-out" programs do not adequately educate students.
D. special education services should not begin until the third grade.

R,C,(201)

38. Which of the following statements regarding handicapped infants and toddlers is/are not true?

A. It is easier to diagnose handicaps in infants than in older children.
B. The law, PL99-459, clearly defines developmental delay.
C. Few infants need special attention.
D. All of the above.

R,D,(204-206)

39. When a child's school work begins to deteriorate, what is the first assumption a teacher should make regarding the cause of the low performance?

A. Physical problems
B. Emotional problems
C. Intellectual functioning problems
D. Peer problems

R,A,(207-208)

40. Which of the following students might qualify for special educational services apart from any adaptations made by the regular classroom teacher?

A. John, who has an average IQ but has difficulty learning to read.
B. Mary, who was absent from school at least one third of the time due to a liver disease.
C. Fred, who comes from a low-income family and has trouble with math.
D. Susan, who is field-dependent and received all C's on her report card.

A,A,(208)

41. Which of the following approaches should the teacher take when exceptional students remain in the regular classroom?

A. Have the exceptional students do the same assignments as the rest of the students but give the exceptional students more immediate feedback.
B. Implement the classroom programs specified in the students' IEPs.
C. Group the exceptional children together and deal with them as a group.
D. Teach aspects of the IEPs that are most relevant to the teacher's competency.

A,B,(208)

42. Which of the following teaching methods is not one of those identified by Madden and Slavin as successful in improving handicapped children's social acceptance and/or achievement in the regular classroom?

A. Discovery learning
B. Social skills training
C. Cooperative learning
D. Individualized instruction

R,A,(208-209)

Essay Questions:

1. Explain the differences between the terms "exceptional", "handicap", and "disability".

Suggested Answer:

The term "exceptional" refers to any student whose performance significantly departs from the average or typical student, either above or below the average. "Handicap" refers to the difficulties faced by a student because of a physical disability or a behavioral characteristic that distinguishes him or her as different from other students. "Disability" refers to a physical problem that leads to a reduction in the ability to perform certain tasks that other students can perform.

U,(166)

2. Identify two benefits of labeling exceptional children and two disadvantages of labeling.

Suggested Answer:

Benefits of labeling include helping professionals communicate in research, promoting student and public awareness, understanding, and acceptance of the handicapped. Disadvantages include the fact that labels may cause others to place limited or unrealistic expectations on the student, and that special education labels have a permanency that is difficult to overcome and makes placement in the regular classroom difficult.

R,(169-170)

3. Briefly describe the classroom teacher's role in the identification and education of the exceptional student.

Suggested Answer:

The classroom teacher has a most important role in the identification and education of the exceptional student. It is usually the classroom teacher who first identifies the student who is at risk for academic failure or who performs exceptionally above the average. It is also the teacher who usually initiates the referral for an IEP and is a member of the IEP team responsible for the development of an educational program for the student. Finally, it is often the teacher herself who is primarily responsible for instructing the handicapped student and for helping the student adjust to the regular classroom.

U,(205-206)

4. What teaching methods can a regular classroom teacher use to improve the learning environment for handicapped students in her class?

Suggested Answer:

The regular classroom teacher can employ a variety of methods to improve the learning environment for handicapped students in his or her class. For example, he or she can provide social skills training for handicapped students, such as those related to making friends, learning to share, and expressing feelings appropriately. The teacher can also use methods such as cooperative learning in which nonhandicapped students are encouraged to work with their handicapped peers. In addition, the teacher can provide individualized instruction for handicapped students when necessary.

A,(207-209)

CHAPTER 6

BEHAVIORAL APPROACHES TO LEARNING

1. The behavioral position regarding the teaching of math to elementary students

    A. views the environment as a controller of behavior.
    B. emphasizes that children must move from concrete experiences with manipulatives to more abstract paper-pencil tasks.
    C. emphasizes the student's level of cognitive development.
    D. focuses on the student's intrinsic motivation for math.

    U,A,(219)

2. According to Pavlov, a dog salivated at the sound of a bell because the bell functioned as the

    A. unconditioned stimulus.
    B. unconditioned response.
    C. conditioned stimulus.
    D. conditioned response.

    R,C,(223)

3. The process of extinction involves

    A. presenting the CS without the US.
    B. a lessening of the frequency of behavior.
    C. allowing behavior to occur without following it with reinforcement.
    D. all of the above.

    R,D,(224)

4. L. Thorndike's theory of learning stressed the

    A. relationship of the unconditioned stimulus to the unconditioned response.
    B. beneficial effects of negative reinforcement on learning.
    C. fact that we learn movements by contiguity in time.
    D. process of forming bonds that facilitate future repetitions of the response.

    R,D,(224-225)

5. Which of the following does <u>not</u> emphasize learning through the simultaneous occurrence of the stimulus and response?

    A. Thorndike
    B. Watson
    C. Pavlov
    D. All of the above

    R,A,(224-225)

6. Which of the following is <u>not</u> an important element of E. L. Thorndike's theory of learning?

    A. Law of effect
    B. Reward
    C. Punishment
    D. Law of exercise

    R,C,(225)

7. The use of timed math drills is an example of the use of which of the following principles?

    A. Pavlov's classical conditioning
    B. Thorndike's law of exercise
    C. Skinner's operant conditioning
    D. Premack's principle

    U,B,(225)

8. In operant conditioning

    A. a specific stimulus initiates a response.
    B. the probability of a response occurring increases with reinforcement.
    C. emotional reactions are considered operants.
    D. the consequences of behavior are relatively unimportant.

    R,B,(226-227)

9. According to Skinner, rewards

    A. are contingent on behavior.
    B. increase the probability of a response.
    C. control behavior in humans.
    D. compensate for services.

    U,D,(226)

10. An important difference between classical and operant conditioning is that in

    A. classical conditioning, a learning situation occurs more often because of immediate reinforcement.
    B. operant conditioning, responses are elicited by stimuli.
    C. classical conditioning, the consequences of behavior carry no weight in learning.
    D. operant conditioning, the reward strengthens the bond between stimulus and response.

    U,C,(227)

11. In terms of operant conditioning in teaching, it is important for students to actively participate in the instruction by giving overt responses so

    A. students will not become inattentive.
    B. the teacher can provide cues and reinforcement to responses.
    C. students will have practice in responding.
    D. the teacher will learn which students have mastered the material.

    U,B,(227)

12. Applied behavior analysis is closely related to which one of the following principles of learning?

    A. Classical conditioning
    B. Operant conditioning
    C. Both A and B
    D. None of the above

    U,B,(227)

13. Mr. Williams is preparing to initiate a behavior modification program for one of his students. He begins by identifying the number of times the student speaks out without permission each ten minutes of a 50 minute period. According to behavioral psychologists, Mr. Williams is

    A. identifying the baseline for misbehavior.
    B. beginning his intervention strategy.
    C. determining the student's zone of proximal development.
    D. using an extinction procedure.

    U,A,(228)

14. The first step in any behavior modification program in the classroom is to

    A. identify positive reinforcers.
    B. identify effective punishers.
    C. define and state operationally the behavior to be changed.
    D. note the frequency of the behavior you are interested in changing.

                  R,C,(227)

15. In operant conditioning, responses may be brought under the control of

    A. discriminative stimuli.
    B. reinforcing stimuli.
    C. unconditioned stimuli.
    D. generalized stimuli.

                  R,A,(229)

16. In educational settings, which of the following is primarily utilized in behavior management systems?

    A. Primary reinforcers
    B. Secondary reinforcers
    C. Intrinsic motivation
    D. Classical conditioning

                  R,B,(232)

17. A stimulus that, when terminated, tends to increase the probability of a response is called a

    A. positive reinforcer.
    B. positive stimulus.
    C. negative reinforcer.
    D. punishment.

                  R,C,(231)

18. A mother repeatedly nags her teenage children to clean up their rooms. Assuming that the nagging is aversive to the children, when they clean up their rooms and the nagging stops they will be

    A. positively reinforced.
    B. negatively reinforced.
    C. punished.
    D. extinguished.

                  A,B,(231)

19. Mrs. Grove has established a behavior management system for Evert, a difficult student. Evert could earn points for good behavior that could be exchanged for free time in the classroom. After two weeks of consistent implementation, Mrs. Grove did not see any change in Evert's behavior and reported to the school psychologist that she had an example for him of a child who does not respond to positive reinforcement. The first factor that Mrs. Grove would be wise to examine is whether

   A. another activity other than free time in the classroom would be reinforcing to Evert.
   B. parents are supporting the behavior management system she is utilizing.
   C. she has attempted to rely on positive reinforcement alone rather than pairing with mild punishment.
   D. she has allowed enough time to evaluate the results.

   A,A,(232-233)

20. A mother says to her daughter: "If you clean your room, you can have the car." Which of the following learning principles is she using?

   A. Classical conditioning
   B. Premack's principle
   C. Primary reinforcement
   D. Social learning

   U,B,(232)

21. Students in Mr. Wright's humanities class have been warned that they will receive unannounced quizzes during the semester. What kind of reinforcement schedule will they be on?

   A. Continuous reinforcement
   B. Variable interval
   C. Fixed ratio
   D. Fixed interval

   U,B,(234)

22. In teaching a new response, one should

   A. begin with intermittent reinforcement; then move to continuous reinforcement.
   B. begin with continuous reinforcement; then move to intermittent reinforcement.
   C. increase rate of reinforcement as the student progresses.
   D. use immediate and specific reinforcement throughout the learning.

   R,B,(234)

23. Schedules of reinforcement result in different

    A. rates of responses.
    B. rates of extinction.
    C. frequencies of reinforcement.
    D. all of these.

                                                    R,D,(234-235)

24. Let's assume you have decided to train your students to stop whatever they are doing and look at you when you give some prearranged signal. If you praise the children who look up at the signal and ignore those who do not, you are attempting to

    A. negatively reinforce.
    B. punish not looking up.
    C. switch to an intermittent schedule of reinforcement.
    D. extinguish response of not looking up and reinforce response of looking up.

                                                    A,D,(234-235)

25. A classroom observer noticed that a student eventually stopped speaking out of turn when the teacher stopped paying attention to her. However, after some time had elapsed, the student starting talking out of turn again. Behavioral psychologists identify this situation as

    A. spontaneous recovery.
    B. time-out.
    C. classical conditioning.
    D. shaping.

                                                    U,A,(235)

26. A teacher wants one of her problem students to complete his entire homework assignment. She begins to praise him for each item of the homework assignment that he does complete. She is practicing the process of

    A. intermittent reinforcement.
    B. extinction.
    C. shaping.
    D. modeling.

                                                    U,C,(235-235)

27. Which of the following is another term for shaping?

    A. Baseline
    B. Spontaneous recovery
    C. Premack Principle
    D. Successive approximations

    R,D,(236)

28. Modeling is important in learning because it allows the learner to

    A. acquire complex behavior by observing others.
    B. discriminate between good and poor behavior.
    C. learn through personal experience and consequences.
    D. all of the above.

    R,A,(231)

29. All of the following are important procedures in shaping except

    A. prompting.
    B. fading.
    C. reinforcement.
    D. time-out.

    U,D,(236)

30. Joseph has observed his friends writing graffiti on the school walls. After several times, he finally brings a can of spray paint and writes on the wall. In terms of observational learning, this is an example of

    A. vicarious reinforcement.
    B. negative reinforcement.
    C. disinhibiting effect.
    D. sublimation.

    A,C,(238)

31. In social learning theory, there is a three-way relationship between personal factors, environmental factors, and behavior. Bandura calls this relationship

    A. an eliciting effect.
    B. reciprocal determinism.
    C. an inhibitory effect.
    D. response generation.

    U,B,(237)

32. According to Bandura, observers are more likely to attend to models who

    A. are perceived to be different.
    B. are perceived to be competent.
    C. appear to be less successful.
    D. imitate their own behavior.

    U,B,(237)

33. In social learning theory, reinforcement is viewed as a

    A. source of information.
    B. strengthener for behavioral responses.
    C. consequence condition of behavior.
    D. factor that bonds observer and observed.

    R,A,(239)

34. During an assembly, Dr. Smith had taken the time to complement a student who had picked up the litter in the playground. As a result, the rest of the students were making an effort to pick up litter found around the school. According to Bandura, this is an example of

    A. self-reinforcement.
    B. motor reproduction.
    C. facilitating effect.
    D. vicarious reinforcement.

    U,D,(239)

35. According to cognitive-behavioral therapy, self-control

    A. can be learned through self-talk.
    B. is not as effective as teacher-administered control.
    C. cannot be taught to children as they get older.
    D. can be quickly taught to older children.

    U,A,(242)

36. When comparing linear and branching programs utilized in programmed instruction

    A. the student writes out answers in branching programs.
    B. frames in linear programs usually contain several paragraphs.
    C. the student responses determine the route he or she follows in branched programs.
    D. linear programs have been found to produce higher achievement.

    R,C,(245)

37. Programmed instruction is based on principles of

  A. intermittent reinforcement.
  B. classical conditioning.
  C. operant conditioning.
  D. modeling.

  R,C,(244)

38. Which of the following types of computer-assisted instruction (CAI) is best suited for teaching students higher-level thinking skills?

  A. Drill-and-practice
  B. Simulation programs
  C. Tutorials
  D. Skill sequence programs

  R,B,(247-248)

39. Computer-managed instruction (CMI) is primarily designed to

  A. teach basic skills.
  B. provide immediate reinforcement during initial learning.
  C. provide students with opportunities to practice new skills.
  D. help teachers monitor and diagnose student progress.

  R,D,(247)

40. Research evaluations of CAI indicate that CAI

  A. has its greatest positive effect on college age students.
  B. is more successful when combined with regular classroom instruction.
  C. is more successful when used alone.
  D. is more successful for teaching higher-level thinking than basic skills.

  R,B,(250)

41. Which of the following statements is supported by a 1988 report on the status of computer competence in the United States?

    A. Students know a great deal about computer applications and programming.
    B. Computer coordinators in school are highly trained.
    C. There are clear racial/ethnic differences in computer competence.
    D. Many students have computer anxiety.

                                                                U,C,(248-249)

42. When evaluating the comparative effectiveness of different types of media on learning, the most important thing to remember is that

    A. it is the instructional design of the learning materials and not the medium itself that affects learning.
    B. it is the effects of the medium itself, more than any other variable, that influences learning.
    C. learners have certain preferences for one type of medium over another.
    D. learning is primarily affected by the learner's attitude toward the medium.

                                                                 U,A,(251)

43. Mastery learning would most likely be advocated by a teacher who

    A. considers differences in student aptitude to be primarily differences in learning rate.
    B. feels that students do best when working alone and at their own rate.
    C. feels that students should work in groups and achieve the same goals at the same time.
    D. all of the above.

                                                                 U,A,(252)

44. In mastery learning, determining student progress and identifying areas where more instruction is needed is accomplished by administering

    A. summative tests.
    B. pretests.
    C. formative tests.
    D. posttests.

                                                             R,C,(252-253)

45. The major differences between mastery learning and Keller's Personalized System of Instruction (PSI) is that the former is _____ based while the latter is _____ based.

A. group, individually
B. individually, group
C. competitively, cooperatively
D. cooperatively, competitively

U,A,(253,258)

46. Mastery learning would probably be least effective in a classroom where

A. students differed only moderately in ability.
B. there was a broad range of individual differences among students.
C. students were young and primarily learning basic skills.
D. students were accustomed to working cooperatively in groups.

U,B,(256)

47. One of the most important characteristics of mastery learning that can be used in regular instruction to help students overcome failure is

A. group instruction.
B. the use of clearly defined instructional objectives.
C. corrective instruction.
D. the division of instruction into small learning units.

R,C,(255)

48. All of the following are components of Keller's Personalized System of Instruction (PSI) except

A. self-pacing.
B. required lectures.
C. proctors.
D. unit mastery examinations.

R,B,(258)

Essay Questions:

1. During a class presentation, Billy became embarrassed when he forgot what he was going to say. Now each time he's to give a speech he complains of a stomachache and asks to be excused. Based on the principles of operant conditioning how would you explain Billy's reaction and what would you do to change it?

Suggested Answer:

By getting sick, Billy is able to avoid an aversive stimulus (giving a speech) and as a result is negatively reinforced. Billy's reaction can be changed in a number of ways, including withholding negative reinforcement (making him give a speech no matter how he feels), giving him positive reinforcement (reward him for giving a speech), shaping his behavior (let him give short speeches at first, then longer ones as he becomes more comfortable), or by having him model the successful performance of the teacher or other students.

A,(226-237)

2. Describe a situation in which modeling would be preferred to operant conditioning for teaching a new behavior.

Suggested Answer:

Modeling would be preferred to operant conditioning in teaching a skill where risk to safety is a factor. For example, teaching a child to properly cross the street is best accomplished by demonstrating and having the child model the skill rather than through trial and error learning, where only correct responses are reinforced.

A,(241)

3. Why should teachers learn to distinguish between different types of reinforcement and punishment?

Suggested Answer:

Learning to distinguish between different types of reinforcement and punishment is important for teachers because each of these can have a different effect on the behavior of students. For example, using positive and negative reinforcement results in increasing a behavior, while punishment has the effect of decreasing it. Also, knowledge of the effects of different types of operant conditioning principles can help teachers do what they have always done more effectively.

U,(233-234)

4. How does time allotted for corrective instruction affect the success of mastery learning?

Suggested Answer:

Time allotted for corrective instruction is a major variable in the success of master learning. If slow learners are to achieve at the same levels as faster learners, slow learners must be given extra time and instruction. If this is not done, mastery learning appears to lose its advantage over nonmastery approaches in producing more learning and less variability in student achievement.

U,(256)

CHAPTER 7

COGNITIVE APPROACHES TO LEARNING

1. Information processing models are primarily concerned with describing how humans

    A. react to environmental stimuli.
    B. think while learning.
    C. behave in social situations.
    D. respond to reinforcement.

    U,B,(268)

2. The first component in the information-processing system is

    A. short-term memory.
    B. long-term memory.
    C. working memory.
    D. short-term sensory store.

    R,D,(268)

3. After being introduced to someone new in class, you repeat the person's name to yourself several times to help you remember it. This process takes place in which component of the information-processing model of memory?

    A. Short-term memory
    B. Working memory
    C. Short-term sensory store
    D. Long-term memory

    U,B,(269)

4. The capacity of short-term memory is about

    A. 2 to 4 items.
    B. 5 to 9 items.
    C. 8 to 10 items.
    D. 11 to 14 items.

    R,B,(269)

5.   In order to remember a telephone number he has just looked up, John repeats the number to himself several times before dialing. This is an example of

A.   chunking.
B.   visualization.
C.   elaboration.
D.   rehearsal.

U,D,(270)

6.   During a third-grade science lesson on weather phenomenon, John suddenly recalls the time he was frightened by a severe electrical storm. This type of recall might best be described as an example of

A.   episodic memory.
B.   short-term memory.
C.   semantic memory.
D.   immediate memory.

U,A,(271)

7.   To help her class prepare for a history test, Mrs. Jones suggests that they underline the key terms in their text. Which of these learning strategies is Mrs. Jones suggesting that her class use?

A.   Rehearsal strategies
B.   Elaboration strategies
C.   Organizational strategies
D.   Comprehension-monitoring strategies

U,A,(274)

8.   The learning strategy that requires the least cognitive effort is

A.   elaboration.
B.   organization.
C.   comprehension-monitoring.
D.   rehearsal.

R,D,(273-274)

9. Mr. Smith helps his science students understand the structure of the atom by comparing it with the structure of the solar system. This analogy is a type of

A. rehearsal strategy.
B. elaboration strategy.
C. organizational strategy.
D. mnemonic strategy.

U,B,(274)

10. The flow of information through the information processing system is controlled by

A. working memory.
B. episodic memory.
C. executive processes.
D. semantic memory.

R,C,(271)

11. Learning strategies are intended to influence the learner's

A. encoding processes.
B. executive processes.
C. chunking processes.
D. information processes.

R,A,(273-274)

12. Mrs. Scot's objective for today is to teach the Greek alphabet. This will require that the students

A. recall information without association with other stimuli.
B. recall information in a particular order.
C. recall information that is associated with some stimulus.
D. relate new information to old knowledge already in memory.

U,C,(277)

13. Roger has decided to wait until the night before the final to study for his history exam. Assuming that he studied adequately, you would expect Roger to

A. do well on the exam but not retain much of what he learned.
B. do well on the exam and retain most of what he learned.
C. do well on the exam but retain only what he recalled on the test.
D. none of the above.

A,A,(278)

14. While at the market, Dick discovers that he has left his grocery list at home. In trying to remember what was on the list, Dick will probably recall best the

A. last part of the list.
B. first part of the list.
C. middle and last part of the list.
D. first and last part of the list.

A,D,(278)

15. Which of the following strategies would you suggest for learning the names of All-Star baseball players and their respective teams?

A. Distributed practice
B. Massed practice
C. Timed practice
D. Serial practice

A,A,(278)

16. Dividing a long list of items into smaller segments for study is termed

A. distributed practice.
B. disjointed learning.
C. part learning.
D. segmented learning.

R,C,(278)

17. Positive transfer is most likely to occur when two tasks are

A. different and require different responses.
B. similar and require the same response.
C. similar but require different responses.
D. different but require the same response.

U,B,(278)

18. In which situation would you expect negative transfer to be the strongest?

A. Learning to play chess after learning to play checkers
B. Learning to play the violin after learning to play the guitar
C. Learning to speak Japanese after learning to speak English
D. Learning to write a poem after learning to write a story

A,A,(278)

19. John has decided to take two foreign language courses this semester, but is upset to learn that they will be offered consecutively on the same day. Being a student of psychology, John realizes that he may have difficulty remembering what he learned in the first class after attending the second class because of

A. suppression effects.
B. proactive inhibition.
C. serial position effects.
D. retroactive inhibition.

A,D,(279)

20. An excellent strategy for reducing the effects of interference on the learning of rote material is

A. sustained learning.
B. massed practice.
C. overlearning.
D. prolonged learning.

U,C,(279)

21. Which of the following techniques is effective for enhancing the meaningfulness of learning material?

A. Elaboration
B. Rehearsal
C. Practice
D. Part-learning

R,A,(279)

22. Mnemonics helps one to learn material that is low in meaningfulness by relating this material to

A. semantic knowledge.
B. short-term memory.
C. auditory responses.
D. the sensory register.

U,A,(279-280)

23. On Monday, Miss Jones taught her kindergarten students the letter "d" and on Tuesday she taught them the letter "b." On Wednesday, however, Miss Jones noticed that many of her students were confusing "b" with "d." This confusion is most likely the result of

    A. retroactive inhibition.
    B. serial position effects.
    C. suppression effects.
    D. proactive inhibition.

    U,D,(279)

24. Mary's music teacher, Mr. Tune, helps her to remember the five lines of the musical staff by reference to the first letter of each word in the phrase, Every Good Boy Does Fine. This sentence mnemonic can be classified under which of the following?

    A. Loci method
    B. Peg-word method
    C. Key-word method
    D. Acronym

    A,D,(280)

25. Dr. Amnesia frequently has trouble recalling the names of his students in his psychology class. One of his students, Johnny Recall, suggests that Dr. Amnesia mentally place the names of his students in a different room of his house, and remember them by mentally going through the house and finding the name associated with each place. Johnny's suggestion is associated with which of the following procedures?

    A. Peg-word method
    B. Key-word method
    C. Loci method
    D. Acronym

    A,C,(280)

26. Research has shown that underlining aids in the recall of information from text. However, underlining is most effective when

    A. done by older children.
    B. students underline only information they find important.
    C. students underline sparingly.
    D. all of the above.

    R,D,(282)

266

27. Note-taking is beneficial for most students except those who have difficulty processing aural information and those

    A. with poor recall.
    B. of average ability.
    C. of low ability.
    D. of high ability.

    R,C,(283)

28. A student can't attend class for a week and asks you if someone in the class could take notes for him. Based on current research on note-taking, you should tell him

    A. that he would benefit from reading another student's notes.
    B. that he would be better off studying the textbook.
    C. that he should ask students what he missed when he returns rather than worrying about class notes.
    D. none of the above.

    A,A,(283-284)

29. Matrix notes are particularly helpful when the instructor lectures about content that can be

    A. compared and contrasted.
    B. organized by many subheads.
    C. easily memorized.
    D. related to personal experiences.

    R,A,(285)

30. Skilled readers

    A. skim reading assignments.
    B. look for facts in a text.
    C. ask questions as they are reading.
    D. all of the above.

    U,D,(286)

31. Mr. Reza handed out questions before the presentation of class material. He was helping students to comprehend the information through the use of

    A. adjunct questions.
    B. encoding strategies.
    C. advanced organizers.
    D. focal questions.

    R,A,(288)

32. Factual questions ask students to recall information verbatim, while higher-order questions ask students to

    A. recall detailed information.
    B. relate or manipulate information.
    C. rehearse information.
    D. recall incidental information.

    R,D,(288)

33. Mr. Hoover would like his American History students to read the Gettysburg Address and to remember both specific <u>and</u> general information about it. With this in mind, which of the following types of questions should he ask?

    A. Prequestions
    B. Factual questions
    C. Review questions
    D. Postquestions

    A,D,(288)

34. All of the following are examples of higher-order questions <u>except one</u>.

    A. How can the limitations of short-term memory be overcome?
    B. How would you account for the effects of adjunct questions in terms of information processing theory?
    C. What are the major components of the information processing system?
    D. Using information processing theory, how would you explain the different effects of elaboration and rehearsal on memory?

    A,C,(288)

35. SQ3R is defined as

    A. study, question, recognize, read, review.
    B. survey, quiz, review, recall, restudy.
    C. survey, question, read, review, recall.
    D. screen, question, read, review, recall.

    R,C,(289)

36. Schemata can be beneficial in learning something new provided the teacher

    A. points out familiar information to students.
    B. makes students aware of unusual or unexpected information.
    C. makes students aware of factual information.
    D. points out relevant information to students.

    U,B,(289)

37. When you use an analogy or comparison to teach new information you are using

   A. a textual schema.
   B. a content schema.
   C. an advance organizer.
   D. an adjunct question.

   R,B,(290)

38. Advance organizers present information before a lesson and are usually presented at

   A. the same level of abstraction as the lesson.
   B. a higher level of abstraction than the lesson.
   C. the same level of generality as the lesson.
   D. a lower level of generality than the lesson.

   R,B,(291)

39. When Mr. Anderson helps Sally to pick out the important material in a text, he is

   A. helping her to regulate her attention.
   B. helping her to select the right information to focus on.
   C. motivating her to attend to important information.
   D. all the above.

   U,D,(293)

40. The primary purpose of procedural knowledge is to

   A. transform information.
   B. structure information.
   C. recognize patterns.
   D. perform a sequence of actions.

   R,A,(294)

41. All of the following are examples of pattern-recognition except

   A. identifying the subject and verb of a sentence.
   B. knowing when to change the form of a verb to agree with its subject.
   C. stating the definition of a subject or verb.
   D. All of the above are examples of pattern-recognition.

   A,C,(295)

42. While at the zoo, little Billy spots a zebra and calls it a "funny looking horse." Billy's mistake is probably due to

   A. proactive inhibition.
   B. overgeneralization.
   C. discrimination.
   D. pattern-recognition.

   A,B,(295-296)

43. Miss English is teaching her students the phonetic rule that a silent e at the end of a word, as in "hate," makes the vowel in that word sound long. A matched nonexample for this word that would help her demonstrate the rule is

   A. sat.
   B. pat.
   C. hat.
   D. mat.

   A,C,(296)

44. Pattern-recognition procedures are learned through a process of

   A. generalization and discrimination.
   B. action-sequences.
   C. abstraction.
   D. feature analysis.

   R,A,(295)

45. A potential source of problems in learning an action-sequence procedure is

   A. limited capacity of working memory.
   B. absence of prerequisite knowledge.
   C. set effect.
   D. all of these.

   R,D,(297)

For items 46-52, mark the appropriate option if the statement best refers to:

   (A) declarative-rote knowledge
   (B) declarative-meaningful knowledge
   (C) procedural pattern-recognition knowledge
   (D) procedural action-sequence knowledge

46. Activating relevant schemata through analogies is an effective strategy for learning this type of knowledge.
   A. (A)
   B. (B)
   C. (C)
   D. (D)

   A,B,(303)

47. Learning the steps involved in the division of two or more place numbers.

   A. (A)
   B. (B)
   C. (C)
   D. (D)

   A,D,(276)

48. Teach to overlearning.

   A. (A)
   B. (B)
   C. (C)
   D. (D)

   R,A,(303)

49. Providing matched nonexamples helps to promote accurate discrimination for this type of knowledge.

   A. (A)
   B. (B)
   C. (C)
   D. (D)

   R,C,(303)

50. Set effect is a major problem.

   A. (A)
   B. (B)
   C. (C)
   D. (D)

   R,D,(297)

51. Student learning to classify examples of igneous rocks.

   A. (A)
   B. (B)
   C. (C)
   D. (D)

   A,C,(277)

52. Mnemonics is an effective strategy for learning this type of knowledge.

   A. (A)
   B. (B)
   C. (C)
   D. (D)

   R,A,(303)

53. Although Sara had learned how to add and subtract two-digit numbers at school, she did not know how much change she should get back at the ice cream parlor. This is probably because

   A. procedural knowledge is more difficult to transfer.
   B. her math teacher emphasized concepts but not how to add and subtract.
   C. procedural knowledge is too abstract to transfer.
   D. declarative knowledge is not task related.

   A,A,(300)

54. Teaching critical thinking skills is fraught with problems because

   A. there is little transfer of the skills to other domains.
   B. there are few gains noted in the research.
   C. only certain students benefit from problem-solving training.
   D. all of the above.

   R,D,(301)

55. In reciprocal teaching the teacher

   A. analyzes each student's thinking abilities.
   B. gradually gives students more responsibility for their learning.
   C. isolates students who distract other students.
   D. instructs students how to use mnemonics for improving rote learning.

   U,B,(314)

56. The teacher's role in direct explanation in the teaching of reading is to

A. explain the process of reading to students.
B. model how to read.
C. use discovery methods.
D. teach decoding skills.

R,A,(315)

57. What behavior is a mathematics teacher attempting to develop when asking the following question in class: "What things can you do to solve more problems correctly?"

A. Combinatorial reasoning
B. Inductive reasoning
C. Product monitoring
D. Process monitoring

U,D,(318)

Essay Questions:

1. Prior to giving a lesson on insects, Mr. Johnson presents his class with a detailed summary of the facts to be taught in the lesson. Is this strategy an example of an advance organizer? Why or why not?

Suggested Answer:

A summary of the facts to be taught in a lesson is not an example of an advance organizer because it is at the same level of abstraction as the material being presented in the lesson. In contrast, an advance organizer presents information at a higher level of abstraction, which provides a general framework of ideas and concepts to which new information can be related.

A,(291-293)

2. Advance organizers appear to be most effective when used to teach information that is poorly structured or when learners lack prerequisite knowledge. What would explain this?

Suggested Answer:

When information is poorly structured advance organizers can be especially effective because they provide learners with an organizational framework that adds coherence and structure to the new material being learned. Advance organizers can also provide learners with relevant background knowledge that can be especially effective for those learners lacking such information.

U,(291-293)

3.   Applying your knowledge of specific learning strategies, describe how you would help a group of students learn the capitals of all fifty states. For each strategy you describe, explain how it is intended to affect student learning.

Suggested Answer:

Responses to this question should include a description of the primary learning strategies for promoting rote learning, that is, spaced and frequent practice sessions, teaching to overlearning, and the use of mnemonics. Also, a description of the effects of these strategies on learning should include references to reducing the negative effects of transfer and interference, and enhancing the meaning of rote-declarative knowledge.

A,(277-282)

4.   Certain types of memory errors, such as recalling information incorrectly, are often attributed to the influence of old schemata. Explain how this occurs, and how students might be helped to avoid such errors.

Suggested Answer:

Schemata are cognitive structures that help organize and process information efficiently. They can, however, have a negative influence on recall, as Bartlett has shown, by causing individuals to distort what they remember to more closely fit their own expectations. The negative influence of schemata can be avoided by helping students attend to the unusual or unexpected in the new information they are learning.

U,(289-293)

5.   Rehearsal and elaboration strategies are often used by learners to help them remember information. How do these strategies differ? Provide an example of each.

Suggested Answer:

Rehearsal strategies involve actively repeating information either by saying or writing it, or focusing attention on its key elements. Examples of these strategies include repeating arbitrary or unrelated factual information aloud, repeating key terms aloud from a lecture or text (shadowing), copying material, taking selective verbatim notes, or underlining important parts. Elaboration strategies involve making connections between new information and what one already knows. Examples of these strategies include forming mental images to associate with the new information, paraphrasing, summarizing, creating analogies, and using mnemonic devices.

U,(279-283)

CHAPTER 8

THE HUMANISTIC PERSPECTIVE

1. Advocates of the humanistic approach to education would most likely select as their concern which one of the following?

   A. Determinism
   B. Results
   C. Empathy
   D. Cognitive structure

   U,C,(322)

2. In adopting a humanistic approach to psychology, one will seek to understand an individual's behavior by focusing on

   A. reinforcement schedules.
   B. his or her perceptual world.
   C. extrinsic motivation.
   D. both A and B.

   U,B,(324)

3. A humanistic teacher would be inclined to accept which of the following as helpful in the management of a destructive child?

   A. Elicit positive behavior and administer tokens.
   B. Model good behavior for the child to imitate.
   C. Try to understand how the student sees the behavior.
   D. None of the above.

   U,C,(324)

4. Combs and other humanistic psychologists are in agreement regarding which of the following aspects of learning?

   A. An individual brings meaning to subject matter.
   B. Learning is essentially a matter of stimulus-response connections.
   C. Individuals learn only that subject matter which they perceive to be within their life spaces.
   D. It is on the structure of the subject matter that efficacy of learning depends.

   U,A,(324)

5. Combs et al. noted that the closer to the self events are perceived to be, the more the events will affect behavior. This might help explain

    A. the unusual behavior of a student.
    B. motivation.
    C. forgetting things that we learn.
    D. all of the above.

    U,D,(324-325)

6. Maslow's theory of how motives are organized is based on which of the following assumptions?

    A. Persons act in ways that are intended to be moral and ethical.
    B. Safety needs must be satisfied before one can be concerned with learning.
    C. Love and belonging take precedence over safety.
    D. True self-actualization is not within the capacity of all persons.

    U,B,(326)

7. According to Maslow, the need to develop one's potential, or to become what one is capable of becoming, is known as
    A. humanism.
    B. self-responsibility.
    C. self-actualization.
    D. self-awareness.

    R,C,(326)

8. Maslow's hierarchy of needs can be separated into two groups. Lower level needs are identified by Maslow as

    A. deficiency.
    B. aesthetic.
    C. self-actualizing.
    D. growth.

    R,A,(326)

9. Among the following classroom outcomes, which is least likely to be emphasized by humanistic educators?

    A. Specific academic competencies
    B. Freedom
    C. Self-awareness
    D. Self-responsibility

    U,A,(324)

10. Kim works hard to complete her homework assignments but then does not turn them in. She knows this will lower her grades, but she persists. What would a perceptual psychologist probably say about this situation?

   A. Her behavior is a purposeful act that to her brings a reward that may be satisfying.
   B. Her behavior tells you that she has been conditioned to respond in such a fashion.
   C. Kim does not want homework in her life space.
   D. There is no rational reason for Kim's behavior.

   A,A,(324)

11. Many humanistic psychologists maintain there is no distinction between cognitive and affective education because

   A. neither is valued by itself.
   B. there is insufficient research to show the difference between the two.
   C. learning involves acquiring information plus giving it personal meaning.
   D. they require the same mental processes.

   U,C,(327)

12. You favor the humanistic viewpoint and implement it to a great degree in your classroom teaching. Which of the following are you most likely to favor?

   A. The students will pursue their own research as much as possible.
   B. Advance organizers will serve to orient the students toward subsequent subject matter.
   C. Teaching will be based on sequential presentation from general to specific subject matter.
   D. Direct instruction will form the basis of your teaching.

   U,A,(327)

13. The author of "Freedom to Learn for the 80's" is
   A. Combs.
   B. Maslow.
   C. Rogers.
   D. Good.

   R,C,(327)

14. Rogers' humanistic principle of "significant learning" is best defined as

    A. learning without threat of criticism and ridicule.
    B. self-initiated learning.
    C. learning perceived by students as relevant to their own needs and purposes.
    D. learning perceived by the teacher as relevant to the students' needs and purposes.

                                                                     U,C,(327)

15. Rogers would agree with all of these instructional strategies except

    A. peer tutoring.
    B. discovery and inquiry learning.
    C. provisions of a variety of instructional materials.
    D. direct instruction.

                                                       R,D,(328-329)

16. Rogers points out that classroom learning can be enhanced by

    A. self-actualization.
    B. advance organizers.
    C. its personalization.
    D. threat.

                                                       R,C,(329-330)

17. Among the following classroom activities, Rogers would be most likely to support a

    A. well-developed classroom lecture.
    B. social studies course with an experiential approach.
    C. good film illustrating major concepts in science.
    D. good programmed textbook for reading.

                                                    U,B,(329)

18. According to Rogers, a teacher who facilitates learning

    A. tells the students exactly what they will learn.
    B. provides many supplementary resources.
    C. gives full responsibility for learning to the students.
    D. directs each stage of the students' learning processes.

                                                    U,B,(329)

19. Humanistic psychologists have found that

    A. socioeconomic status has a greater impact on school achievement than personal values.
    B. values should not be included into the classroom environment.
    C. schools would do well to incorporate health care into their curriculum.
    D. personal development is the responsibility of the parents alone.

    R,C,(331)

20. Teachers who engage in values clarification are dealing with

    A. indoctrination.
    B. leadership skills.
    C. attitudes.
    D. concept formation.

    U,C,(333)

21. The program called values clarification is based on the premise that

    A. young people have a good concept of what their values are.
    B. decision and choice making skills are a natural part of teenage development.
    C. the content of values and process of valuing are one and the same.
    D. exercises involving feelings and beliefs may increase the salience of personal values.

    U,D,(333)

22. Which of the following is <u>not</u> a criticism of teaching values clarification in schools?

    A. There isn't any one set of values better than another.
    B. There may be conflict between the teacher's and students' values.
    C. Students may make statements they feel are socially acceptable and may not really explore their own value system in depth.
    D. Examining values may direct students to new insights about how they view choices and make decisions.

    R,D,(334)

23. A theory of moral development based on belief that morality is a set of rational principles for making judgments about how to behave has been developed by

A. Kohlberg.
B. Bem.
C. Rotter.
D. Weiner.

R,A,(334)

24. According to the theory of moral reasoning, children reason at the preconventional stage in terms of

A. what they can get away with.
B. meeting external social expectations.
C. the authority of others.
D. ethical principles.

R,A,(335)

25. According to Kohlberg, autonomous or "principled level" values refer to

A. motivation due to sense of duty.
B. self-chosen moral principles.
C. motivation due to self-interests.
D. social order expectations.

R,B,(337)

26. According to Kohlberg, "law-and-order orientation" decisions are based on

A. individual expectations for praise or punishment.
B. personal expectations of some returned benefit.
C. a sense of duty for maintaining social order.
D. a sense of human dignity and equality.

R,C,(337)

27. Which of the following statements about Kohlberg's theory of moral reasoning is true?

    A. A student's particular response to a problem situation reveals his or her stage of moral development.
    B. Discussing problems at a person's present level of reasoning is the most effective way to increase moral judgments.
    C. Students can choose the same resolution for a dilemma for entirely different reasons.
    D. None of the above.

                                                                 R,C,(337)

28. It is best to present moral dilemmas for class discussion at

    A. the students' present level of moral reasoning.
    B. a stage below the students' level of moral reasoning.
    C. a stage above the students' level of moral reasoning.
    D. none of the above.

                                                                 R,C,(338)

29. The morality of Ghandi and Thoreau attained the highest stage of moral development, designated

    A. law and order.
    B. punishment and obedience.
    C. universal ethical.
    D. social contract, legalistic.

                                                                 A,C,(336)

30. Students refusing to copy materials stolen from a teacher's test file may have been motivated by

    A. avoiding punishment.
    B. conformity to shared standards, rights, and duties.
    C. maintaining the law, even at personal expense.
    D. all of the above.

                                                         A,D,(336-338)

31. Cognitive development appears to _____ development of moral reasoning.

    A. supersede
    B. undermine and gradually replace
    C. parallel or relate to
    D. conflict with

    U,C,(334)

32. Children are more likely than teenagers to

    A. say the means are as important as the ends.
    B. refuse parental justice.
    C. condemn an ill consequence regardless of intent.
    D. refuse teacher intervention.

    U,C,(335)

33. A student realizes that there is a problem situation in which he must act. He makes a decision as to the course of action but has difficulty acting on the judgment he makes. This student is having difficulty with which of the following components influencing the production of moral behavior?

    A. Moral sensitivity
    B. Moral judgment
    C. Moral motivation
    D. Moral character

    U,C,(338)

34. Which of the following is not a criticism of Kohlberg's theory of moral reasoning?

    A. Kohlberg underemphasizes the importance of rules in maintaining society.
    B. Kohlberg places unrealistic demands on teachers.
    C. Kohlberg overemphasizes the affective influence of the role of morality.
    D. Kohlberg developed his theory on the basis of his investigation with males.

    R,C,(338)

35. Discussions involving moral dilemmas may use in-depth questions. These strategies encourage

    A. understanding of the moral dilemma.
    B. expressions of points of view concerning the dilemma.
    C. statements concerning the moral aspects of the dilemma.
    D. confrontations with different points of view.

    R,D,(339)

36. Compared with indirect approaches, direct approaches to moral education are less concerned with which of the following statements?

    A. How students think about moral issues
    B. How students behave
    C. Teaching moral behavior
    D. Developing moral standards

    R,A,(342)

37. How is an open classroom structured?

    A. Each student has his or her own work area.
    B. The room is divided into activity centers.
    C. Most of the walls in the class are removed.
    D. The teacher's desk is in the front of the room.

    R,B,(334)

38. Which of the following statements is not true regarding cooperative learning?

    A. Students are given rewards based on their group performance.
    B. Students work in small groups or learning teams that remain stable in composition for several weeks.
    C. Students are more likely to attribute failure to lack of effort than to ability when working in cooperative settings.
    D. Students are more likely to attribute failure to inability than to lack of effort when working in cooperative settings.

    R,D(346)

39. In which cooperative learning situation or technique is academic material divided equally among students who in turn study their part and then teach it to other student members of their team?

    A. Student Teams-Achievement Divisions
    B. Teams-Games-Tournaments
    C. Jigsaw
    D. Group Investigation

    R,C,(348)

40. Mrs. Sanborn wants to ensure that her students have the skills that interact appropriately in group settings. In attempting to teach interpersonal skills, she tries to stimulate academic controversy by encouraging her students to challenge each other's ideas and reasoning. Mrs. Sanborn's techniques are best representative of which of the following skills?

   A. Functioning
   B. Formulating
   C. Fermenting
   D. Forming

   A,C,(353)

41. The most effective response in small group interaction is giving

   A. explanations.
   B. terminal help.
   C. reinforcement to all students.
   D. reinforcement to low-achieving students.

   R,A,(350)

42. According to Webb's research on group composition, it is best to formulate groups comprising

   A. more boys than girls.
   B. more girls than boys.
   C. all low-achieving students.
   D. students with a moderate range of ability.

   R,D,(351)

43. Which of the following is a serious problem that can diminish the effectiveness of cooperative groups?

   A. Spending time explaining answers
   B. Status differences in group interaction
   C. Groups comprising five students
   D. None of the above

   R,B,(351)

Essay Questions:

1. Discuss why a teacher would want to use cooperative learning in her classroom.

Suggested Answer:

Cooperative learning may diminish the impact of failure for low-achieving students. There is evidence that when students fail in cooperative groups, they are more likely to attribute their failure to lack of effort than ability. Second, cooperative learning is effective in improving race relations among students. Third, mainstreamed handicapped students are more likely to be accepted in cooperative learning settings than in individualized or competitive learning environments.

A,(346-354)

2. Discuss three criticisms of affective or humanistic educational programs.

Suggested Answer:

Affective or humanistic education is often criticized because it lacks clear direction or purpose. Also, it is frequently based on experiential activities that lack organization and sound theoretical orientation. In addition, measurement and evaluation of affective programs are often inadequate and result in a poor understanding of the factors that influence affective behavior and development.

R,(354-355)

3. Discuss the criticisms of educational approaches to moral education or character development during the last three decades and discuss recent educational approaches in this area.

Suggested Answer:

The major approaches to moral education (i.e., values clarification and Kohlberg's stages of moral reasoning) emphasized the importance of student discussion of moral issues to help them understand their values or improve their reasoning. Since moral reasoning is not related to moral behavior, many educators believe that more attention should be given to programs to involve students in their school and community. That is to say, if schools can encourage students to help others and act in socially responsible ways, students will make more progress in the area of moral or character education than simply discussing issues in class. Secondly, in the early programs, teachers generally took a neutral position on moral issues encouraging students to develop their own opinions. Many educators now believe that teachers should play a more direct role by developing standards and teaching moral behavior.

R,(331-339)

4. Discuss the factors that can lead to a reduction in the effectiveness of cooperative learning.

Suggested Answer:

Teachers must consider how students interact in groups as well as the individual differences of students in each group. Webb has pointed out that if students don't receive help when they ask for it, they will attain less information. Therefore, it is necessary to teach students how to interact in groups, especially how to help others. Also, Cohen's research indicates that status factors can influence the nature of student interaction whereby students respond to each other in terms of their race, gender, or culture rather than their expertise on a subject. Therefore, it is important that teachers take steps to reduce the impact of status factors in group interaction. Providing opportunities for all group members to experience different assigned roles is one way to try to change competence expectations held for low status students.

R,(349-355)

CHAPTER 9

PLANNING FOR INSTRUCTION

1. Which of the following statements best describes an instructional goal of survival competencies?

   A. Understanding political issues such as states' rights
   B. The correct use of banking services involved in personal money management
   C. The development of positive interaction with peers
   D. Knowledge of the history of civilization and its application to today's society

   U,B,(367-368)

2. One of the most crucial issues in instructional planning involves the identification of

   A. teaching activity objectives.
   B. learning process objectives.
   C. implied instructional objectives.
   D. explicit instructional objectives.

   R,D,(368)

3. Which of the following best exemplifies a behavioral objective?

   A. The student will write an acceptable essay for the school paper.
   B. The student will attend a journalism workshop, keep notes on the session, and report back to the class on developing a by-line.
   C. The student will visit the local newspaper.
   D. The student will develop written language skills at about his or her grade level.

   U,A,(368)

4. Which of the following would not be considered a major component in writing instructional objectives?

   A. The behavioral terms indicating the type of task required
   B. The situation or condition under which the behavior would be performed
   C. The activity or process used by the student in problem solving
   D. The criterion level of performance used to evaluate the success of the performance or product

   R,C,(368-372)

5. In writing a specific objective, it is essential that the outcome be

   A. significant.
   B. at grade level.
   C. quantifiable.
   D. timed.

   R,C,(371)

6. Which of the following is probably <u>not</u> an appropriate verb to use when writing behavioral objectives?

   A. Discriminates
   B. Contrasts
   C. Appreciates
   D. Matches

   U,C,(371)

7. The department chairperson asks you to write explicit instructional objectives. You write the following objective: "The student accurately identifies the noun and the verb in ten sentences." The department chairperson most likely will regard the objective as

   A. acceptable.
   B. too explicit.
   C. incomplete.
   D. a process objective.

   A,A,(371)

8. Which of the following statements does <u>not</u> pertain to the benefits of an alternative approach to writing instructional objectives?

   A. The teacher can state a general instructional objective and then clarify the objective by listing only a sample of the specific types of performance needed to attain the goal.
   B. An alternative approach may actually increase the amount of work for the teacher yet help the teacher plan more effectively for instruction.
   C. If a specific standard or criterion is not stated, the teacher can vary the standard without rewriting the objectives.
   D. An alternative approach allows the teacher to have different standards for different groups of students or to have lower standards at the beginning of a unit and higher at the end.

   R,C,(372-373)

9. All of the following are arguments often voiced in support of using instructional objectives except one.

    A. Instructional objectives help teachers become more precise in their evaluation of student performance.
    B. Instructional objectives give teachers greater freedom in planning what and how they are to teach.
    C. Students more clearly understand what is expected of them when the objectives of a lesson or course are stated.
    D. Instructional objectives often lead to more efficient learning.
                                                                    R,B,(373)

10. The student will tour the County Museum. This is an example of an

    A. explicit objective.
    B. expressive objective.
    C. objective stated in terms of student outcomes.
    D. objective that is "student-oriented."
                                                                    U,B,(374)

11. Which of the following is not true regarding planning strategies that are alternatives to instructional objectives?

    A. Many experienced teachers do not use instructional objectives in planning.
    B. Expressive objectives encourage exploration by individual students.
    C. Better teaching results from alternative planning strategies.
    D. Not all teaching goals have to be translated into instructional objectives.
                                                                    U,C,(375)

12. Which of the following is not true regarding teacher use of instructional objective planning?

    A. Research evidence indicates that planning by objectives is a helpful approach for both teachers and students.
    B. Most experienced teachers use instructional objectives in planning.
    C. Research has not adequately prescribed alternate approaches to objective planning.
    D. Beginning teachers need the structure of a method of planning to develop alternative teaching strategies.
                                                                    U,B,(375)

13. A teacher should keep in mind the importance of writing objectives that are

    A. consistent with traditional education.
    B. consistent with progressive education.
    C. consistent with the students' abilities.
    D. relevant to vocational goals.

    R,C,(376)

14. The process of identifying the subskills needed for problem solving according to a hierarchy is known as

    A. a curriculum guide.
    B. the level of difficulty.
    C. a task analysis.
    D. the taxonomy.

    R,C,(376)

15. The purpose of the "Taxonomy of Educational Objectives" is to

    A. define and classify the various types of educational objectives.
    B. determine minimum educational objectives for each subject.
    C. select general goals for public education.
    D. both A and C.

    R,A,(379)

16. The cognitive, affective, and psychomotor domains

    A. are congruent.
    B. are independent.
    C. are hierarchies.
    D. relate to both A and C.

    U,C,(379)

17. The "Taxonomy of Educational Objectives" in the affective domain is organized from receiving to characterization of value complex, along a dimension of increasing

    A. values.
    B. knowledge.
    C. verbalization.
    D. internalization.

    U,D,(379)

18. The main learning outcome in a subject field such as science is in the _____ domain; the outcome in physical education is in the _____ domain; the outcomes of learning associated with moral education are part of the _____ domain.

    A. affective, psychomotor, cognitive
    B. psychomotor, affective, cognitive
    C. cognitive, psychomotor, affective
    D. cognitive, affective, psychomotor

    R,C,(379-380)

19. All of the following are benefits of using the "Taxonomy of Educational Objectives" for classroom application except one.

    A. Descriptions, instructional objectives, and specific learning outcomes are given for cognitive and affective domains.
    B. Because of the taxonomy, it is now possible to write objectives for and measure complex skills rather than for just the recall of basic facts.
    C. Teachers who overemphasize knowledge and comprehension questions can improve their questioning behavior from high-level question examples given.
    D. Students can learn higher levels of thinking through the effective quality of questions provided in the taxonomy.

    U,A,(379-380)

20. In the cognitive domain, one observes that the "Taxonomy of Educational Objectives" is ordered by increasing

    A. complexity.
    B. significance.
    C. semi-abstraction.
    D. knowledge.

    U,A,(Table 9.2,380)

21. Which of the following categories of cognitive objectives listed below does not belong?

    A. Knowledge
    B. Emitting
    C. Analysis
    D. Comprehension

    R,B,(Table 9.2,380)

22. At which level in the cognitive domain is the following term: "Using your knowledge of biological and chemical principles, develop an effective approach for identifying the source of DDT in the marine food chain."

    A. Analysis
    B. Synthesis
    C. Evaluation
    D. Application

    U,B,(Table 9.2,380)

23. In a political science class, an instructor asks his students to identify elements of propaganda in a political speech. This objective would be an example of which of the following categories in the cognitive domain?

    A. Knowledge
    B. Application
    C. Analysis
    D. Synthesis

    A,C,(Table 9.2,380)

24. After having learned to make change in class, students go on a field trip to a store to try out their newly learned skill. In the cognitive domain this would be an example of

    A. Application.
    B. Analysis.
    C. Evaluation.
    D. Comprehension.

    A,A,(Table 9.2,380)

25. The process of organization in the affective domain is closest to which process level in the cognitive domain?

    A. Synthesis
    B. Evaluation
    C. Application
    D. Knowledge

    U,A,(Table 9.3,381)

26. Which of the following objectives would be classified at the receiving level of the affective domain?

    A. The student reads his assignment on time.
    B. The student practices the rules of safety in chemistry.
    C. The student receives visitors at his home.
    D. The student watches a film on poverty in America.

    A,D,(Table 9.3,381)

27. Although George has worked for only two months as a salesman, he has already been made assistant sales manager. This promotion is the result of his industry, punctuality, and ability to work on his own. In the affective domain this would be an example of

    A. receiving.
    B. organization.
    C. responding.
    D. value complex.

    A,D,(Table 9.3,381)

28. Which of the following statements is true regarding a unit plan?

    A. A unit plan is a specific individual lesson plan.
    B. Unit planning provides a narrow framework for a short period of time.
    C. In considering the overall goal of the unit, very specific outcomes should be delineated.
    D. Unit planning is often viewed as more important than daily lesson planning.

    U,D,(384)

29. In developing a unit plan, a teacher should first

    A. outline the major concepts or ideas in the unit.
    B. write specific objectives for the unit.
    C. consider the overall goal or purpose of the unit.
    D. determine the instructional procedures for teaching the unit.

    R,C,(384)

30. In which of the following grades does homework have the greatest positive effect on achievement?

A. Upper-level elementary school grades
B. Junior high school grades
C. High school grades
D. Lower-level elementary school grades

U,C,(387)

31. Which of the following is not true about homework?

A. Homework is better for learning simple rather than complex tasks.
B. It seems that 1 to 2 hours a night is best for junior high students.
C. Homework should not be assigned on new topics if the students are young.
D. Continuous grading of homework is better than intermittent grading.

U,D,(388)

32. A lesson plan includes the goal of identifying all of the following except

A. the content of the lesson in outline form.
B. the characteristics of individual students to be taught.
C. the instructional procedures; how the lesson will be taught.
D. evaluation procedures, and assessing student performance.

R,B,(390)

33. After having read the research on direct instruction, Mr. Good is anxious to use this teaching approach in his fourth grade classroom. To gain maximum benefit from this approach, however, he should use direct instruction for all of the following except

A. helping his students gain an appreciation of early American music.
B. teaching two-place multiplication.
C. helping his students learn the rules for dividing a word into syllables.
D. teaching the steps for operating a computer.

A,A,(390)

34. According to your text, direct instruction is best suited for teaching

A. creativity.
B. basic skills.
C. comprehension.
D. abstract thinking.

R,B,(390)

35. Proponents of direct instruction suggest that a lesson begin with

    A. guided practice.
    B. presentation of new material.
    C. a review of what students have recently been taught.
    D. an assessment of students' comprehension.

R,C,(391)

36. Which of the following is <u>not</u> characteristic of direct instruction?

    A. Frequent review
    B. Teacher-centered learning
    C. Student-centered learning
    D. Guided practice

U,C,(391)

For items 37-41, mark the appropriate option if the statement best illustrates

    (A) anticipatory set
    (B) modeling
    (C) guided practice
    (D) independent practice
    (E) closure

37. "Today we are going to learn to divide fractions."

    A. (A)
    B. (B)
    C. (C)
    D. (D)
    E. (E)

A,A,(392-393)

38. "OK, class, follow along as I do this problem on the board."

    A. (A)
    B. (B)
    C. (C)
    D. (D)
    E. (E)

A,B,(393)

39. "David, come up to the board so I can check to see how you do this problem."

    A. (A)
    B. (B)
    C. (C)
    D. (D)
    E. (E)

    A,C,(393-394)

40. "Before we finish, I'd like to check to see who understands how to divide fractions and who doesn't." Let's take a little test."

    A. (A)
    B. (B)
    C. (C)
    D. (D)
    E. (E)

    A,E,(394)

41. "Tonight for homework, I'd like you to do this set of problems."

    A. (A)
    B. (B)
    C. (C)
    D. (D)
    E. (E)

    A,D,(394)

42. Closure is best defined as

    A. the point at which you end a lesson.
    B. a summary of the lesson describing to students what they have learned.
    C. tying the different elements of the lesson together.
    D. a time for students to demonstrate what they have learned.

    R,D,(394)

43. Closure is probably not particularly important for a lesson on

    A. solving quadratic equations.
    B. conjugating Spanish verbs.
    C. learning to use a computer.
    D. understanding modern art.

    A,D,(394)

44. Discovery learning methods are best used

    A. as supplements to direct instruction.
    B. for teaching basic skills.
    C. for students with low motivation.
    D. for less able students.

    U,A,(396)

45. Which of the following techniques would be least characteristic of the discovery approach?

    A. Permitting mistakes
    B. Allowing students to ask questions
    C. Introducing disturbing data
    D. Stating behavioral objectives

    U,D,(396)

46. Teaching students to develop strategies for manipulating and processing information is characteristic of _____ learning.

    A. discovery
    B. inquiry
    C. rote
    D. expository

    R,B,(396)

47. A teacher using the inquiry learning approach would most likely begin her lesson by

    A. formulating a hypothesis for the students to consider.
    B. defining important concepts related to the lesson.
    C. helping her students identify a problem from which to develop a hypothesis.
    D. providing her students with a summary of the information to be presented in the lesson.

    U,C,(397)

48. Cooperative learning requires that

    A. all students have high general ability.
    B. all students are prepared for their roles.
    C. instructional objectives be written.
    D. evaluation be on a group basis.

    U,B,(402)

Essay Questions:

1. Define the term "instructional (performance or behavioral) objective" and distinguish between implicit and explicit behavioral objectives.

Suggested Answer:

Instructional objectives are precise statements of what the student will be able to do as a result of instruction. Objectives are stated in terms of behavior that can be observed and measured to determine whether the objectives have been attained. Implicit objectives are general descriptions of learning outcomes, whereas explicit objectives identify specific student learning outcomes.

R,(368-370)

2. How does the use of expressive objectives relate to traditional instructional objectives? Give an example.

Suggested Answer:

Critics of instructional objectives argue against the need for precise stating of every objective. They propose the use of expressive objectives that identify situations in which students work but do not specify what the students are to learn from the situations. Expressive objectives allow students to explore and focus on issues that are of particular interest or importance to them personally. For example, on a trip to an art museum, the students may explore the environment and achieve their own idiosyncratic learning interpretations and outcomes.

U,(374-375)

3. Describe the importance and purpose of task analysis.

Suggested Answer:

Task analysis affords the teacher the opportunity to identify the subskills of a task in an hierarchical outline. This outline is important in helping the teacher plan the order of content presentation for a lesson so that all important aspects of the lesson are included and there is no confusion on the part of the students. By delineating or developing a task analysis before instruction begins, the teacher can also help determine which students do not have adequate entry-level behavior or subskills or which skills have already been mastered. The teacher can also prepare students for learning higher-order skills that come after providing the foundation of subordinate skills.

U,(376-378)

4. Distinguish between a daily lesson plan and a unit plan.

Suggested Answer:

A daily lesson plan is a specific detailed outline of the objectives, content, procedures, and evaluation of a single instructional period. A unit plan, on the other hand, is a detailed outline for a series of interrelated lessons or plans on a certain topic of study lasting from two to four weeks.

R,(388)

5. It is usually suggested that direct instruction be modified for high ability learners. What is the reason for this suggestion, and what type of modifications are usually made?

Suggested Answer:

Direct instruction is a highly supportive teaching method that explicitly guides learners through each step of the learning process. High ability learners, however, usually benefit most from less structured and explicit teaching because of their own well-developed skills and abilities. Direct instruction, then, is usually modified for these learners by increasing the instructional pace, while decreasing the amount of review, practice, and feedback.

A,(390-392)

CHAPTER 10

MOTIVATION

1. Kate has an internal locus of control. Which of the following is <u>least</u> likely to characterize her behavior?

    A. Her level of participation in class discussions is high.
    B. She usually acts on her own without soliciting the opinions of others.
    C. She is well liked by her teachers.
    D. She does not think studying for a test will help her succeed.

    A,D,(415)

2. If you were concerned above all else about promoting internal locus of control in your children, you would be

    A. warm and affectionate.
    B. vigilant and objective.
    C. strict and affectionate.
    D. supportive and disparaging.

    U,A,(415)

3. Coleman's data on school desegregation imply that as the number of white students in a predominantly black school increases, the

    A. black students' self-concepts go down.
    B. black students' academic achievement will increase.
    C. affective tone of the school will change.
    D. white students' academic achievement will increase.

    U,B,(415)

4. Students who are motivated to avoid failure rather than to achieve success are more likely to choose

    A. only very difficult tasks.
    B. only very easy tasks.
    C. either very difficult or very easy tasks.
    D. moderately difficult tasks.

    U,C,(416)

5. Students who are motivated by the need to achieve rather than the need to avoid failure are more likely to have had parents who

   A. rewarded success and punished failure.
   B. were vague about what behaviors were inappropriate.
   C. focused on overcoming weaknesses.
   D. did not overly punish their children when they failed.

   U,D,(416)

6. A causal attribution to "effort" is

   A. external and stable.
   B. internal and unstable.
   C. internal and stable.
   D. external and unstable.

   R,B,(417)

7. Attributions to a lack of ability after a failure condition appear to

   A. augment expectancies for success.
   B. reduce expectancies for success.
   C. have little impact on expectancies for success.
   D. nullify the failure condition.

   U,B,(417)

8. Learned helplessness is evident in which of these situations?

   A. A student tries again after failing to achieve a particular goal the first time.
   B. A student has learned to achieve goals by investing effort.
   C. A student has learned that he or she has no control over the outcome of events.
   D. A student is motivated to avoid failure.

   U,C,(418)

9. According to Covington's theory of self-worth, if a student doesn't try, or doesn't expend much effort studying and fails, she is

   A. trying to avoid success.
   B. protecting her self-esteem, and avoiding negative inferences to her lack of ability.
   C. experiencing more shame than if she had tried hard.
   D. risking a loss of self-esteem and avoiding negative sanctions from her teacher.

   A,B,(419)

10. Which of the following statements best characterizes the self-efficacy theory of motivation?

   A. A good paper will lead to a higher grade.
   B. I do not have the necessary knowledge to write a good term paper.
   C. When teachers dislike you there is no way you will get the best grade.
   D. More time spent studying will result in higher scores on tests.

   A,B,(421-422)

11. Mr. Crabtree recognizes that one of his students, Jim, has had little encouragement from home and is poorly motivated in school. He does not expect Jim to be able to pass his science class. Which of the following is true?

   A. Jim's achievement will inevitably be affected by Mr. Crabtree's lowered expectation.
   B. Mr. Crabtree must somehow communicate his expectations to Jim in order for them to affect Jim's performance.
   C. Mr. Crabtree will probably devote extra time to Jim in order to overcome his expectation.
   D. There is little chance that Mr. Crabtree's expectation will influence his behavior toward Jim.

   U,B,(424)

12. In considering self-fulfilling prophecy, which of the following is not true?

   A. Individual differences of students influence the effects of teacher expectations.
   B. A teacher's expectations often influence how students behave in the classroom and how much the students learn.
   C. High-achieving students are more often criticized for failure than low-achieving students.
   D. Teachers often spend less time waiting for low-expectation students to answer than high-expectation students.

   R,C,(424-425)

13. Which of the following statements about teacher expectations is not true?

   A. Teacher expectations influence the expectations that students have for their own achievement.
   B. Teacher expectations are generally accurate.
   C. The differences between teacher behavior toward high and low achievers are the result of teacher expectations.
   D. Teacher expectations give children clues about how intelligent they are.

   U,C,(425)

14. If a teacher praises a student for "neat work" rather than for his or her performance on the learning task itself, the student will tend to

   A. feel proud of his or her work.
   B. feel that the teacher thinks the student is too stupid to perform well.
   C. increase his or her effort on the next assignment.
   D. expect to succeed in the future.

   U,B,(426)

15. All of the following factors appear to be related to teachers developing a sense of efficacy except the quality of their

   A. teacher education.
   B. teacher-parent relations.
   C. collegial relations with fellow teachers.
   D. family relations.

   R,D,(427)

16. Which of the following is one of the consequences of mastery learning goals in the classroom?

   A. Students will tend to select tasks that conceal low ability.
   B. Teachers tend to support the use of the learning strategies they are teaching.
   C. Students will be more motivated to compete for better grades.
   D. The goal of studying tends to be self-improvement.

   U,D,(428)

17. Jill has interests and abilities quite different from many of the students in her class. She would most likely benefit from being with a teacher who developed a(n)

   A. unidimensional classroom.
   B. multidimensional classroom.
   C. competitive classroom.
   D. structured classroom.

   U,B,(429)

18. A secondary school teacher is trying to motivate one of her students who appears to be bright, yet is low-achieving and not much interested in school. The student also occasionally assumes the role of the clown. Which of these prescriptions should the teacher use to motivate the student and help him to accept responsibility?

A. Have the student lead a classroom discussion or chair a student committee.
B. Assign the student to teach one lesson to the entire class in an area of his choice.
C. Present a problem situation and have the student present and explain the solution for the class.
D. All of the above.

A,D,(430)

19. A fourth grade teacher has a personal philosophy that children are naturally curious and that the best way to encourage learning is through a process of self-discovery. This teacher is likely to use methods that encourage

A. intrinsic motivation.
B. extrinsic motivation.
C. imitation.
D. competition.

A,A,(430-431)

20. A teacher who uses authoritarian or punitive methods to maintain involvement in classroom tasks, but who wants to encourage students to explore the subject independently should be aware of the research on

A. extrinsic motivation.
B. continuing motivation.
C. sex differences.
D. none of these.

R,B,(432)

21. In a fifth-grade social science class, the teacher often divides his students into small groups in which the students in each group discuss, plan, and create different individual projects for entire group presentation. This is basically an example of a(n) _____ goal structure.

A. competitive
B. cooperative
C. individualistic
D. extrinsic

U,B,(433)

305

22. In a competitive classroom setting where students work against each other to achieve goals, student self-assessment becomes based on

   A. ability, not effort.
   B. effort, not ability.
   C. both ability and effort.
   D. neither ability nor effort.

   U,A,(434)

23. As a classroom teacher, you want to ensure that your students are using an effort attribution in assessing their achievement, one in which each student can judge his or her progress according to individual performance. Which of the following goal structure settings would you implement to ensure that your students are experiencing this kind of mastery orientation in their learning?

   A. A competitive goal structure setting
   B. A cooperative goal structure setting
   C. A noncompetitive-individualistic goal structure setting
   D. None of the above

   U,C,(434)

24. Which of the following is <u>true</u> regarding how various goal structures influence the way students evaluate their performance?

   A. In competitive structures, students are very much concerned about their previous performance.
   B. In competitive structures, students are primarily concerned with whether or not they were successful on the present task.
   C. In individualized settings, present performance primarily influences a student's affective reactions.
   D. In individualized settings, past performance is ignored by students in their evaluation of present performance.

   R,B,(435)

25. Frequent evaluation

   A. encourages students to complete tasks.
   B. lowers test anxiety.
   C. encourages failure avoidance.
   D. counteracts the negative effects of competition.

   U,C,(435-436)

26. Which of the following situations does <u>not</u> typify the classroom behavior of an anxious student?

   A. Chooses and performs more successfully on easy tasks
   B. Does well on tasks requiring short-term memory
   C. Performs best when learning material is well organized
   D. Is overly preoccupied with negative self-references

   R,B,(437)

27. Competition may be detrimental to learning for

   A. low anxiety students.
   B. high self-concept students.
   C. high anxiety students.
   D. moderately anxious students.

   U,C,(437)

28. Research studies suggest that student anxiety may be linked to

   A. certain family experiences occurring during the child's early years.
   B. unpleasant preschool and elementary school experiences.
   C. racial-ethnic minority status.
   D. all of the above.

   R,D,(437)

29. An extremely anxious child will likely have a

   A. slow conceptual tempo
   B. high intelligence test score.
   C. low self-concept.
   D. field-dependent orientation.

   R,C,(438)

30. An anxious student is most likely to be successful in

   A. group projects.
   B. open classrooms.
   C. more structured learning situations.
   D. classroom discussions.

   R,C,(439)

31. Researchers have found that as anxiety increases, intelligence test scores

    A. decrease.
    B. increase.
    C. do not change.
    D. increase at the same rate.

    R,A,(440)

32. Which of the following is not conducive in helping students to deal with test anxiety?

    A. Reduce the emphasis on letter grades by replacing them with reports of student achievement, effort, and strengths and weaknesses.
    B. Use tasks and test items that emphasize short-term memory skills.
    C. Establish a program for teaching test-taking skills and encouraging parental support.
    D. Modify testing procedures by increasing time limits and changing instructions.

    U,B,(440-441)

33. Which of the following statements about the relative importance of motivation and metacognitive skills is true?

    A. Metacognitive skills are more critical than motivation.
    B. Motivation is more critical than metacognitive skills.
    C. Metacognitive skills and motivation are both equally important.
    D. Metacognitive skills can compensate for low self-esteem.

    R,C,(445)

Essay Questions:

1. How does Weiner's attribution theory differ from Rotter's locus of control theory?

Suggested Answer:

   Rotter's locus of control theory refers to how students perceive the link between their behavior and its consequences and whether or not they accept responsibility for their actions. Weiner's attribution theory refers to the inference (attribution) one makes about the causes of success or failure in an achievement situation, that is, ability, effort, task difficulty, or luck. This theory includes locus of control as one dimension, but also adds stability as another dimension.

   U,(414-418)

2. Describe how teacher expectations relate to or affect self-fulfilling prophecies.

Suggested Answer:

Teacher expectations are beliefs that teachers have regarding students' present and future achievement and behavior. The teacher's expectations can lead to self-fulfilling prophecies, which is the process in which a teacher's expectations determine how that teacher relates to and treats students. These expectations can, in time, influence students' classroom behavior, the quality and quantity of what they learn, and how they feel about themselves.

U,(422-424)

3. How does a teacher's self-efficacy relate to or affect student learning? How is a teacher's self-efficacy maintained?

Suggested Answer:

Recent research has indicated that teachers who have a greater sense of efficacy regarding their ability to affect student learning produce higher achievement gains in their students. It has been found that teachers who have received good training in dealing with a diversity of students and who have the support of their colleagues seem to develop the belief that they can solve classroom problems and help students learn. Working cooperatively with parents and having good interpersonal relations with colleagues also appears to enhance and maintain teachers' self-efficacy.

U,(427-428)

4. How do you think an autonomy-oriented versus a control-oriented teacher would affect students' self-esteem and intrinsic motivation?

Suggested Answer:

An autonomy-oriented teacher would probably believe in students' intrinsic motivation and would use a self-discovery approach to education, in which he or she would support students in solving their own problems according to their own interests. A control-oriented teacher, however, would probably believe more in extrinsic motivation and use a more structured, directive approach, in which he or she would use rewards and control techniques in learning. For most students, their belief in their ability to achieve and their self-esteem or self-worth would probably be greater in the autonomy-oriented teacher's classroom than in the classroom of a control-oriented teacher.

U,(431)

5. Describe some of the possible classroom behavior manifested by an anxious student.

Suggested Answer:

An anxious student may avoid evaluative situations and choose to perform easy tasks where he or she has a greater chance of being successful. This student may have difficulty with tasks requiring detailed responses, short-term memory, or with timed tasks that require quick completion. An anxious student may also have difficulty with material that is unstructured or nondirective. Specific symptoms of anxiety may include: nail biting, sweating, severe headaches or stomach disorders, irregularity in speech and motor coordination, restlessness, and general distraction.
R,(437-439)

CHAPTER 11

CLASSROOM MANAGEMENT AND DISCIPLINE

1. As a teacher preparing for class in September, which of the following should you do <u>first</u> in developing an effective classroom management system?

    A. Determine expected student behaviors.
    B. Identify consequences for positive or negative student behavior.
    C. Translate expectations for student behaviors into procedures and rules.
    D. Determine a method for communicating your management system to your students.

    A,A,(455)

2. Based on the classroom management research of Evertson and Emmer, the preferred teaching method to use during the first few weeks of school is

    A. small group instruction.
    B. whole group instruction.
    C. individualized instruction.
    D. a combination of small group and individualized instruction.

    R,B,(457)

3. Which of the following strategies is likely to be the most effective in teaching students appropriate classroom behaviors?

    A. A detailed explanation of classroom rules and procedures
    B. A posted list of classroom rules and procedures
    C. Modeling of classroom rules and procedures by the teacher or students
    D. In-class discussion of classroom rules and procedures

    A,C,(458)

4. Considering classroom management and student misbehavior, it is important to understand

    A. that student misbehavior seldom results from specific behaviors.
    B. the need for the teacher to explain the reasons why inappropriate behavior cannot be tolerated.
    C. teachers should expect that students will be able to endure lulls in the classroom routine and/or lesson without misbehaving.
    D. the need for the teacher to prevent and avoid misbehavior from occurring in the first place.

    U,D,(458)

5. More effective classroom managers

    A. set rules after discussing them with students.
    B. assume that students have no previous knowledge of how to behave in a classroom.
    C. spend time giving detailed instructions to students.
    D. do not drill students in rules and routines.

    U,C,(458)

6. Which of the following is least characteristic of effective classroom managers?

    A. Communicating clear expectations for student behavior
    B. Dealing effectively with transitions from one activity to the next
    C. Good administrative record keeping
    D. Understanding student needs and concerns

    R,C,(458)

7. Miss Bright requires all of her students to maintain an assignment notebook in which they record the dates their assignments are due and whether or not their work has been completed. In terms of classroom management, this strategy should best help to improve student

    A. motivation.
    B. interest.
    C. cooperation.
    D. accountability.

    A,D,(459-460)

8. Which of the following is a criticism of assertive discipline?

    A. It requires a lot of planning on the part of the teacher.
    B. It requires input from every student at the planning stage.
    C. It does not encourage self-discipline.
    D. It is too hard on students who break a rule.

    U,C,(461)

9. Kounin uses the term "with-it-ness" to describe a teacher's ability to

    A. know what's going on in the classroom at all times.
    B. empathize with the student's emotional and affective needs.
    C. be well organized and prepared to teach.
    D. provide adequate consequences for student behaviors.

    R,A,(462)

10. For teachers, the major advantage in practicing "with-it-ness" is the ability to

    A. move smoothly from one classroom activity to the next.
    B. maintain continuity and momentum in lessons.
    C. keep students engaged in seatwork.
    D. prevent student misbehavior before it occurs.

    R,D,(462)

11. Mrs. Jones has difficulty monitoring her class while teaching a smaller group of students a reading lesson. Mrs. Jones' problem could best be described as poor

    A. "continuity."
    B. "signaling."
    C. "overlapping."
    D. "momentum."

    U,C,(462)

12. Variety and challenge in seatwork is found to be

    A. negatively correlated to student learning.
    B. unrelated to student involvement.
    C. unrelated to student learning.
    D. positively correlated to student learning.

    R,D,(463)

13. During a math lesson, Mr. Smith notices several students quietly trading notes at the back of the room. Rather than confronting the students, Mr. Smith waits until the lesson is over to deal with the problem. In Kounin's terms, Mr. Smith is demonstrating the skill of

A. "overlapping."
B. "continuity."
C. "signaling."
D. "empathizing."

U,B,(463)

14. The time a student spends on academic tasks while performing at a high rate of success is called

A. allocated time.
B. time-on-task.
C. academic learning time.
D. engaged time.

R,C,(464)

15. David is a low-achieving student. When doing seatwork you would probably expect him to

A. complete the easy parts of the assignment first and save the more difficult parts for last.
B. ask for help when he didn't understand something.
C. wonder what the purpose of the assignment was.
D. be more concerned with completing the assignment than getting it right.

U,D,(466)

16. Monitoring seatwork can be made more effective by

A. giving students additional time to complete their work.
B. asking students to explain their answers.
C. having students work rapidly until they are finished.
D. checking seatwork only after it's completed.

R,B,(468)

17. Which of the following is <u>not</u> a characteristic of a token economy?

   A. Tokens can be exchanged for reinforcers.
   B. Students vote to award tokens to others.
   C. A "reward menu" lists reinforced behaviors.
   D. Desirable behaviors are clearly identified.

   U,B,(470-471)

18. Which of the following best describes a "contingency contract"?

   A. The contingencies of reinforcement are recorded in writing or in a verbal statement.
   B. About 70 percent reinforcement is given on a predetermined schedule of contingency.
   C. Primary reinforcers are exchanged for secondary reinforcers.
   D. Peer reinforcement is scheduled so that all contingencies are systematized.

   R,A,(471)

19. Practice of social skills is most effective when it occurs in

   A. one context.
   B. the presence of the students' parents.
   C. conjunction with problem-solving activities.
   D. a variety of settings.

   U,D,(475)

20. A teacher who is interested in improving his students' social skills decides to apply McGinnis's Skill-streaming program. He task-analyzes a skill into specific behavioral steps and demonstrates each step to his class. This procedure is called

   A. stimulus generalization.
   B. modeling.
   C. performance feedback.
   D. practice.

   U,B,(475-476)

315

21. Monitoring and feedback to students on their practice of social skills is essential because

   A. it shows the student that the teacher is serious about these skills.
   B. if a student is practicing a skill incorrectly, it will be difficult to modify once it has become automatic.
   C. it builds the students' confidence.
   D. it allows the teacher to evaluate how well he or she has taught the skill.

   U,B,(476-477)

22. Let's assume you have decided to train your students to stop whatever they are doing and look at you when you give some prearranged signal. If you praise the children who look up at the signal and ignore those who do not, you are attempting to

   A. negatively reinforce.
   B. punish not looking up.
   C. switch to an intermittent schedule of reinforcement.
   D. extinguish response of not looking up and reinforce response of looking up.

   A,D,(478)

23. If a student's misbehavior is the result of frustration he is experiencing with a task that is too difficult for him, the teacher would be wise to change his behavior by

   A. changing the stimulus environment by breaking the task into easier components.
   B. ignoring his misbehavior and reinforcing other students.
   C. punishing his misbehavior.
   D. having the student model appropriate behavior.

   U,A,(479)

24. When utilizing punishment, you should remember

   A. that emotional side effects are rare.
   B. it is not very effective in stopping behavior.
   C. to reinforce the alternative appropriate behavior.
   D. a positive approach is always better.

   R,C,(479)

25. If a teacher tells a student to stand in the corner with his or her face to the wall, which of the following time-out procedures is the teacher employing?

   A. Observational time-out
   B. Exclusion time-out
   C. Seclusion time-out
   D. Reinforcement time-out

   A,B,(480)

26. A major criticism regarding the use of behavior modification techniques in schools is that

   A. the effect of these techniques is only temporary.
   B. they require an inordinate amount of a teacher's time to implement.
   C. they work with only certain types of students.
   D. they are often used to make students conform to poor or inadequate learning environments.

   R,D,(482)

27. Gordon's Teacher Effectiveness Training most closely resembles the ideas of

   A. Maslow.
   B. Rogers.
   C. Combs.
   D. Johnson.

   R,B,(483)

28. According to TET, a teacher should summarize or paraphrase what a student says in an effort to encourage the student to feel understood and to communicate honestly and directly. This approach is known as

   A. sympathy.
   B. active listening.
   C. effectiveness.
   D. empathy.

   R,B,(483)

29. In attempting to apply TET principles to solving students' problems, a teacher should adhere to all of the following except

    A. determine problem ownership.
    B. use passive listening.
    C. use acknowledgement responses.
    D. use evaluative questions.

    U,D,(483)

30. Which of the following is not a characteristic of I-messages?

    A. A nonblaming, nonjudgmental description of the student's behavior
    B. A description of the tangible effect the behavior has on the teacher
    C. A description of the tangible effect the behavior is having on the student
    D. A description of how the behavior makes the teacher feel

    R,C,(486)

31. All of the following statements are true regarding Glasser's Reality Therapy (RT) except one.

    A. The basic RT principle states that human problems arise when primary needs of love and worth are unfulfilled.
    B. RT evolved from Glasser's work with delinquent adolescents.
    C. Glasser believes that need deficiency results in disruptive behaviors in which the individual is alienated from reality.
    D. The primary goal of RT is to help meet individual needs in a way responsible and sensitive only to the self.

    R,D,(489)

32. A fifth-grade student periodically disrupts the classroom with his acting-out behavior. The teacher is attempting to apply Glasser's RT principles to help this student. The teacher helps the student understand the effects of his behavior on others and to accept responsibility for his actions. Which of the following RT strategies is the teacher using?

    A. Planning responsible behavior
    B. Evaluating behavior
    C. Focusing on current behavior
    D. Commitment

    A,B,(489)

318

33. Glaser's system of "lead management" for administration of schools is based on the assumption that motivation

   A. requires self-esteem.
   B. comes from external events.
   C. requires consistent leadership.
   D. comes from within the person.

   R,C,(490)

34. Glasser promotes the use of classroom meetings for the dissolution of classroom management problems. Which of the following types of classroom meetings should be used in solving individual and group problems of the class?

   A. The social-problem-solving meeting
   B. The open-ended meeting
   C. The student-teacher conflict meeting
   D. The educational-diagnostic meeting

   R,A,(491)

35. Regarding the use of classroom meetings, Glasser emphasizes all of the following except one.

   A. Meetings should be held on a regular basis.
   B. Any problem relevant to the group or an individual is appropriate for discussion.
   C. Students' reactions and comments should be periodically evaluated by the teacher.
   D. One should not expect that any problem can be solved in a single meeting.

   R,C,(492)

Essay Questions:

1. How would you explain the apparent relationship between classroom management, student engaged time, and student achievement?

Suggested Answer:

   Research indicates that the more time a student spends engaged in an academic task, the greater the student's achievement. It is also known that when a classroom is well organized and managed, there are more opportunities for students to engage in learning. Thus, better classroom management leads to greater student engagement, which in turn results in increased student achievement.

   U,(462-465)

319

2. If you were a teacher of low ability students, what strategies would you use to help your students do their seatwork?

Suggested Answer:

A number of strategies can be used with low ability students to help them with seatwork. For example, they should be assigned work that is at the right level of difficulty for them. They should also be told the purpose of the seatwork and given strategies for completing the assigned task. In addition, they should be closely monitored during seatwork, with the seatwork being evaluated as soon as possible after its completion. Finally, they should be asked to explain their answers.

A,(466-468)

3. How are I-messages effective in helping to change a student's undesirable behavior?

Suggested Answer:

I-messages are effective in helping to change a student's undesirable behavior because they are only minimally negative, and do not upset the teacher-student relationship. I-messages also clearly place the responsibility for the student's undesirable behavior with the student, and point out the adverse effect the behavior is having on the teacher. When the student realizes this, it should motivate the student to change.

U,(484-487)

4. Briefly describe Glasser's recommendations for conducting a classroom meeting.

Suggested Answer:

Classroom meetings should be held with the teacher and students seated in a circle and should be of short duration. The teacher should use open-ended questions and begin by introducing a topic. The teacher should explain that there are no right or wrong answers and be nonjudgmental in his or her reactions. Any problem that is relevant to the group or to a student should be acceptable for discussion and a solution sought without fault-finding. The teacher can periodically paraphrase or summarize the students' reactions and comments, and stress that problems cannot always be solved in a single meeting.

R,(491-492)

CHAPTER 12

STANDARDIZED AND TEACHER-MADE
MEASUREMENT INSTRUMENTS

1. During the semester, Mrs. Newton periodically tests her students to monitor their progress. She uses the results of such tests to identify areas where she may need to change or modify her instruction. The type of evaluation used by Mrs. Newton is called

    A. summative.
    B. normative.
    C. diagnostic.
    D. formative.

    U,D,(507)

2. Mr. Evans is concerned about George, a student in his class who is having difficulty mastering three-place multiplication. To better understand George's problem, which type of evaluation should Mr. Evans use?

    A. Placement
    B. Summative
    C. Formative
    D. Diagnostic

    U,D,(507-508)

3. The major difference between norm-referenced and criterion-referenced tests is in the

    A. format of the test.
    B. content of the test.
    C. interpretation of results.
    D. method of record keeping.

    R,C,(508)

4. A distinction between norm-referenced tests and criterion-referenced tests is that

A. norm-referenced tests cover broad general curricular objectives, and criterion-referenced tests cover specific curricular objectives.
B. norm-referenced tests cover specific curricular objectives and criterion-referenced tests cover broad general curricular objectives.
C. norm-referenced tests cover curricular objectives while criterion-referenced tests cover program objectives.
D. teachers usually prefer norm-referenced tests while students prefer criterion-referenced tests.

R,A,(509)

5. On a criterion-referenced test, one would expect a

A. broad range of scores.
B. narrow range of scores.
C. normal distribution of scores.
D. both A and C are correct.

U,B,(509)

6. In criterion-referenced tests, the performance of an individual is evaluated by a comparison of his or her score with

A. national norm scores.
B. a matched individual.
C. an absolute standard.
D. local norm scores.

R,C,(509)

7. Which of these would be least appropriate in appraising the content validity of a standardized test in English for high school pupils?

A. Correlation with high school marks
B. Analysis of the content of high school English textbooks
C. Examination of objectives in secondary English curricula
D. Pooled judgment of a group of experts

A,A,(510-511)

8. For which of the following tests would construct validity play the largest part in evaluation of the instrument?

   A. A proficiency test for aviation mechanics
   B. A selection test designed to select typists
   C. An achievement test in high school social studies
   D. A test designed to appraise self-concept

   A,D,(511)

9. A psychologist administers a standardized interest inventory and correlates the student scores with teacher's ratings of the students' interests obtained the same day. This enables one to establish the _____ of the test.

   A. predictive validity
   B. concurrent validity
   C. equivalent form reliability
   D. test-retest reliability

   A,B,(511)

10. Which type of validity is most essential for a classroom achievement test?

   A. Construct
   B. Criterion-related
   C. Content
   D. Internal Consistency

   R,C,(511)

11. Which of the following statements is the best definition of a highly reliable test?

   A. Two scores for the same examinee agree closely with each other.
   B. Good students make much higher scores on the test than poor students.
   C. There is a normal distribution of scores on the test.
   D. Most of the items in the test are difficult.

   U,A,(511-512)

12. Increasing test length would most greatly increase

   A. validity.
   B. reliability.
   C. item difficulty.
   D. item discrimination.

   U,B,(513)

13. A school district is interested in evaluating a new experimental reading program. The most appropriate form of evaluation to use for this purpose would be

   A. achievement tests.
   B. placement tests.
   C. aptitude tests.
   D. diagnostic tests.

   A,A,(514)

14. One feature of a standardized test that is not usually typical of a teacher-made test is

   A. raw scores that can be converted to percentile ranks or T-scores.
   B. a specific, uniform procedure for test administration and scoring.
   C. the need for careful score interpretation.
   D. the use of objective test items.

   R,B,(514)

15. What is the main distinction between an aptitude test and an achievement test?

   A. The kind of items included in the test
   B. The number of scores reported
   C. The accuracy of the scores reported
   D. The use to which the scores are put

   U,D,(516)

16. In evaluating an achievement test for possible use in your school, the most important consideration is whether the test

   A. is based upon a thorough survey of teaching practices over the whole country.
   B. matches in content the objectives of instruction in your school.
   C. has sufficiently high predictive validity.
   D. has sufficiently high test-retest reliability.

   U,B,(517)

17. If a teacher wishes to obtain a critical review of a standardized test he plans to use with his class, he should consult the

   A. publisher's catalog.
   B. test manual issued by the publisher.
   C. Review of Educational Research.
   D. Mental Measurements Yearbook.

   R,D,(517)

18. A special education teacher who wants to determine areas of learning difficulty in a student should use a(n) _____ test.

    A. individual achievement
    B. readiness
    C. intelligence
    D. diagnostic

    A,D,(518)

19. As states embark upon legally mandated programs for testing minimum competency, the most difficult problem will be that of

    A. achieving a sound definition of what constitutes minimum competency.
    B. developing test exercises that correspond to the agreed-upon definition.
    C. developing tests that are easy enough to be passed by a minimally competent person.
    D. preventing schools from teaching to the tests.

    U,A,(520)

20. Critics of minimum competency testing for teachers argue that such testing fails to validly measure

    A. academic skills.
    B. teaching ability.
    C. basic skills.
    D. academic ability.

    R,B,(522)

21. All of the following are examples of test-taking skills except

    A. content preparation.
    B. time management.
    C. guessing strategies.
    D. avoiding errors.

    R,A,(523)

22. Indicate the one principle that seems to run through all of the criticisms of standardized testing mentioned by the author of your textbook.

    A. The results are not used to the advantage of the learner.
    B. Test items tend to oversimplify the material.
    C. Teachers do not know how to write good test items.
    D. Tests require only details and not broad, general ideas.

    U,A,(525-527)

23. What would be the most likely outcome if there were no published standardized tests?

    A. Students would learn more because they would not have to worry about grades.
    B. Colleges would find it easier to select appropriate students for admission.
    C. It would be more difficult to compare students in one school with those in another.
    D. Teachers would not know what their students were learning.

    A,C,(528)

24. The major difference between teacher-made tests and standardized achievement tests is in their

    A. content coverage.
    B. predictive validity.
    C. measurement of different types of cognitive processes.
    D. need for different types of reliability.

    R,A,(528)

25. For which of the following would a teacher-made test be more suitable than a standardized test?

    A. Selecting recipients of a national scholarship
    B. Placement of students in a reading program
    C. Determining the relative effectiveness of three teachers using three different textbooks
    d. Assigning course grades

    A,D,(528)

26. An advantage of "objective" tests over essay tests is that

    A. they take less time to prepare.
    B. the sampling content can be wider.
    C. they require less technical knowledge.
    D. they are easier to interpret in terms of objectives of instruction.

    U,B,(529)

27. What is the first decision made by the test constructor?

    A. Characteristics of the students taking the test
    B. Number of test items to use
    C. Types of test items to use
    D. Purpose of the test

    A,D,(530)

28. In constructing a table of specifications for a classroom test, the number of test items allotted to each cell should be

   A. varied each term so that students are unable to detect the amount of emphasis given to each area on the test.
   B. approximately equal so that no particular objective will receive undue emphasis.
   C. balanced between recall and higher level learning outcomes.
   D. determined by the emphasis given during instruction.

   U,D,(531)

29. Which of the following test attributes is most likely to be improved by use of a table of specifications?

   A. Difficulty
   B. Test-retest reliability
   C. Content validity
   D. Predictive validity

   U,C,(531)

30. Probably the most difficult task in the construction of multiple-choice test items is

   A. writing unambiguous stems.
   B. identifying the central problem.
   C. finding several plausible but wrong answers.
   D. making the stem long enough to cover all possibilities.

   U,C,(533)

For items 31 to 36, mark the appropriate option if the statement best refers to a(n):

   (A) essay item
   (B) matching item
   (C) multiple-choice item
   (D) true-false item
   (E) completion item

31. This type of item objectively assesses knowledge at all levels of complexity.

   A. (A)
   B. (B)
   C. (C)
   D. (D)
   E. (E)

   R,C,(533)

32. A social studies teacher wants to know if his pupils can recognize the capital of five states.

    A. (A)
    B. (B)
    C. (C)
    D. (D)
    E. (E)

    A,B,(534)

33. An English teacher has been teaching his classes new vocabulary words. He is interested in knowing whether or not his students can recall the words if they are given the definition.

    A. (A)
    B. (B)
    C. (C)
    D. (D)
    E. (E)

    A,E,(534)

34. This type of item requires recall and yet restricts the type of response students can make.

    A. (A)
    B. (B)
    C. (C)
    D. (D)
    E. (E)

    R,E,(534)

35. Guessing has the most effect on this type of item.

    A. (A)
    B. (B)
    C. (C)
    D. (D)
    E. (E)

    R,D,(535)

36. Subjectivity is the major problem with this type of item.

    A. (A)
    B. (B)
    C. (C)
    D. (D)
    E. (E)

    R,A,(537)

37. For which of the following learning outcomes is the essay test item <u>most</u> appropriate?

    A. Ability to analyze facts and principles
    B. Ability to organize and integrate ideas
    C. Demonstrate understanding of principles
    D. Ability to sort and interpret data

    A,B,(536)

38. In the scoring of essay examinations, all the following are generally considered desirable practices <u>except</u> to

    A. reduce the grade for poor spelling and penmanship.
    B. prepare a scoring key and standards in advance.
    C. remove or cover pupils' names from the papers.
    D. use the same standards for all students.

    U,A,(536-537)

39. As the item difficulty increases toward 1.00, one can also expect an increase in

    A. item discrimination.
    B. guessing.
    C. test difficulty.
    D. none of these.

    U,D,(540)

Essay Questions:

1. Explain why it would be inappropriate to consider the results of an academic achievement test as a valid measure of a student's intelligence.

Suggested Answer:

   The results of an academic achievement test should not be considered a valid measure of a student's intelligence because this type of test is designed to assess specific school-related knowledge only, not general intellectual ability. Intelligence tests, such as Wechsler, provide more valid measures of intelligence for they are primarily meant to measure a student's learning potential rather than acquired knowledge.

U,(514)

2. In administering a standardized achievement test, Mr. Rogers misread the directions and mistakenly gave his students an extra fifteen minutes to complete the test. What effect, if any does this situation have on the test results?

Suggested Answer:

Standardized tests are designed to be used to make comparisons among large groups of students. For these comparisons to be valid, test administration and scoring procedures must be kept uniform. By giving his students extra time, Mr. Rogers failed to do this, thereby invalidating the comparison of his students' scores to those of other students who took the test under standardized conditions.

A,(528)

3. Miss Miller is disappointed because her students scored poorly on a standardized math achievement test, despite doing very well on math tests created by Miss Miller herself. Based on what you know about standardized and teacher-made tests, how would you explain the difference in student performance between the two tests?

Suggested Answer:

The difference in student performance is most likely due to the subject-matter content assessed by each test. Since standardized tests assess broad curriculum objectives they seldom fit the specific content and objectives selected by a teacher for his or her own particular class. The students did poorly on the achievement test probably because they were tested on material never covered in class. On the other hand, their performance on Miss Miller's own tests was better because her tests more closely matched the material she presented.

U,(528)

CHAPTER 13

ANALYZING TEST SCORES AND REPORTING STUDENT PROGRESS

1. A frequency distribution represents a _____ summary of test scores.

   A. graphic
   B. tabular
   C. numeric
   D. standardized

   R,B,(548)

2. What is the mean of these scores: 534, 500, 483, and 551.

   A. 500
   B. 517
   C. 582
   D. None of these

   A,B,(549)

3. For the distribution 15, 17, 18, 19, 20, 21, and 52, which would be the most desirable measure of central tendency?

   A. The median, because it is affected less by extreme scores.
   B. The mean, because it uses all the scores in computation.
   C. The median, because it is easier to compute.
   D. The mean, because it is the average.

   A,A,(549)

4. When the standard deviation for a group of test scores is small, the

   A. scores will be close to the center of the distribution.
   B. scores will spread out widely.
   C. test will be hard.
   D. test will be easy.

   U,A,(550)

5. What is the standard deviation for this set of four scores: 5, 5, 1, and 1.

   A. 1
   B. 2
   C. 3
   D. None of these

   A,B,(551)

6. Your child receives a raw score of 52 on a test in spelling. This tells you

   A. that he should get a B.
   B. that he did better than half the class.
   C. that he answered 52% of the questions correctly.
   D. nothing about his achievement.

   A,D,(551)

7. Sue's parents come in for a conference and ask you to explain what is meant by her percentile rank of 72 on a mathematics test. What is the best reply?

   A. She did better than 72% of all the members of the class.
   B. She did better than 72% of all the students who took the test.
   C. She did not do as well as 28% of all the students who took the test.
   D. She got 72% of the questions correct.

   A,B,(552)

8. The 50th percentile is always the same as the

   A. median.
   B. mode.
   C. mean.
   D. none of these.

   R,A,(552)

9. Mrs. Jones has just received the percentile ranks of her students on a national achievement test. She asks you whether she should calculate the mean percentile rank for her class. You should advise her

   A. yes, because the mean is a very stable measure of central tendency.
   B. yes, because the mean can be easily computed and interpreted.
   C. no, because the data are not equally spaced.
   D. no, because the mean percentile rank does not convey much information.

   A,C,(552)

10. A teacher should be careful in interpreting grade equivalents because they

    A. cannot be added.
    B. are not very stable.
    C. do not have a one-to-one correspondence with the number of items correct.
    D. all of the above.

                                        A,D,(553)

11. One good reason for using standard scores is to be able to compare

    A. the students' standing in the class.
    B. scores at the beginning and end of a course.
    C. raw scores with derived scores.
    D. scores on different tests.

                                        U,D,(553)

12. If one desires to give equal weight to several tests when combining scores, the best results will be obtained if one uses

    A. percentages.
    B. percentile scores.
    C. raw scores.
    D. standard scores.

                                        A,D,(553)

13. Which of the following standard scores is the largest?

    A. $z = 1.6$
    B. $T = 57$
    C. stanine $= 4$
    D. Deviation IQ $= 110$

                                        A,A,(553)

14. A z score has a mean of _____ and a standard deviation of _____.

    A. 0; 16
    B. 50; 10
    C. 0; 1
    D. 100; 15

                                        R,C,(553)

15. Tina's T score is 60, Tony has a T score of 40. If the distribution of scores is normal, how many scores fall between Tina's and Tony's?

    A. 16%
    B. 34%
    C. 68%
    D. 84%

    A,C,(554)

16. Assuming a normal curve, about what percentage of scores will fall one standard deviation above and below the mean?

    A. 34%
    B. 50%
    C. 68%
    D. 99%

    R,C,(554)

17. Nancy's teacher told her that she could have either a z score of zero (0.00) or a stanine score of 5. Which would you advise her to take?

    A. The stanine of 5, because it is higher.
    B. The z score of 0.00, since it is more accurate.
    C. Neither, because evaluation should be objective.
    D. Either, since they represent the same level of ability.

    U,D,(554)

18. If we know that the standard error of measurement for an IQ test is + or - 5, how would a score of 98 for Ted and 101 for Tammie be best interpreted?

    A. Tammie probably has higher ability than Ted.
    B. Tammie probably has ability equal to Ted.
    C. Ted probably has lower ability than Tammie.
    D. No interpretation is possible in this case.

    A,B,(556)

19. It is often recommended that teachers avoid looking at a student's cumulative record until they have had a chance to work with the student because

    A. cumulative records contain little relevant information that can be of help to teachers.
    B. the information in cumulative records is often wrong.
    C. the information in cumulative records may lead teachers to develop false expectations about students.
    D. the information in cumulative records is often difficult to interpret.

    R,C,(560)

20. One precaution to take in evaluating information from a cumulative record is to

    A. disregard teachers' comments.
    B. avoid making cause and effect relationships about certain information.
    C. look for patterns of strengths and weaknesses in different academic areas.
    D. none of the above.

    R,B,(562)

21. The rationale for grading on the curve is that

    A. only a few students deserve A's or F's while most students deserve B's, C's, or D's.
    B. student achievement and aptitude is assumed to be normally distributed.
    C. the normal curve has been empirically verified.
    D. parents and students understand their meaning.

    U,B,(563)

22. For two tests to be of equal weight in determining a final grade, they must

    A. be equal in difficulty.
    B. have the same number of points.
    C. test similar content.
    D. be of similar variability.

    R,D,(564)

23. Which of the following grading schemes is most closely associated with a mastery of criterion-referenced testing concept?

    A. Basing grades on predetermined levels of achievement
    B. The inspection method
    C. Basing grades on the normal distribution
    D. Basing grades on norms from standardized achievement tests

    A,A,(565)

24. The pass-fail grading system would probably be <u>least</u> suited for evaluating performance in a course

    A. where students are required to achieve a high level of competency.
    B. like art appreciation, where mastery of subject matter is not the primary goal of instruction.
    C. where information on how students are learning is only moderately important.
    D. taken by students for their own self-improvement.

    U,A,(568)

25. In evaluating a teacher's performance in parent conferences, a negative rating would most likely be given if the teacher

    A. discussed progress with reference to the student's record from the previous year.
    B. was firm in asserting that the student had some problems.
    C. spoke only in general terms about the student's progress.
    D. specifically described aspects of the student's achievement.

    U,C,(571)

26. Which of these would not be considered an appropriate strategy for sharing information with parents during a parent conference?

    A. Begin by describing the student's weak points.
    B. Be cautious about giving advice.
    C. Use language that parents can understand.
    D. Encourage parents to participate in the conference.

    R,A,(571)

27. The usefulness of school marks might be improved by

    A. increasing the number of A's and B's.
    B. consistently grading on the curve.
    C. defining clearly what the marks mean.
    D. eliminating all information except actual written scores.

    U,C,(574)

28. Letter grades are not an effective means for comparing student performance across classes because

   A. students in each class may differ in ability.
   B. educational achievement is difficult to measure.
   C. letter grades are frequently a source of student anxiety.
   D. letter grades do not mean the same in all classes.

   R,D,(574)

29. All of the following are arguments cited by <u>opponents</u> of the letter-grade system <u>except one</u>.

   A. Self-esteem can be negatively affected by evaluation in school.
   B. Letter grades are not objective measures of student achievement.
   C. Letter grades don't ensure competency.
   D. Letter grades prepare students for competition in the real world.

   R,D,(574)

30. All of the following are arguments cited by <u>proponents</u> of the letter-grade system <u>except one</u>.

   A. They are needed to report academic progress to parents.
   B. High school grades don't always predict success in college or in business.
   C. They help students become competitive.
   D. They help colleges select the best students.

   R,B,(575)

31. Other things being equal, the benefits of retention seem to be greatest for

   A. children in the early elementary grades.
   B. children in the late elementary grades.
   C. boys rather than girls.
   D. children with physical disabilities.

   R,A,(576)

Essay Questions:

1. Bob is delighted because it appears that he has outdone Ray, his arch rival, on the history final. Taking the same test, but in different classes, Bob scored at the 96th percentile and Ray at the 93rd. Is Bob correct in assuming that he outperformed Ray on the final? Is there another way to verify Bob's claim?

Suggested Answer:

Bob is incorrect in assuming that he outperformed Ray on the final because their percentile rankings are not directly comparable. Since they took the test in separate classes, their rankings are only comparable to students within their own respective classes. Another way to verify Bob's claim would be to compare their scores on the test itself. Because they took the same test, this would allow for a direct comparison of their performance.

A,(552)

2. How can a teacher guard against forming false expectations about a student based on information in that student's cumulative record?

Suggested Answer:

To guard against forming false expectations, a teacher can wait until he or she has worked with a student before looking at the cumulative record. This will give the teacher a chance to see how the student actually behaves or performs before accepting the opinions of others about that student. Also, a teacher can make sure that he or she is adequately trained to evaluate and interpret the information in the cumulative record. If not, the teacher can seek the advice of those who are trained, such as the school psychologist.

U,(560-562)

3. Although proponents of letter grades argue that grades are an effective means of communicating a student's academic status, what aspects of grades would tend to weaken this argument?

Suggested Answer:

First of all, grades are only a relative measure of student achievement, which means that letter grades are not comparable across classes or subjects. An A in one class may be worth only a C in another. Also, letter grades are not objective, as they are often influenced by the personal feelings of the teacher toward the student being graded. Finally, grades are not always true indicators of competency, for they are often used by teachers to indicate other characteristics of students, such as willingness to cooperate and expend effort.

U,(572-575)

4. As a principal, you are asked by one of the sixth-grade teachers at your school for advice concerning the retention of one of his students. The student's parents are opposed to the retention because of their child's age, but the teacher feels the student could benefit by repeating the grade because of poor work. Based on what is known about the promotion and retention of students, what advice

would you offer in resolving this situation?

Suggested Answer:

The student would probably benefit most by being promoted. Research on the effects of retention shows that, in general, it fails to lead to either improved achievement or better personal adjustment. Retention is usually beneficial only for students in the earlier grades. Other alternatives to retention can be suggested, such as identifying the student's problem areas and addressing these by giving the student specific remedial instruction in the next grade level.

A,(575-576)